Praise for *Preemptive Love*

"Courtney gives an honest, and at times poignant, account of his efforts to establish the Preemptive Love Coalition in Iraq, whose aim is to save children with life-threatening heart defects by selling *klash,* a locally made Kurdish shoe. Courtney relates his riveting story through the inner thoughts of both patients and adversaries, describing events like the chemical bombing of Halabja and the attack of a roadside bomber from a personal perspective. Ending with the building of the Remedy Mission, which allows children to receive lifesaving surgery in Iraq, this true story of people coming together to live the doctrine of 'love first; ask questions later' by building bridges and saving lives is powerfully inspiring, touching, and, unfortunately, urgently relevant."

—*Publishers Weekly*

"In *Preemptive Love*, Courtney deftly chronicles his journey to help children obtain lifesaving surgeries in battered regions where hospitals had long been gutted and clinics closed. In the process, he finds that his family's strategy of defeating hate and prejudice with unconditional love heals hearts beyond the ones he set out to fix. Courtney's moving story gives us some of the best news to come out of Iraq in ages."

—Lorraine Ali, *Los Angeles Times*

"This is a wonderful book with a powerful, time-tested message: love wins. But Jeremy Courtney and his wife aren't just writing about love in theory or theology. They are showing us all the power of God's love in practice, evidenced through the love of His people for others very different from themselves. As a former U.S. diplomat and Ivy League professor, I highly recommend this book. But more important, as a human being looking for God's love in this war-torn and weary world, I thank God for this book."

—The Honorable Gregory W. Slayton,
author of the national bestseller *Be a Better Dad Today!*

"Jeremy Courtney weaves the compelling, true story of grace in the midst of violence! He and his colleagues risk touching the pain of Iraqi children plagued by heart defects and their families who scramble to get care for them. They all risk betrayal in order to achieve healing. In the process, they discover opportunities for releasing love and hope into a torn world."

—Sister Simone Campbell, executive director of NETWORK, founder of Nuns on the Bus

"*Preemptive Love* is a beautiful and inspiring book about the power of love in a time of war and the capacity of personal interactions, based on love, to break through all the geopolitical strategizing and local suspicions to build trust and, in the case of Jeremy and Jessica Courtney, to save lives."

—Joe Lieberman, former U.S. senator, author of *The Gift of Rest*

"Jeremy Courtney's story, and that of the Preemptive Love Coalition, will help you redefine and reimagine what love really means. *Preemptive Love* will inspire you to dream of a love that risks everything. It is the kind of story and radical surrender the world is longing to see in those who profess to love like Jesus."

—Ken Wytsma, founder of the Justice Conference, author of *Pursuing Justice: The Call to Live and Die for Bigger Things*, president of Kilns College

"Compelling! While the rest of us fold our arms and complain about the situation in the Middle East, Courtney proves that one family can begin an avalanche of change."

—Leigh Saxon, coordinator of Mission Waco– Mission World Health Clinic

"I'm a cynic. I have to be in my line of work. But the world of cynicism isn't one that Jeremy and Jessica inhabit. And Iraq's broken children are all the better for it. . . . I am also a diehard agnostic. And while Courtney writes of his faith as a powerful motivating factor in what he does, he doesn't preach. This is just one man's journey, told from the heart. What *Preemptive Love* is, above all else, is a book of adventure, tragedy, suffering and hope, and the incredible and indomitable power of human compassion. . . . A thoroughly gripping and moving tale of what motivates one group of people to help the children who suffered the most in Iraq."

Alex Hannaford, journalist and author of
Last of the Rock Romantics

"There's enough intrigue, betrayal, death, bombings, and more to fill a blockbuster novel, but this is not fiction. It's a 'warts and all' look at Christianity in action in the trenches, an honest, unflinching look at the cost of living out what you believe. Complacent Christians be warned: this is not just a book, it's a wake-up call. How many of us are bold enough to 'love first; ask questions later'? That is the challenge of *Preemptive Love*."

—Crosswalk.com

"Jeremy Courtney is doing some of the most redemptive work on the planet, providing lifesaving surgeries for Iraqi children. The motto, 'Love first; ask questions later,' is a brilliant critique of preemptive war. Jeremy has become a close friend over the years, and many of us have been waiting for this book like kids on Christmas morning. From TED talks, to megachurches, to Congress and the UN, Jeremy's message that 'violence unmakes the world, and love remakes it' has been transforming hearts and minds. Now that message is in your hands. Share it with the world."

—Shane Claiborne, author, activist, and preemptive lover,
www.thesimpleway.org

"Jeremy Courtney clearly identifies the need for compassion and forgiveness; spreading this message is his mission. He has shown his love and generosity to many of Iraq's neediest children. *Preemptive Love* is a story of caring for and bringing healing to those who have suffered violence and war. Courtney is moved by faith and acts with grace and love."

—Imam Mohamed Magid, imam of ADAMS Center Virginia and president of the Islamic Society of North America

"The story of *Preemptive Love* is so awe-inspiringly powerful it could rewrite the hardwiring that holds humanity hostage. Our perpetual fears and resulting violence stunt evolution; we are a primitive species, still. But Courtney and his Preemptive Love cohorts are lights revealing humanity's greater, true self. As living, breathing examples of agape they raze the walls that blind and divide us."

—Greg Barrett, journalist and author

"I could not put this book down. *Preemptive Love* brings you to the streets of Iraq and into the hearts of children, shouting the powerful message that love has the capacity to remake our world."

—Peter Greer, president and CEO of HOPE International and author of *The Spiritual Danger of Doing Good*

"Jeremy Courtney is a prophet who has undertaken the task of reminding those of us discouraged by the brokenness and fear of this world to choose something greater. Courtney believes in a Real World, the kind of world God always intended for us, one that right now, in the midst of violence and hate, is being remade by love. And, like a true prophet, he invites us to join him in the remaking."

—Micha Boyett, author of *Found: A Story of Questions, Grace and Everyday Prayer*

"Read this book to challenge your stereotypes of Iraq, Islam, and the Middle East more broadly. Read it to learn about the people of Iraq. Read it for the sheer pleasure of Courtney's stunning prose. Read it to be inspired by the notion that preemptive love is possible. Read it to remember what matters. Whatever you do, just read it."

—Tim Høiland, journalist

Preemptive Love

pursuing peace ONE HEART *at a time*

JEREMY COURTNEY

HOWARD BOOKS
A DIVISION OF SIMON & SCHUSTER, INC.

New York   Nashville   London   Toronto   Sydney   New Delhi

Howard Books
A Division of Simon & Schuster, Inc.
1230 Avenue of the Americas
New York, NY 10020

Copyright © 2013 by Jeremy Courtney

Scripture quotations are taken from King James Version of the Bible (Public Domain)
and the HOLY BIBLE, NEW INTERNATIONAL VERSION ®.
Copyright © 1973, 1978, 1984 Biblica. Used by permission of Zondervan.
All rights reserved.

First Howard Books trade paperback edition September 2014

HOWARD and colophon are trademarks of Simon & Schuster, Inc.

For information about special discounts for bulk purchases, please contact
Simon & Schuster Special Sales at 1-866-506-1949 or business@simonandschuster.com.

The Simon & Schuster Speakers Bureau can bring authors to your live event. For more
information or to book an event, contact the Simon & Schuster Speakers Bureau at
1-866-248-3049 or visit our website at www.simonspeakers.com.

Designed by Claudia Martinez
Cover design by Bruce Gore
Cover front photographs: top by Mario Mattei, bottom by Matthew Willingham

Manufactured in the United States of America

3   5   7   9   10   8   6   4

The Library of Congress has cataloged the hardcover edition as follows:
Courtney, Jeremy.
Preemptive Love / Jeremy Courtney.
p. cm.
Includes bibliographical references.
1. Charities, Medical—Iraq. 2. Courtney, Jeremy. 3. Preemptive Love Coalition.
4. Cardiology—Iraq. 5. Non-governmental organizations—Iraq. 6. Iraq War, 2003–2011.
7. Postwar reconstruction—Iraq. I. Title.
HV687.5.I72C68 2013
956.7044'31—dc23
[B]
2013005270

ISBN 978-1-4767-3346-3
ISBN 978-1-4767-3365-4 (pbk)
ISBN 978-1-4767-3347-0 (ebook)

To Jessica, Emma, and Micah,
that you would be perfected in love, free from fear.

With thanks to our Remedy Mission partners at Living Light International, the International Children's Heart Foundation, and For Hearts and Souls.

You healed the hearts of our children, not just physically, but also spiritually. You created for their relatives the true happiness which has become so hard to get nowadays. And you healed the reputation of your country and your people. That is how you uncovered the bright truth of who you really are . . . When you come back, you will find the gates of our hearts are already open to you, as are the gates of our Holy City.

—HIS EMINENCE SHEIKH KHALISY

Contents

Caveat Emptor

One of the old literary canards holds that all memoir is fiction. I suspect most of those who say this are unmarried. There is always more truth than that which can be ascertained in real time.

My honest intention is to make sense of how it all felt to me while living through it and how it feels now, living in its afterglow (and moving into new oddities). Where there is discrepancy, I've likely made composite sketches or somehow noted my uncertainty. Names, ages, places, and other identifying details may or may not have been changed at any point to protect those who did not sign up to be in my book, because let's face it, the great lure of this story rests largely in the fact that Iraq is a scary, dangerous place, and too many identifying details can land the very people I love in danger.

Can you trust me and my version of this real-life story? Absolutely. Every word of this is exactly as I experienced it then and experience it today. Let's call this an entirely reliable, factually true-to-life, imaginative memoir . . . of sorts.

At times, great memoirs can seem like fiction. Our story here might actually be stranger than fiction, and it is going to require you to take a great risk in reading it, in those moments when you must choose to doubt it as fiction and remain the same, or believe it as truth and be transformed.

But if you are brave enough to believe this story—and you dare to believe it for you and for us all—I give you my word, we will never be the same!

This is not a story about Iraq, her children, or my family at all; we would be stage props in a grand ballet. But I will leave it to you to take the risk and see for yourself what it's all about.

Jeremy Courtney
December 6, 2012
Basra, Iraq

CHAPTER 1

Chai in an Iraqi Hotel

How many times have I sat behind the ominous blast walls in this Iraqi hotel? Will I really be protected if a car bomb goes off outside? (I would get that answer soon enough.) The gaudy orange decor was offensive at first, but I eventually resigned myself to it. It can be so difficult to see things for what they are, even more so to see what they could be.

I never had a room there at the hotel. Unlike most of the journalists and aid workers who frequented the hotel, I wasn't on assignment. With our families expressing deep concern over the targeted killing of Christians in Iraq, Kurdish-Arab tensions on the rise, and the Sunni-Shia civil war in full effect, my wife, Jessica, and I felt compelled to take our beautiful baby girl and move to Iraq.

We lived in a house down the street from the hotel, in a neighborhood called Peace.

In the winter, when the neighborhood only had about three hours of electricity per day, our home was frigid and dark. But it taught us an invaluable lesson: *we don't need power to live in Peace.*

Sure, we longed for power. It would have made everything easier! We even bought a small gasoline generator to run the lights and our computers, but using it was like announcing, "We have money, and you don't!" So after a few can't-live-without-it moments, we decided not to use it again.

The spring was pleasant, but by the summer our house had become a brick oven. Jessica was pregnant with our son while trying to care for our daughter. Most days she navigated life in Iraq with little or no water and electricity. Without a working knowledge of local languages or a car to get around the city, she felt like a prisoner. It was becoming increasingly clear that we had not chosen an easy path, and our marriage was suffering.

One thing that simultaneously made my life better and her life worse was the hotel up the road with its Hollywood classics on the lobby big screen, air-conditioning, and table-side tea service. The hotel served as an office for my work with war widows, but also as a place of retreat from the difficulties of life outside. It gave respite. It was an oasis, far away from some of the difficulties of life in Iraq. If my clothes smelled of burned coffee and other men's cigarettes when I walked in the front door, Jessica knew where I'd been. And I could pretty much guarantee I wasn't getting that "Honey, I'm home" hug. If there is one thing Jessica cannot abide, it is the feeling that everyone is not getting their fair share. And she certainly was not getting hers.

It was Jessica's beauty and her utter lack of pretension that first drew me to her in college. But it was her passion for fairness that kept me close. Sure, I found it easy to mock ("Life's not fair!") as I awkwardly groped for attention and security with a woman who was utterly out of my league. But there is something completely enchanting about a woman who believes that life *should* be fair, not for her own sake, but for the sake of everyone else. Still, talk is cheap. Few women are serious enough about fairness and justice to run toward the broken, forgotten people of the world. That's Jess. She doesn't have a vapid bone in her body. And it was ultimately her character and conviction that compelled us to move to Iraq.

But conviction and naivety are good friends. We nearly destroyed our marriage trying to help everyone else. Like a Scud missile through the roof, our marriage came crashing down around us during a terrifying yelling match in 120-degree heat where I thought my life was ending. But things were about to turn around.

I imagine it took days for him to get up the nerve to approach me. He probably had to talk himself into it, given the changing perspectives on Americans in Iraq and our inability to speak each other's language. He may have even rehearsed his speech a few times.

I had been visiting his hotel café for months. We were familiar with one another, even friendly. But on this particular day, he had a favor to ask. In and of itself, this was not unique. I was constantly asked to give money, sponsor a green card, or teach English. Most of the Iraqis I knew were very accustomed to being rejected for these things. There was not often a lot of push-back or sense of entitlement for many of the favors we were asked to bestow. But this guy was different. I remember him being fairly solemn—as if it really mattered and he wanted to get it right.

As he nervously asked for permission to present his request, I remember thinking . . .

Nothing. I don't remember thinking anything. This was just another conversation for me. I had not been building up to this for days. I did not have anything riding on this conversation. I certainly did not know that his request would change my life forever.

"Can you help my cousin?" he said. "His daughter was born with a huge hole in her heart, and no one in all of Iraq can save her life. Can you help?"

If you are like me, you hear heroic stories and you wonder, *What would I do in that situation? I'm sure I would wear the white hat and save the day.*

My answer to his earnest appeal came quite easily.

"I can't help you. I don't know anything about that."

I did not need any rehearsal time. My list of justifications was waiting at the gate to be unleashed.

- I'm not a doctor.
- I've never done that before.
- I don't know anything about sending children abroad for treatment.
- I don't have that kind of money.
- My organization does not handle situations like that.

At this response, my friend (he was obviously more a friend to me than I was to him) could have attacked my character, quoted how much money I had spent on coffee and tea over the past months, lambasted me for my hypocrisy, or come at me just for being an American. Instead, he did the exact opposite. Rather than condemn me, he praised me. Like Jessica and her conviction that the world *should* be fair, he was totally disarming.

He appealed to my obvious desire to make things right in the world and said, "Mr. Jeremy, you are an American, right? Clearly you didn't move your family to Iraq to say no to people. You want to help people. You are a good Christian. You did not move here to say no. You moved here to say yes. Please say yes to my cousin, Mr. Jeremy."

There was so much fear in my initial rejection of his need. I was so unsure of myself and where I stood in the world. I was not a leader in my organization, and my marriage demonstrated how lame a leader I was in my own home as well. I was so vulnerable to any number of attacks that he could have launched. He could have won the argument by laying waste to me and my attempt to hold his family's suffering at arm's length. But he was interested in more than scoring points for the home team. He saw a *life* in the balance—a little four-year-old girl whose mommy and daddy loved her very much. He did not care to be "right"—he cared about saving her life.

And his insight cut my hardening heart and made me alive again. I did move to Iraq to help people. I did *not* move to Iraq to say no. I was convinced that I could make a difference, and I intended to say yes as often as I could.

Jessica always says, "You catch more bees with honey than vinegar." He clearly believed the same thing. I reversed my answer. He disarmed me, and I said, "Yes!"

A few days later I was back in the hotel lobby to meet with the cousin and read the medical reports. I had no idea what I was doing. I couldn't read a medical report to save my life. I didn't have a background in social work. I was a complete novice.

As the cousin walked through the door of the café, my heart melted. He had brought his little girl with him—the best decision he could have made. When I saw her, I thought of my little brown-eyed girl, Emma. Was there anything I wouldn't do to save her life? How many doors would I knock on? How long would I beg? To what degree would I debase myself to see her live?

I was a goner before the meeting ever began.

I stood up to greet the man—a kindhearted father a few years my senior. He was shorter than I; I think he had a mustache. He was gentle, respectful, and very guarded, as though a single misstep on his part could cost his daughter her life.

I realized how little I understood about the world, about power distribution, and about how it feels to be completely at the mercy of another.

It's amazing how many thoughts can go through your mind in a few minutes. As I think back on that meeting, I have this image of myself begging on the street corner for money to pay for my daughter's surgery. I don't think I've ever done anything altruistic in my life. Everything I do is probably motivated by some sense of guilt or out of a desire to stave off my own demise. It is hard for me to ascertain whether I was compelled to help this dear man because I saw him in need or because I conjured up an image of myself in need.

We regularly tell one another to "put yourself in their place" or "walk a mile in their shoes." I saw myself standing in his shoes, on the corner, begging for change with my little girl in my arms. I was terrified. But I don't think I was terrified primarily for him. I think I was terrified for myself.

Whatever the case, I was moved by the idea that this little girl could die without someone who would take the risk and intervene. And I knew I would want someone to take a risk for me if I was the one holding my Emma in search of surgery.

The medical reports were unclear to me. The field of pediatric cardiology was nonexistent in Iraq as a subspecialty at that time. My impression was that she had a hole in her heart. That sounded bad enough to get my attention—it seemed reasonable enough to assume that major organs were not supposed to have extra holes in them. If the reports had been more technically accurate, they would have flown over my head altogether. But the idea of this little princess struggling to walk and play and breathe because of a life-threatening hole in her heart was enough to inspire me to jump in with both feet.

I had not named it yet—that passion and joy that caused me to suspend my questions and fears. My military friends had mantras like "Better to be judged by twelve than carried by six" and "Shoot first; ask questions later." But I had watched Iraq destroy nearly all the people who allowed themselves to live in a constant state of suspicion or cynicism. So I adopted my own motto: "Love first; ask questions later." Today I call it preemptive love.

Nothing had changed in my actual capacity to help this dear family. I still wasn't a doctor. I still didn't know anything about sending children abroad for treatment. I was wealthier than he was, but I still didn't have enough money to pay for her surgery on my own. And my team was still focused on helping war widows—not medical treatment for children. What had changed was my heart. I moved from a policy of risk management and calculated charity to a way of life that seemed much more like the Jesus I had grown up hearing about on my nona's lap as my nono preached from the Bible.

I promised to take the medical reports and knock on a few doors and make a few phone calls to friends. If I had one thing, it was a network of foreigners who might have access to better information than I. But I also made one more promise: I looked the father in the eyes and promised him that I would fail; I promised him that I was not going to be the one to turn up any results.

This may seem like a strange, even cruel thing to promise. But I had seen enough good intentions during my brief time in Iraq to know that good intentions are not enough. I had seen Americans swoop in and promise the moon and then fail to deliver. They always meant well. I wanted to help. But I did not want to be one more person to make promises that I could not keep. So I did the opposite.

Underpromise, overdeliver.

He gave me the medical files and a CD of data in a manila envelope. I imagine he went home and celebrated with his family. This was the closest they had come yet to saving their daughter's life. I hoped his family looked at him differently that night—with pride and with confidence that he could get the job done to protect and provide.

Deep down, I hoped that helping this little girl would cause Jessica to look at me again with pride and trust that I could protect and provide for our family. After the rush of emotions wore off, helping this little girl became a mostly perfunctory task for me. I still had Hollywood visions of lifesaving, and this did not fit the bill. I was younger and more naive than I am now, and I did not yet realize that paperwork saves lives. *Police officers* save lives. *Firefighters* save lives. *Surgeons* save lives. But people who push paper around? Well, I would do what was required of me, but I certainly did not see it as a task that was likely to make much of a difference.

As I made my inquiries of foreigners in the community who were experts in their fields, I started learning shocking details and claims about the legacy of birth defects in Iraq. Every major Iraqi community had a different story to account for the apparently high rate of birth defects. Still, their stories from north to south and across ethnic and religious lines had one thing in common: almost everyone interpreted their sick and malformed children through the lens of various violent acts that were done to them by "the evil other"—that sometimes-hard-to-define group of people who are, at their core, not like us. Almost all my interviews and encounters flatly ignored the more mundane factors and known causes that are common worldwide. Instead, most derived a cathartic sense of meaning for their child's sickness by concluding it was a result of war and violence.

And this was not without good cause, as I would learn in coming months.

I had recently met a guy named Cody who worked for a different field office—the Halabja office—inside our broader relief and development organization. He was fresh off the plane from California. I remember thinking he was both daring and perhaps a bit of a pie-in-the-sky dreamer when I saw him walking around with a book of poetry in the language of the local greats.

Surely he can't read that? Hmph. Show-off!

The details of what happened next are a little hazy. But we don't always know the major junctions at which our lives will change. I must have been casually getting to know Cody and the work they did all the way out there in the Halabja office. Knowing Cody the way I do today, I can guess that he probably gave me some impassioned sermon about rehabilitating people still suffering from Saddam's chemical bombardment in 1988.

Saddam's chemical bombardment of Halabja in 1988? My mind trailed off as Cody talked. I could not recall that I had ever heard anything about it. It is only now in retrospect that I can understand how ignorant and offensive that is to my Kurdish friends. At the time, however, it simply wasn't on my radar. Unlike many of my colleagues (including my wife, who studied the events in graduate school), it was not a factor that compelled me to feel compassion for the Kurds, nor did it cause me to move to Iraq in hopes of making a difference. I vaguely remember Jessica's late-night retellings of Saddam's atrocities as she would read her books or verbally process the mind-blowing lecture of the day by Dr. Marc Ellis at Baylor University. But the gassing of Halabja never got under my skin—never seeped into my soul—the way it did for others. I was busy studying theology at the time.

Then Cody mentioned something about trying to help children with heart defects. He had my full attention.

I told him the story of my encounter with the little girl in the hotel lobby, and Cody began to connect me with others on his team who had a little more experience helping kids with broken hearts. He snowed me under with a lot of things that I didn't understand—something about collecting medical files from across the region and sending them out to doctors in Jordan for evaluation. He mentioned a desk in their office that was piled up—his hand went above his eyes like an elevator—with reports from hundreds of children who were waiting in line for lifesaving heart surgery.

Waiting in line . . . I've never had to wait in line for much of anything. I've waited in a waiting room before. But I had an array of *Highlights* magazines and a comfy-enough chair to sit in at least. I've waited on hold with the credit card company while I flipped through an array of television stations. I've waited for food at fancy restaurants—but I always had a reservation for the table itself before my wife and I even arrived. There were a number of times in Austin, Texas—the Live Music Capital of the World—when I waited in line for a concert, but I already had my tickets in hand. My entrance was guaranteed. I've never truly waited in line the way these mothers and fathers did.

At that time, there were few diagnostic tools available in Iraq. Most cardiologists and pediatricians in the country—particularly in the Halabja region, where Cody worked—were diagnosing heart defects blindly with a stethoscope while the rest of the developed world was using ultrasounds, magnetic resonance imaging (MRI), computerized tomography (CT) scans, and catheterizations. There are a few phenomenal doctors out there who can perceive anatomical malformations by placing an ear on a child's chest, but there is nothing like a qualified doctor really *seeing* a problem when it comes time to solicit support to save your child's life.

Most doctors in Iraq never really knew what was wrong with their heart patients. In spite of the fact that there are scores of distinct heart defects and defect combinations, the vast majority of the population still says their child has a "hole in her heart"—a product of each doctor's inability to truly see and understand what was going on inside a child's body after decades of sanctions, war, and mass exodus among the country's most knowledgeable medical experts. Like any father or mother looking out for the interest of their family, a huge number of Iraq's medical elite escaped Iraq as soon as they saw the writing on the wall—in the late 1970s as Saddam Hussein ascended in power and became more caustic toward Iran, in the late 1980s as Saddam bankrupted the country and ultimately invaded Kuwait, and throughout the sanctions era as children starved to death and the UN pursued its doctrine of "containment" to its most extreme ends. Many of those doctors who *could* escape did. Of those who stayed, many were assassinated in the sectarian divide that opened upon the fall of Saddam.

When a child's medical report landed on the pile on the corner desk in Cody's office, the vast majority of them simply said "needs surgery"— hardly a viable medical diagnosis upon which to base the triage of children.

So as these parents waited in line, they were not merely waiting for lifesaving surgery. They were actually waiting for a proper diagnosis, living each day with a child who couldn't walk to school or whose skin was blackish-blue from a lack of oxygen. Obtaining a proper diagnosis was a bit like playing Russian roulette, a one-in-six chance that a child would be severe enough to catch someone's attention and rise to the top of the waiting list. Of course, if they were "lucky" enough to actually have a heart defect that demanded immediate attention, it often meant the child was very sick and very risky. I would soon learn that these were exactly the kind of children that aid offices like Cody's and the charitable hospitals with whom they worked were most unlikely to accept.

Paradoxically, the kinds of children that the hospitals and aid groups often prefer to help are the children who are sometimes least likely to find their way to a doctor's office in the first place. They are the ones who have ticking time bombs in their chests that absolutely must be repaired, but they lack the blackish-blue skin and lips, the deformed finger- and toenails, or the obvious exhaustion and breathing problems that result from certain defects. When war, terrorism, and underdevelopment create an impediment to routine checkups and proper diagnoses, these preferred children are the very ones who never make it onto the list at all.

I remember the day I visited Cody's office and saw the pile of reports. It was an overwhelming sight. I gave my manila envelope to Cody's friend as he explained a little more about how they had to wait on the once-a-week commercial flight into and out of our city to send a stack of files to a partner organization in Jordan. There was no FedEx or DHL. In Jordan, doctors would peruse the files and select those who seemed likely to fit their final selection criteria. If there were hundreds of cases for consideration, a group of twenty would be selected to come to Jordan for a real diagnostic evaluation. It wasn't clear to me who paid for the travel or how long it took to organize a massive trip to Jordan at a time when Jordan was claiming millions of refugees from the Iraq War. Who handled the visa applications? Who guaranteed the patients' return to Iraq?

In any case, upon arrival in Jordan, a portion of the twenty would be found to be too risky. A few might actually be given a clean bill of health—maybe there was a misdiagnosis or a self-correction of one of the more minor defects. Those who were determined to need surgery would receive their official diagnosis and be told that the organization would try to help provide surgery for them within the coming year.

Depending on available funding, a few were taken immediately to surgery and the rest of the group returned to Iraq to sit and contemplate their lot. By my later estimations, almost all of them returned to wait in line again, regardless of what the doctors in Jordan said. If their child was too risky, then they had to keep searching for solutions elsewhere. But we also learned that a "clean bill of health" was an incredibly difficult thing to accept once you've resigned yourself to the idea that your child is living on the brink of death.

What if the doctors in Jordan were wrong? Is this Jordanian subterfuge because I'm Iraqi? Arab subterfuge because I'm Kurdish? My child is probably still sick—I should never give up until I find someone willing to give my child the surgery I know he needs.

Even those who were selected for surgery would often doubt the intentions of the organization or would play the field to see if there was any way to expedite the surgery through another avenue.

Why take any risks after all that we've seen in the last few decades?

I looked at the towering stacks of files on the desk. They reminded me of the collapsing Twin Towers on September 11, one of the driving forces that had helped land me in Iraq in the first place. It was hard to imagine someone getting on a commercial flight with a bag full of files. At once it seemed innovative and harkened back to images of the Pony Express. But what would become of those who were literally lost in the shuffle? I think I remember seeing an envelope that had inadvertently fallen under a nearby table. Was it full of receipts from last week's team retreat? Or was there a paper inside with a photo of a blue baby stapled to it that said, "Needs surgery"? He probably wouldn't have been offended if I asked. But what did I know about saving lives?

Firefighters, surgeons, sure . . . but people who push paper around?

CHAPTER 2

The Sky Rained Death

I really wish I could tell you the name of the father and his daughter whom I met that day in the hotel lobby. I know it would help you relate to her and her family's situation a lot better and make my claim that this encounter forever changed my life much more believable. I wish I could tell you the name of their cousin who approached me in the café and asked for my help. (I'm pretty sure it began with a *B*.) But the truth is, this was real life, and nothing was scripted. I'm embarrassed that I can't name them or place them in a crowd. But I wasn't a social worker, and I missed some obvious things, like making photocopies of their files before they disappeared in a black duffel bag on the Iraqi Pony Express out of the country. I did not understand the impact the encounter would have on me.

Here is what I do know: they were a Kurdish family from the area around Halabja—the Kurdish city near Iran about which I knew so little. The mere mention of Halabja evokes all manner of Kurdish nationalism, pride, and—at its worst—anti-Arab sentiments. Halabja is mostly unknown (except for the few times American presidents have cynically cited it to justify military actions).

This is the version of the story you can find in almost any Kurdish tea shop: On March 16, 1988, Saddam Hussein's military dropped chemical weapons on the seventy thousand residents of Halabja. Five thousand people died instantly. Another twenty thousand people were seriously injured and directly exposed to the chemical weapons. Kurds still see rates of birth defects and cancers that rival that of Hiroshima.

The real story is even more troubling.

Nasreen and her younger sister, Rangeen, were doing their best to maintain an atmosphere of hospitality as they stepped outside to prepare food for their thirty or forty relatives the day the sky rained death. Why should the family's honor be a casualty of war along with everyone else?

Nasreen noticed the first helicopter around ten thirty that morning, but it was not attacking. The men inside were just taking pictures.

Nasreen had been only sixteen years old when her father had given her in marriage to her thirty-year-old cousin Bakhtiar, a local physician's assistant, just a few months prior. It was nearing the end of the Iran-Iraq War as her large family holed up in the cellar beneath the house. Most of the city's seventy thousand other residents were similarly waiting for an Iraqi counterattack as punishment for Kurdish collusion with the Iranian Revolutionary Guard against Saddam Hussein in Baghdad. In the days leading up to March 16, Iraqi soldiers had experienced a serious defeat outside of Halabja. More than a thousand troops—including their officers—were captured by the Iranians. They were forced to retreat.

Of all the ground Iraq could have lost in the war, Lake Darbandikhan outside of Halabja had to be among the most strategic. If it was captured, Baghdad would lose a significant portion of its water supply, plus all the electricity generated by the lake. On March 15, as Iranian troops shouted, "God is great! Khomeini is our leader!" through the streets of Halabja,[1] Baghdad punted on the option of sending in troop reinforcements. They had "an entirely different strategy in mind."[2]

Nasreen made lunch in fear. The helicopter surveilling her neighborhood did little to ease her mind.

The bombardment started around eleven that morning. Nasreen and Rangeen rushed to join the others in the cellar. For three hours they holed up in the dark underneath the house, supposing it to be the safest place to avoid the explosions and shrapnel.

The human mind can tend to so many things at once—how many more things is a young woman charged with when caring for her family? Nasreen's new husband, Bakhtiar, was outside the city, so she prayed God would keep him safe and reunite them soon. And how many times did she think of her food burning outside during the raid? It's exactly the kind of thing Jessica would obsess over, even as the bombs were falling.

When the attack let up in the early afternoon, Nasreen emerged from beneath the house to get the food.

What's that strange smell? she wondered. It was terrible, like garbage. And then sweet, like apples. Her friends would later tell journalists that the sky smelled like garlic or eggs. To this day, residents of Halabja are known to have an aversion to smells that remind them of the day the sky rained death.

"At the end of the bombing," she said, "the sound changed. It wasn't so loud. It was like pieces of metal just dropping without exploding. We didn't know why it was so quiet."

We now know that the shells contained chemical agents that dispersed upon impact—Baghdad's response to the Iranian "liberation of Halabja."

Everywhere she looked, Nasreen saw traces of this new, silent killer. "It was very quiet, but the animals were dying." She looked in on the partridge that her dad kept in the house. Inside the cage, the bird was dying, lying on its side. The sheep and goats were dying. She went back to the cellar to sound the alarm.

"Something is wrong with the air!"

Her family began to panic. Without knowing what awaited them outside, they were not eager to leave the shelter. But it was becoming increasingly clear that they were getting sick. Nasreen felt a stabbing pain in her eyes. Children began vomiting. Then the old people started throwing up. Shelters became gas chambers as Saddam's poison gas, heavier than the air, clung to the ground and seeped into cellars across the city.

When liquid began coming out of people's eyes, Nasreen's uncle said it was time to leave the cellar. They decided to run.

When Nasreen emerged the second time from the cellar—this time with a few relatives—she saw their cow lying on its side and breathing heavily. Had it been running away from the gas? Or was it simply suffocating? The Kurdish celebration of spring and new life was just around the corner, but now the leaves were falling off the trees. Chemical clouds clung to the ground, searching out the water wells, infecting every living thing in sight.

They headed upwind in an effort to escape the effects of this unknown killer. The children were too exhausted to walk after relentless vomiting episodes. Family members took turns carrying the children as long as they could, even as they grew thirsty, and the ooze from their eyes and the clouds on the ground forced them to wash their faces. But was the water safe? The white powder that now appeared on the ground gave them pause, but some drank anyway.

Nasreen and her family ran toward Anab—one of the recently created concentration communities—an abysmal place of relocation to which the Iraqi Army forced the Kurds after destroying the surrounding villages. On the way, people began showing different symptoms. One person's skin started bubbling after she touched some of the white powder. Meanwhile, overhead, the bombing continued as they fled.

Hope of salvation came when a neighbor pulled up in a truck and allowed Nasreen and her family to climb in the back. But as they drove, they began to see horror greater than the sickness of the birds, cows, and trees.

"We saw people lying frozen on the ground. There was a small baby on the ground, away from her mother. I thought they were both sleeping. But she had dropped the baby and then died. And I think the baby tried to crawl away, but it died, too. It looked like everyone was sleeping."[3]

Then, as surely as hope had appeared, it vanished like a chemical cloud. The truck driver eased to the side of the road and totally abandoned the truck, Nasreen and her family, and even his own wife.

"Flee if you can!" he said.

What were these chemicals capable of? Why would someone abandon his family?

So Nasreen and the children were back on foot.

Did Bakhtiar survive the attack? she wondered. But survival itself was a moving target if the chemicals in the air and on the ground could cause parents to abandon their children and husbands their wives.

Do I want to survive under these conditions? Do I want to reunite with a husband whose mind might be so far gone that he would abandon me and walk away?

The long trek to Anab was chaotic. Parents were forced to make utilitarian decisions about which children to save and which children to leave behind. All around, people were dying. How does a parent cope with such a reality?

People became hysterical with fear whenever their child would dawdle or refuse to walk any farther. Ultimately, many children were abandoned, and the elderly as well. Other children ran for the hills, screaming and crying, "We can't see! My eyes are bleeding!" They were going blind.

Tragically, the mass exodus from Halabja to Anab caused Nasreen to become separated from her mother and father. At sixteen, married but alone, Nasreen became responsible for leading her cousins and siblings through one of the most horrific atrocities in the history of the world.

Then, under the mind-altering effects of the poison gas, she inadvertently circled around and led her group back into Halabja's gas chambers. When a stranger found Nasreen they were led out of the city again to a small mosque set upon a hill. For a moment they were sheltered, exhausted and hungry. With air raids still under way, they wondered if the mosque might be a target and later moved to a nearby house.

People would later describe the scene as "life frozen . . . like watching a film and suddenly it hangs on one frame. It was a new kind of death. . . . You went into . . . a kitchen and you saw the body of a woman holding a knife where she had been cutting a carrot."[4]

By this point it was evening, and everyone was getting hungry.

Meanwhile, Bakhtiar desperately searched the city and the road to Anab for his wife. But he wasn't searching to be reunited. He assumed she was already dead like so many others; he just wanted to find her so he could give her a proper burial. Bakhtiar seems to have survived as he reentered the city by calling upon the knowledge he had gained as a physician's assistant and giving himself an injection of atropine after scouring the remains of a local health clinic. Atropine is a drug often given as an antidote for the symptoms that Nasreen and Bakhtiar were seeing all around them, including vomiting, watery and oozing eyes, difficulty breathing, and heart irregularities. He brought an extra syringe along with him as he went about the city looking to bury his new wife.

How long would you look for your spouse's body among throngs of others? How long would you last before you decided it was a lost cause? And what kind of plan works best? Do you save time—cover more ground—by looking for clothes and head scarves that look familiar? Or do you actually bend down and brush the hair back from the face of every young woman lying dead in the street? Is it haram to remove the head covering of another man's daughter or wife in search of your own?

I sometimes lie awake at night and wonder how many bodies I could flip over before going insane. How long would I search for Jessica? Emma? Micah? Would I devote the same time and passion to each search? At what point would I join the truck driver and simply walk away from those I love the most? Those questions haunt me . . . but they are just questions for me. For my Kurdish friends from Halabja, however, this was reality.

Bakhtiar never gave up. After untold hours of failure to locate Nasreen's body, someone said they had seen her and some kids headed for the mosque on the hill.

"Nasreeeeeeeeen!" he called. He headed up the hill.

When he drew near, he heard crying inside the house near the mosque. To his great relief, he found Nasreen alive, but all was not well.

Nasreen had gone blind while searching for food and drink for the group. She had found a container of milk and inched her way back to the children, feeling along the walls and the ground as she went. As everyone else was also apparently blind by that point, she groped for their faces, letting her fingers find the softness of their lips, and gave them drink.

Bakhtiar tried to wash the poison off the children at the nearby well. Given the house's distance from Halabja and its elevation, the water was probably not polluted like the wells the family had used earlier. But still the task proved extremely difficult. Not only were they blind—requiring Bakhtiar to lead or even carry them in his own arms to the well—but the poison had reached their nervous systems and was destroying their motor skills.

To make matters worse, one of Bakhtiar's neighbors—a woman named Asme who holed up in the mosque with the others—was yelling and smashing her head into the wall, unable to breathe. The poison had completely overtaken her. Bakhtiar remembered his last syringe of atropine. In a moment of amazing selflessness, he injected Asme with the only antidote that could save her life.

But it was too late. Asme passed away shortly after receiving the injection.

"I should have used it for Nasreen," Bakhtiar chided himself, wondering if he had made the right choice, knowing his own wife would not receive another chance.

But help was on the way. Iranian troops reentered the city and began administering aid to those caught in the bombardment. Thousands were buried while survivors were evacuated for treatment in Iran. By God's providence, Nasreen and other members of her family were found and transported for treatment to a hospital in Tehran.

"Where are my mom and dad?" she asked Bakhtiar. He had his suspicions, but he genuinely did not know the truth. He stalled, avoided the question, and ultimately changed the subject every time it came up.

Nasreen was blind for twenty days. When she regained her sight, she began combing through books of photographs of the dead from Halabja that were compiled by the Iranian Red Crescent Society. One day, Nasreen found her mother's photo. She eventually learned that her father was alive, but he was permanently blind. Her sister Rangeen and four other brothers and sisters were dead.

Her physical recovery in Iran was an emotional affair. She was grateful to be alive yet deeply mourning the loss of her mother, five siblings, and countless family and friends. And then her health took a serious turn for the worse. Nasreen began menstruating profusely. She tried to hide it, as did many of the other female victims in the hospital who were experiencing similar symptoms. Although she was among medical professionals, her conservative culture made talking about such things feel like an impossibility.

"I cannot stop bleeding," one woman finally confessed. This emboldened another to confide, and then another. Eventually Nasreen joined the throng of women who received drugs to stop the bleeding. But bringing the subject to light had only opened Pandora's box. Doctors told her that her womb was barren and she would never have children.

Nasreen was devastated. What sixteen-year-old, young married woman who has just lost her mother and five brothers and sisters can stomach the promise of her own infertility? She would never be able to bring laughter into the world to replace all the sadness. Her daddy— who had just lost so much—would be so disappointed. And what of Bakhtiar? Every Kurdish man dreams of having a son to whom he can give his name.

Here she had survived one of the world's worst acts of chemical warfare—the "Chemical Rain"—but what was she supposed to be looking forward to?

My Kurdish friends have confided that the horror of these attacks ultimately meant Iraqi fighter planes could have dropped something as harmless as sugar or mere "air" on the population, and they would have gone mad for fear of suffering the same fate their brothers, sisters, and cousins did in Halabja. It is a widely held notion that Saddam's chemical attacks—including the less famous ones at Penjwin and Haj Umran that preceded Halabja—were mostly about creating unfathomable terror in revolutionary Kurds and the Iranian military with whom Iraq was officially at war. The fear alone would accomplish more than the casualties.

Iran reached its limit by summer 1988. The international community—including France, Germany, Italy, and the USA—had so thoroughly rallied behind Saddam Hussein, there was little chance for Iranian success. On July 20 Iran accepted the United Nations' cease-fire resolution.

Amidst the chaos of continued Iraqi reprisals against the Kurds, Nasreen and Bakhtiar returned home to Kurdistan in Iraq. The year would continue with Saddam Hussein perpetrating further chemical attacks around Bahdinan on August 25 and four days later in the Bazi Gorge, where nearly three thousand were gassed, killed, and ultimately burned. Seventy-seven villages were gassed in this August campaign alone.[5] This went on until October.[6]

While Nasreen and so many of her friends and family suffered these horrific gassings, the international response was a deafening silence. It was this deafening silence—and the reasons behind it—that captured my attention and propelled me fully into the way of preemptive love.[7]

I was eleven years old when I first met the Kurds of Iraq, sitting on my living room floor in Austin, Texas. (I was the one sitting on the floor; the Kurds themselves were on TV, variously featured on *NBC Nightly News* with Tom Brokaw or *ABC World News Tonight* with Peter Jennings.) The Kurds versus the notorious Saddam Hussein is probably the earliest, most entrenched memory I have of good versus evil. The innocent Kurds with their AK-47s hiding in the mountains against evil Saddam and his one-million-man military.

This was 1991, and the Iranian threat had been sufficiently quashed after eight years of war. Moreover, Saddam Hussein had just invaded

Kuwait, and the war drums were beating loudly. As a young boy, I remember being enthralled by green night-vision images of Scud missiles obliterating Iraqi targets. There was not a lot of room in our Reagan Republican community for discussion of our own complicity in years of material support for Saddam Hussein's regime in Baghdad, including furnishing him with chemical and biological agents. To this day I find it incredibly ironic that Kurds so hailed U.S. intervention in Iraq in 2003 when it was the U.S. who had backed Saddam Hussein throughout the Iran-Iraq War, turning a blind eye to his chemical attacks against Iranian troops inside Iraq and ultimately against tens of thousands of Kurds across the country.

But history is littered with inconvenient atrocities. Why should 1988 be dragged again into the present day? It sounds like a question I would ask Jessica repeatedly throughout our latter years of college as she pursued her degree in history. She quickly memorized the maxims that all history buffs trot out for ignoramuses like me. For me it comes back to Nasreen.

Two years after the attack on Halabja—indeed, two years after doctors in Tehran told her that she was barren and would never have children—she gave birth to a boy named Arazoo (Kurdish for "hope"). Against all the odds—having survived all the pain and loss—Bakhtiar and Nasreen enjoyed the bliss of parenthood. Nasreen was only eighteen years old, but life had seasoned her and matured her beyond imagination. Arazoo was healthy, and days passed with all the usual infant fanfare: first eye contact, first smile, late-night nursing, obsessing over sneezes and coughs. Two years on, and the people of Halabja were bringing forth new life again. The city was being rebuilt—dubbed "New Halabja." Still, this was not how things were supposed to be. Nasreen had always dreamed of raising her kids with her mom at her side. Instead, she was blind again, groping her way through all these new experiences without a guide.

And then the unthinkable happened.

Hope died. Arazoo was born with a hole in his heart that choked his body of much-needed oxygen. He was just three months old when he was buried in the poisoned soil that had already claimed the lives of so many family members before him.

Nasreen, Bakhtiar, and Arazoo grab me and demand my focus, because there are thousands more like them. The Halabja attacks are commonly held to have claimed five thousand lives on March 16, 1988. Another twenty thousand in the city are alleged to have been exposed on the day of the Chemical Rain. As thousands of families continued to suffer aftereffects of the poison gas, as babies were spontaneously aborted or delivered prematurely, and as countless children were diagnosed with heart and other birth defects, it became increasingly clear that the death toll from Saddam's chemical warfare could not be strictly limited to the 1980s. Across the border, Iranian soldiers were experiencing the same realities.

When this news reached geneticist Dr. Christine Gosden, she traveled to the area to conduct research on the soil and the symptoms among the still-living population. Even by the time she arrived in 1998—ten years after the bulk of the attacks—her work revealed the presence of mustard gas and the nerve agents sarin, tabun, and VX.[8] She said:

> What I found was far worse than anything I had suspected . . . I compared the frequency of these conditions such as infertility, congenital malformations, and cancers . . . in those who were in Halabja at the time with an unexposed population from a city in the same region. We found the frequencies in Halabja are at least three to four times greater, even ten years after the attack . . .
>
> I found that there was also a total lack of access to pediatric surgery to repair the major heart defects . . . This meant that children in Halabja are dying of heart failure when children with the same heart defects could have had surgery and would probably have survived in Britain or the United States.[9]

In 1993, the human rights group Middle East Watch said, "Only when those responsible . . . are brought to justice will the work end."[10] Saddam and "Chemical" Ali are now dead. But Christine Gosden, Arazoo, and the girl in the hotel lobby each stand to remind us that the work is far from over—and justice is far from accomplished—as long as there is a total lack of access to pediatric surgery and children are dying while *waiting in line* in Iraq when they would have probably survived elsewhere.

This is why Jessica, Cody, and Michelle—a single girl living in our house who would one day become Cody's wife—and I started the Preemptive Love Coalition.

CHAPTER 3

The Iranian Bard and His Beautiful Shoes

Our new friend Ebo (pronounced Ee-bow) was a well-to-do Iranian living and working in Iraq. He was passionate about German engineering (he drove a BMW and dealt in high-end audio equipment with names like Neumann and Schoeps), wore Italian jeans, and smoked petite Bahmans from the state-owned Iranian tobacco company.

He was a renaissance man.

But the skeptics in our orbit just couldn't accept him at face value.

"What better cover for an Iranian spy?" they said.

I can hardly blame them for their fears. The United States had just raided the Iranian proto-consulate in Erbil in an effort to detain two senior Iranian functionaries. The news in America was rife with stories of Iran's material support for attacks on American troops. Pundits and prophets were crying foul over a botched war in Iraq as the country spiraled further into an intractable civil war between Sunnis and Shias. And there was much ado about the porous border region through which foreign fighters were coming (and escaping) and the high-dollar investments Iran was making to install deep-cover intelligence officers in cities like Baghdad and Najaf, and across Iraq. Though many claimed

President George W. Bush was on a campaign against Islam, by many accounts, the war on Iraq had actually done nothing short of strengthening our greatest enemy in the region: the Islamic Republic of Iran.

Within days of my meeting Ebo, the Iranian government captured fifteen British sailors and marines operating under the mandate of the United Nations in the Persian Gulf and treated them as enemy combatants. Some time later, eyewitnesses saw three Americans who were hiking through the mountains near Halabja—in Iraq—arrested illegally by Iranian police who crossed the Iraq-Iran border. The two guys in the group were held captive and subjected to kangaroo court proceedings in Iran for over two years. Official state-sponsored neurosis was on the rise in Iran.

Was my new friend Ebo *really* the businessman he claimed to be? My Iraqi neighbors and friends have always believed me to be CIA. Could I accept Ebo at face value, or should I hedge my bets like so many of my friends and cautiously hold him at arm's length in case he was some kind of Iranian spook plotting to kidnap me and my family when the time was right? These were the explicit questions—and implicit fears— friends and family expressed as I began to learn for the first time what Jesus meant when he said, "Love your enemies."

I didn't know it at the time, but in just five years, my new friend Ebo would be a headline-making icon of terrorism across Iraq and Iran in a way no one ever would have guessed. But that's a story for another time. For now, I just knew I was learning more clearly how to choose love first.

"Come on, man!" he said.

I set my tulip-shaped tea glass in its decorative saucer and stood to leave.

"Why don't you just start a church here?" he said.

I sat back down. "Why would you say that?" I asked. "Aren't you a Muslim?"

Ebo chuckled as he let off some expletives about Islam and the cursed revolution back at home in Iran, and urged me again to create a counterweight to "fascist Islam's" growing influence in Iraq before it was too late by opening a church.

As a Zionist Reagan Republican born in 1979—the year of the Islamic Revolution in Iran that overthrew the despotic Pahlavi dynasty— I knew everything I needed to know about Iran and its people. They were, of course, mostly lunatic Muslims who were all hell-bent on acquiring nuclear weapons in order to wipe Israel off the map and spread their uniquely apocalyptic brand of Shia Muslim terror. Shortly before I moved to Iraq, Iran was enrolled in the Axis of Evil, a grown-up version of a similar "members only" club I founded in grade school for all my classmates with whom I refused to speak. Like all my enemies (homosexuals, pro-choicers, Muslims, and anyone who wore blue during election season), Iranians were a faceless people summed up by the dour expressions of their supreme leader, Ayatollah Khomeini.

Though Saddam's chemical attacks against Iran caused loss of life for decades, I was not taught to consider, let alone sympathize with, the plight of the people of Iran. And then I met Ebo, with his love of cinema, his utter disdain for all things Islam, and his urgent desire that I become the first founding friar of a post-Saddam Christian church in Iraq. He was totally different from our well-guarded stereotypes. And so, in spite of the warnings from wise and well-intentioned friends, I threw caution to the wind and befriended my first "enemy."

Ebo's father was a well-to-do television producer in Tehran in the golden era before the Iranian Revolution. Ebo grew up in the educated upper class, metropolitan, open-minded. Among other shows, his father produced Iranian bandstand television, hobnobbing with the best of Iran's musical superstars. For Ebo's dad and his rock-star friends, the day Ayatollah Khomeini came to power in 1979 was the day the music died. Khomeini knew what many dictatorial leaders seem to know and what many of us in the comfortable middle class seem to forget: a song can start a riot. He shut down the television shows and radio programs that featured pop, folk, protest, and other styles of music. In this way, Ebo's contempt for Islam was very personal; he considered it a cancer occupying the space where deep pride in his father's profession and status in life had once reigned.

I guess it's not surprising then that one of the most course-altering nights of my life came with Ebo, doing what his dad taught him to do in thumbing his nose at the Islamic Revolution by tracking an Iranian folk band through the mountains of dissident "Kurdistan" in search of a song.

Spring was emerging from the coffin of winter when Ebo called me to join up with the caravan of a musical troupe from Tehran fronted by one of Ebo's good friends.

"Oh, and bring your guitar!" he said as we hung up.

Before I lost all my hair (which is another Ebo story altogether), I was something of a bard myself, traveling across the plains of West Texas to the Hill Country in search of anyone who would listen to my songs and join me in a sing-along. My entire childhood is tattooed with indelible memories of my nono preaching in various churches across Texas and the United States with my dad at his side leading the congregation in song. Music filled our home in some of the most beautiful ways imaginable growing up. But where my dad hymned his praise directly to God and led others to join in, my songs were often cautionary tales, populated parables. Less angelic, more "voice in the wilderness."

It must have been midnight when Ebo and I met up with the band in the hotel lobby that cold spring night. Spread across the foyer was an entourage of singers, percussionists, woodwind players, and stringed instrumentalists. I took special note of the double-bellied *tar*—the steel-stringed Persian grandfather of the Martin dreadnought in my hand. The *tar* represented ancient knowledge and ingenuity, with three sets of strings set at octave intervals strung over two sound holes that were carefully covered with a thin animal hide to enhance the resonance of the otherwise small-bodied instrument. The *tar* has often been the protest instrument of choice throughout a number of Persian dynasties for its ability to inspire angst on a quiet scale, being much more portable and subtler than the Persian *qanun*.

After some formalities and introductions, the hotel lobby transformed and evoked the bandstand party days of Ebo's youth as conversation gave way to chorus. Clearly this was not the first time the band had moved in and occupied a city for the night. They had no compunction about overrunning the hotel's lobby, and those gathered around certainly didn't seem to mind. The first few songs were odes to long-gone days when they had the freedom to worship Ahura Mazda and the freedom to be proudly Kurdish or Azeri without fear of public hanging or brutal disappearance. Many of the songs ultimately proclaimed the greatness of an alternate kingdom, a nation greater than the Islamic Republic of Iran. They were Kurds singing about a fantasy place called Kurdistan, where cousins from all over the world would gather under a single flag for the first time in ages.

Their vision had so much color: the yellow hues of twenty-one sunbeams to light the way, the green of the Alborz mountains, the red of martyrs' blood, and the white of righteous relationships. Imagining the boldness of throwing off tyrannical shackles and declaring the supremacy of a different leader challenged me to reconsider my own assumptions and allegiances. Could Jessica and I have a life that was larger than our nationalistic rhetoric? Could we learn to love the ones we were supposed to hate? Was there even a kingdom on earth where people were truly welcomed—not just for citizenship, but for the fullest possible participation and blessing, without regard to ethnicity, gender, or past history? If a place like that existed, I knew that was where I belonged.

The singing stopped. Everyone was looking at me expectantly. The *tar* player repeated his question, "Will you play us a song?" Lost in thought as I was, thinking about this far country; contemplating the way my Iranian, Iraqi, Syrian, and Turkish Kurdish friends had been subjected to unspeakable forms of torture; considering the Iraqi Arabs filling the lobby and how many of them barely escaped daily suicide bombings, targeted killings, and ethnic purging, I grabbed my guitar and began an old Southern standard:

> *Through many dangers, toils, and snares*
> *I have already come*
> *His grace has brought us safe thus far*
> *And grace will lead me home*

I vamped for a few seconds and tried to gauge the room before picking up the pace and singing another verse. The *tar* virtuoso began improvising a jangly melody over the mahogany rhythm of my folk guitar. A mustached guy in the corner picked up an enormous tambourine and pounded the leather face of it like his life depended on it. Half the band began clapping in the syncopated rhythms of a Sadat-era Egyptian TV drama.

> *When we've been there ten thousand years*
> *Bright shining like the sun*

Black-haired ladies in sequined robes joined in on cue. They didn't understand the words I was singing or the parallels between their idyllic homeland and mine. They were angelic nonetheless.

If the best art does indeed come from pain, confusion, fear, or despair, it seemed those of us gathered in this hotel lobby from across Iraq and Iran who had been primed to hate and fear one another were in the ideal position to create something that renewed hope, restored visions of relationships remade, and instilled the boldness to rail against the prevailing authorities that demanded our allegiance. In that moment, right as I was about to fulfill Ebo's earlier request to start a church with a revivalist altar call that would have made my nono proud, the *tar*ist swung his feet around the arm of the couch, and I noticed the most unique pair of handmade designer shoes I'd ever seen.

We drew the music to a close with rousing laughter and applause. It was an amazing moment! As our conversation resumed, I had to ask, "Where did you get those shoes?"

I expected to hear of an uppity European designer whose name I could barely pronounce. Instead, I was met with stares of indignation from around the room.

"Are you serious? How do you not know about *our* shoes? These are Kurdish shoes. We make them ourselves! They are called *klash*."

I'll be honest: having lived and traveled across the Middle East with Turks, Arabs, Kurds, and Persians for nearly a decade, there are very few things for which domestic production inspires in me a lot of confidence. While individual families often prove to be very adept at innovating for their specific needs, scaling and standardizing this innovation into a successful mass-production business has often been better achieved by counterparts in China, Korea, and Japan. But modern Chinese manufacturing had nothing on these shoes!

"We will take you to the bazaar tomorrow and get you a pair!" Ebo said.

I don't want to mislead you. Our journey to love first and ask questions later—to save lives behind enemy lines—did not only begin with that cute, desperate little girl and her father in the hotel lobby. It didn't begin with the towers of backlogged children in Cody Fisher's office; it was not entirely altruistic. In many ways, it started with a late-night jam session and my outsized interest in a one-of-a-kind pair of gleaming white, hand-stitched shoes.

Ebo picked me up the next day, and we visited a distant cousin of one of the band members—a cobbler—in the deep recesses of the bazaar's Soap Makers' Quarter. White yarn was strewn across the cement floor. Bricks of bubble-gum-sized red and blue cotton fabric were stacked knee-high randomly throughout the shop. I nearly tripped over a box of wooden blocks. Some of them were precariously crammed into pairs of these finished knit shoes, causing the flexible cloth sole to bend far beyond its natural shape into the downward grasp of an eagle's claw. This was retail and factory floor in one, all in a ten-foot-square corner shop. The walls were made out of PVC—barely enough to withstand a storm. A wooden tree stump was cemented into the floor, the ultimate chopping block, glassy smooth, as if shellacked, from years of beating by the handheld hammers that the cobbler used to pound his shoes into shape.

I heard the guys say "handmade" in the hotel the night before, but actually seeing handmade shoes come to life from scratch was, quite literally, a life-changing experience. In the courtyard of a house down the road a man used a sawed-off rusty oil barrel, his shepherd's crook, and various dyes to color large sheets of cotton just thicker than cheesecloth. In the corner shade of his quadrangle, he ripped the dried sheets into ribbons the width of yardsticks and cut them to length with a butcher knife. These bedsheets would soon form the impenetrable sole of the world's longest-running handmade shoe (first created six centuries before Christ by local accounts).

The shoemakers I met over my subsequent trips to the Soap Makers' Quarter—friends like Uncle Barzan, Sa'dun, Khalil, and Aram—each regaled me with the same stories of Italian designers and Chinese factory men who beheld the glory of the *klash* and wanted to know how to mass-produce it or improve upon it. The inevitable punch line of every telling—which it seems I've heard hundreds of times now over the years—was something like, "But no matter how hard the Italians tried, they could not improve it!" or "No matter how the Chinese tried, they could not mass-produce it!" We would all share a good belly laugh at the arrogance of the Western know-it-all or the naivety of the Asian cost-cutter. A new round of tea was poured for all to celebrate the icon of Kurdishness—the *klash*.

The Hawrami Kurds of Iraq and Iran stood guard over a three-thousand-year-old trade around which entire families would orient their lives. *Klash* making had traditionally been an in-house trade, with each nuclear family seeing the entire process to completion under one roof and selling the shoes from their front porch or shop in the bazaar. After the fall of the Ottoman Empire, contiguous "Kurdistan" was divided between what we know today as Armenia, Iran, Iraq, Syria, and Turkey. Kurdish groups in each new country have dealt with their minority status and nationalist aspirations in their own ways, but Kurds universally across the Middle East have experienced a great amount of persecution and suffering since the Treaty of Versailles was signed.

As many of my Kurdish friends took up arms to reclaim a Kurdish homeland from the soil of Iran and Iraq, they were met with fierce retribution from Saddam Hussein: the splintering of families, dispersed across the country, and ultimately hundreds of thousands of people going to sleep each night without a clue why their loved ones had suddenly disappeared. The fallout and suffering from this era had effects that reached far beyond the small Hawraman region and our *klash*-cobbling friends, but it forever contributed to a fundamental change in their way of life. With elderly fathers and mothers left at home as the boys went off to war, shoemaking as a major source of income could no longer live strictly in-house.

By the time I arrived on the scene, with my interest in buying a single pair of shoes to honor my rock-star friends, a nation with fifty thousand shoemakers in the Hawraman mountains had been reduced to just a tenth of that. Between the decades of revolutionary fighting, war with Iran, and modernization, fathers and sons no longer worked under the same roof caring strictly for the same nuclear family as they once did back in the village. My Hawrami friends talk of leaving their homes as Iranian soldiers entered through the mountains and took up residence in Kurdish villages inside Iraq to fight Saddam Hussein. The first of Saddam's chemical attacks that were known—even sponsored—by the United States were attacks on Iranian troops in Iraqi-Kurdish villages at Penjwin and Haj Umran. Like Nasreen and Bakhtiar after the day the sky rained death in 1988, many of the Hawrami Kurds still braving the war on the border finally retreated and settled in Sulaymaniyah or farther west.

While much of the world was becoming more Toyotacized and lean in its production methodologies, Kurdish shoemaking had become one of the world's most inefficient production lines, transferring works-in-progress on the backs of pack mules or in the trunks of beat-up, rusted-out, white-and-orange-striped taxis to far-flung cousins now hours away, where they added to the next stage in the shoes' development. After these men added their hours of work to a single pair of shoes—forming the skeleton of the cloth sole by threading hand-cut leather straight from the bull they had butchered for that day's lunch—they would pack up a couple hundred finished soles and send them downstream to another village, where their auntie or grandmother would begin knitting hand-spun yarn into the pliable upper of a shoe in between cleaning the house, making the day's meal, and keeping the household fueled with chai.

On and on the process went, passing through some four to six different hands, across as many villages, with each person in the family selling the unfinished product to the next cousin, having added value that only they could. By the time the shoes arrived in the store where I was sitting with Ebo, they had gone through forty hours of actual labor, not to mention the hours spent in transit and sitting idly between production stages. They were a work of beauty to hold in your hands and wear on your feet. For the Hawrami Kurds, they were so much more than shoes— they were a history book, a bulwark of family heritage, guardian of the Hawrami way of life. They staved off the worst parts of modernization and resisted the forces that cause so many traditional family networks to totally dissolve.

I had lived in the country for a few months by this point, but I had not seen the shoes until the *tar* player caught my eye the night before. Part of this was due to the fact that I arrived in winter and the cloth sole of the *klash* does not take kindly to winter rain. The other part had to do with the fact that I spent most of my time with men in their twenties, and they were far more likely to consider the shoe a relic of the past—an old man's shoe. But it was new to me. I gladly bought a pair, feeling as though I had been let in on a secret that no one else knew about.

It cannot often be said that a pair of shoes changed someone's life. It may be just Dorothy, Cinderella, and me. Immediately, upon walking out of that shop, I had an extra something in my step. Wherever I went, if Kurds were there, I was welcomed in with joy. Shopkeepers would point from across the street at my feet, yelling things like "Hey, American, you like Kurdish shoe?"

I was pulled into countless shops selling stationery, black-market electronics, and pirated DVDs as people would pour in to see the American wearing Kurdish *klash*. As far as making relationships, learning languages, and getting an on-the-ground understanding of culture in the Kurdish areas of Iraq, nothing got my foot in the door more than being a young American in an old man's shoe. You'd think I'd wrapped myself in the Kurdish flag, so great was the welcome I received when I met Kurds in my *klash*.

When I bought my first pair of *klash* I was warned against treating them like any other pair of shoes. It had the foreboding of a Grimm's fairy tale, as though something terrible would befall me and my family if I did not heed my shoemaker's caution. Unlike most shoes that men and women around the world wear, *klash* are not made with a right or a left foot. The leather strips woven between the cloth strips to form the skeleton of the sole are strung in such a way as to accommodate either the right foot or the left foot. When the aunties and grandmothers gather around their tea and televisions to knit the sparkling white upper portion of the shoe, they are careful to knit exact replicas, rather than the mirror images that would seem necessary to accommodate each foot's natural arch.

The goal in caring for your *klash,* then, is to keep them pointing straight ahead rather than allowing them to curve and conform to one side or the other. *Klash* should never be allowed to be strictly "left" or strictly "right," for that would run them into the ground and render them useless much more quickly than those shoes that spend an equal amount of time on each side.

We routinely encapsulate very important ideas with foot phrases like "the shoe's on the other foot," "digging your heels in," "walking a mile in another's shoes," and "putting your best foot forward." Whether he knew it or not, the shopkeeper had given me a shoe analogy I would never forget.

Before I met Ebo, I was shaped by a worldview that was decidedly one-sided. Opposing ideas were cast as oil and water. I was nurtured on Orientalism and the "clash of civilizations." When Jessica and I moved from small-town Texas to the Middle East and undertook raising our kids there, we began to experience for the first time how imaginary the distinctions between "East" and "West" actually are, how some of the world's most liberal activists are Muslims and its nastiest terrorists are sometimes Christians. Of course, there are a good number of imaginary ideas that shape the world and how we each behave in it. But all imaginary things can ultimately be reimagined. And that, for me, has become one of the great goals of my life—to call people forth into a new country that is neither East nor West, a far country come near to all the last-in-liners, where former enemies from the east and west, north and south, feast together.

While many friends around the globe were digging their trenches deeper where they already stood, my new pair of shoes was calling me to keep walking, and to do so in a way that refused to conform to the arbitrary sides we sometimes make up for our various sparring matches. Yes, I recognize that there are real political, theological, and philosophical differences that warrant serious debate. But I don't want to be easily summed up as a "left-leaning liberal" so that the far right can ignore me and brand me immoral. And I don't want to be summed up as a "right-leaning conservative" so that the far left can ignore me and brand me a religious nut.

Our souls, like Kurdish *klash,* require the discipline of spending time on both sides in order to not get warped, in order to stay straight.

I no longer accept the zero-sum worldview that says we cannot simultaneously be on the side of the Democrats and Republicans; Americans, Israelis, and Iranians; Jews and Palestinians; Sunnis and Shias, Arabs, Kurds, and Turks. I choose them all.

I don't lean left or right. I lean in. I lean forward, because that's where love lives.

CHAPTER 4

Buy Shoes. Save Lives.

While I was still working to help war widows, Jessica and I attended a conference at a famous retreat center for wealthy Arabs and the nation's political parties. One night, in between meetings, I struck up a conversation with a guy who still had sleep in his eyes and looked a little green. I was immediately struck by his passion. One of the first questions we all wanted to ask in those days was "How did you come to be in Iraq?" Although most of our stories boiled down to "I want to make a difference" or "I think God was telling me to go," many had taken very circuitous routes.

This guy recalled being in high school, sitting in the parking lot listening to the radio as the second plane hit the south tower of the World Trade Center on September 11, 2001. His emotions had been a blend of horror and hatred. Like many young men, he reached out to the military recruiters on campus, who saw record numbers of applications in the months following the attacks. He wanted a gun, and he wanted to take care of Islamo-fascism once and for all.

Unlike some of his friends, he did not immediately deploy to Afghanistan (or Iraq a few years later). He did not even end up enlisting. He focused for the next few years on finishing school, until an earthquake in Pakistan during the Muslim holy month of Ramadan caused him to see Muslims in a totally different light—this time, in the light of God's love and compassion. He watched the death toll reach seventy-five thousand and saw Pakistani Muslims entrusting themselves to God in the midst of such tragedy. As he heard one old man talk about staying faithful to his daytime fasting while moving rubble to look for bodies, he felt for the first time that he had more in common with Muslims than perhaps he had once understood. Where his nation's tragedy a few years prior had initially caused hatred and a bloodthirsty retribution, their nation's tragedy was now causing compassion. He began his second effort to enlist, this time motivated by a God-given desire to help Muslims, not a fear-driven desire to *get* them.

Now in Iraq in the middle of the war, this guy would soon become one of my best friends. That night of the jam session in the hotel lobby, I sensed the time had come to create something that renewed hope and offered a new life. The day Jessica and I met Cody Fisher was, in many ways, the most important piece of the puzzle.

Somewhere in between stories, Cody commented on my shoes.

"Where did you get those?"

"Are you serious?" I replied, trying to baptize him in my embarrassment over asking the same question a few months prior. "How do you not know about *these* shoes? These are Kurdish shoes. They make them themselves! They're called *klash*.

"I'll take you to the bazaar tomorrow and get you a pair!" I said.

Over the next few weeks Cody and I spent a lot of time together. We took our cameras to the Soap Makers' Quarter and bought him his own pair of *klash,* making us two of the easiest-to-talk-to Americans in the Kurdish cities. We made a short documentary on the *klash*-making process. And Cody began explaining to me more and more about his group's work in Halabja, the prevalence of children in need of lifesaving heart surgery, and the ways they were trying to interface with international surgery centers to send a few children per year to get the treatment they could not receive anywhere in Iraq.

Cody shared that his office wasn't doing anything to actually *fund* heart surgeries and that they were limited to helping send files to doctors abroad, serving as a frontline triage center, and playing a role in the logistics if a child was actually selected for treatment by the international centers.

Loving our new *klash* as we both did, we began scheming together.

"What if we sold these shoes to our friends back home and used the profit to actually pay for more children to get the surgeries they needed?"

I had just recently met the little girl and her father in the hotel lobby. Knocking around with her medical reports had led me back to Cody and his friends, who were focused on the issue. But, to be honest, their efforts seemed to lack the very thing that was most needed to save these lives. Not personnel, not passion, and not money. But vision. Toward what grand goal were we pursuing heart surgery for these children? Just to save one? It certainly had value, but it really wasn't enough for Jess and me.

Invoking a phrase that we often use with one another to keep our marriage on track, we simply looked at each other and said, "Too small!" Those two words have moved mountains for us throughout the course of our relationship. Whether praying about where we would live and what careers we would pursue or contemplating how to respond to suicide bombers in our office and fatwas calling for our death, "Too small!" challenges our protectionist impulses, which often serve to keep risk, failure, and danger at bay. We're convinced that almost all the good things God has to give us come somewhere beyond the edges of "Too small!," out where people lose their lives and become alive to a new way of seeing the world.

As Cody, Jessica, and I spent more time together contemplating the massive list of children in need of surgery, we began talking about what it would take to "eradicate the backlog." We never settled for saving just one. We never dabbled. Fueled by a conviction that tomorrow always has the possibility of being better than today, we were doggedly optimistic in the face of those who considered the continued downward spiral of Iraq a foregone conclusion.

My work in Iraq to that point had largely been centered on writing grant proposals—the supplicant process of asking rich, powerful entities like the Department of Defense, the United States Agency for International Development, or the Bill & Melinda Gates Foundation to consider the merit and impact of my project and invest in it financially. The grants awarded were often large enough to keep small, upstart organizations believing that just a single gift would make all the difference in the world for the impact of their work. But the time required to actually write a proposal took away valuable time from pursuing many other, surer types of funding. Moreover, the process was exceedingly opaque, and you rarely learned anything about yourself or your organization that could help you improve for the future from the inevitable denial letter. For me, grant writing was one of the worst jobs imaginable.

When it came to Cody, Jessica, and I dreaming about forging a new path that would do more than handle the requisite paperwork for these children, I knew immediately that I did not want the economic engine of our program to be beholden to grant writing and official aid money. There was certainly a lot of official U.S. government aid money in Iraq to go around.[1] But getting our hands on the money would have meant putting all our effort into a single channel and marrying our program to a few people whose bottom-line agenda was necessarily different from ours.

We decided to do the exact opposite. Rather than waiting on glacial governments to pick our needle proposal out of the haystack and fund our initiative, we wanted to flip the official aid model on its head and distribute the funding responsibility to thousands of consumers across the United States and, ultimately, the world.

To the bemusement of many, we didn't do any market research, and we didn't have a business plan. In our minds, a war was waging, and children from north to south were waiting in line for lifesaving heart surgeries.

How large is your niche market? Who are your competitors? What is your marketing plan? How many staff do you need to carry out this operation between America and Iraq? What is your break-even point, and how long would it be before you begin using your profits to actually send Iraqi children to lifesaving heart surgeries?

I don't mean to say that we did not care about these questions. We did. But we were developing this habit of loving first and asking questions later. Each day in Iraq we became better and better at loving our way into situations and commitments and letting the questions come to us once we were in a "no turning back now" posture of love.

People smarter than I have challenged our way of life and called us naive for thinking that the world won't eat us alive this way. The truth is, we've done the math on it, and staying alive is not what we call living. The experts may be right. Our preemptive-love mantra might be terrible foreign policy for the U.S. government and large corporations, but our story proves over and over again that "love first" is an amazing way to live as an individual and a community!

As young twentysomethings who had never held down professional jobs, we were still paying off school loans and did not have a lot of money to start our little shoe company. And we were living in *Iraq*—not America—so hopping from meeting to meeting to raise venture capital wasn't exactly an option either. Luckily, unlike many start-ups, our product was already in production. We did not require any overhead to launch our production facility, and the war headlines from Baghdad and Fallujah did a fair amount to bring the general theme of our cause into the homes of people across the world each and every day through television, newspapers, and various Internet sources.

I started a website, ahead of any official business filings, financial investments, hires, etc., as a way of testing the waters for our idea. Jessica and I had a few thousand dollars—our life savings at that time if I remember correctly—that we were willing to go all-in with, but we wanted to at least see a few people commit to the *klash* and these Iraqi kids we were growing to love before we purchased a container of handmade shoes and were left footing the bill alone. You've heard about people moving overseas and "going native." Maybe our sense of what was cool nowadays was woefully off.

We put photos of the shoes online under the banner "Buy Shoes. Save Lives" and each sent out a mass call to our friends and family, inviting them to go beyond the headlines of doom and gloom about Iraq. We promised them that they could actually make a difference in the lives of the children they were hearing about each day.

Within days our arbitrary goals were shattered, and we had enough money in the bank to go buy all the shoes we needed and more. Jess and I threw our life savings into the pot, Cody did the same, and Buy Shoes. Save Lives., a for-profit shoe company that would one day be folded into the Preemptive Love Coalition, was born!

In spite of all the external excitement about starting something new, leaving the organization we had been working with, and saving lives, Jess and I were dying on the inside. We did our best in public meetings to put on a smile, like a boxer who looks tough and confident after retreating to his corner, but at the end of each meeting the bell rang again and we found ourselves back at home and at each other's throats.

I was living a dream in many ways. Iraqi and Kurdish newspapers and photographers were following our story. Cody and I were out in the bazaar each day making new business contacts, sharing our vision of businesses giving back to their communities. Jessica, on the other hand, was living a nightmare. With Jessica in her third trimester under the scorching Iraqi sun and with only a few hours of electricity each day, the odds seemed stacked against us. But there was more than pregnancy at play. We were forced finally to come face-to-face with long-standing problems in our marriage, many of which had to do with questions of identity, vocational and domestic expectations of one another, and, perhaps at the most fundamental level, whether or not we would need to move the goalpost a little bit closer with regard to the things we had been mocking as "too small!"

In our effort to live on the edge, it seemed we were about to fall off entirely. So Jessica and Emma (our toddler) boarded a plane late in the summer and retreated to the States for a vacation. To be honest, when I put them on that plane, I wasn't sure I would ever see them again in Iraq. When I stayed back to buy shoes, traveling from village to village along the mountainous Iraqi border with Iran, which, by all local accounts, still held latent cells of al-Qaeda-linked terrorists, it was not entirely clear to me what I was even doing. Was I busying myself with activity to avoid reckoning with the relational problems in our home? Was I spending our life savings in the hopes of buying our way into significance? Or was it really as simple as buying shoes and saving lives?

In September, shortly after I had reunited with my family in the States, Cody sent me a message about an older child, Aras, who was well beyond his prime for getting the surgery he needed. He was approaching the age of inoperability and would almost certainly die young if he was not helped fast. Like many of the earliest children who came across our path, Aras and his family were from Halabja. Had his father's exposure to mustard gas fundamentally altered his ability to give birth to healthy children? Both anecdotal evidence across the region and later studies[2] would suggest that was the case.

While I trekked across America peddling shoes and T-shirts to university campuses, church gatherings, and rock concerts, Cody traveled back to Halabja a number of times to forge trust and friendship with Aras and his family. Throughout September and October Cody sent me photos and updates on Aras. We had never had a specific child whose life we could impact as clearly as his. We looked at our sales projections and began planning to give away our first major donation, clear the backlog of one more child, and send Aras to his lifesaving heart surgery.

And then it happened! Less than four months after launching our website and sinking our life savings into a risky business idea, we went against what all our advisers were telling us to do and gave away almost every dollar to save Aras's life.

Our sagacious, successful advisers rightly said, "It's far too soon. You must invest in your business, or you will never be able to sustain this!"

Knowing we fly a lot, our advisory board used the airplane metaphor of applying the oxygen mask to ourselves before trying to save others. But following the rules that had made them successful in their various fields carried little weight with us. We were operating with a different metric for success, a different bottom line. What we were doing looked a lot like traditional business and required many of the same components, but our driving force was always going to be doing whatever was required to eradicate the backlog. And we figured we needed to get started sooner rather than later. After all, we had sold all these shoes on a promise to our customers: *If you like our shoes enough to hand over $100, we will send Aras to get heart surgery.* It felt wrong to tell people wherever I went, "Aras needs urgent surgery!" only to sit on the money once it was available in the name of paving the way for a better business model.

Instead, we drained our bank account, paid for Aras to have surgery, and used our various channels to tell everyone what they had accomplished. With U.S. soldiers dying every week and ongoing speculation about the complete futility of the war, our good news from Iraq spread more quickly than we could have hoped for. New sales poured in. New press coverage followed. Within three weeks we wrote another check to send Hedi to surgery, and on the heels of Christmas sales a month later, wrapping up our second quarter as a company, we paid for Dilshad and Hussein to get their surgeries before the close of the year.

We had a lot of questions that would soon need answering, but pre-emptive love was working, saving lives and sowing peace wherever we went.

Actually, that's not entirely true. Not everyone in Iraq was happy with our solutions for these children. For some, the outcome of a life saved was not good enough. For some, it mattered a great deal where the surgery was performed and who was saving the life.

I forgot to mention we were sending these Muslim children to Israel.

CHAPTER 5

Fatwa

You are never ready for the day you wake up to find that a fatwa has been issued by prominent Muslim scholars calling for your death.

A fatwa is simply one Islamic scholar's nonbinding opinion on Islamic law. But when Iran's Ayatollah Khomeini took to state radio in 1989 to denounce Salman Rushdie's book *The Satanic Verses,* the idea of a fatwa as a death warrant was permanently seared into the minds of Westerners.

"I am informing all brave Muslims of the world that the author of *The Satanic Verses,* a text written, edited, and published against Islam, the Prophet of Islam, and the Qur'an, along with all the editors and publishers aware of its contents, are condemned to death," Khomeini said in his official ruling.

A few days later, the president of Iran seemed conciliatory when, in a Friday sermon, he said, "If Rushdie repents and . . . apologizes to the Muslims of the world . . . people might forgive him."

The next day Rushdie apologized and tried to make peace, denying that the book was written as blasphemy against Islam. Per usual, Khomeini was implacable.

"Even if Rushdie repents and becomes the most pious man of his time, it is still the duty of all Muslims to use their lives, wealth, and efforts to dispatch him to hell."

Oddly, Khomeini's fatwa did not include a legal justification at all—just his own musings. In fact, Khomeini's death sentence actually violated Islamic law by overreaching into countries that do not operate under Islamic law, by refusing Rushdie the right to confront his accuser in an Islamic court of law, and by circumventing Rushdie's right to defend himself. Khomeini also went further than Islamic law allows by calling for the death of "all the editors and publishers aware of its contents," conflating actual blasphemy with the distribution of blasphemous materials, and by seeking to hold non-Muslims in contempt of Islamic law.

When the phone call reached my office in Iraq warning me that a fatwa had been issued against us and our work, calling for punishment and death, memories of Rushdie came to mind.

What would this mean for my wife and kids? For our team? For our work?

Ours was not a fatwa on charges of blasphemy, although, in the vein of Khomeini, a clear legal reasoning was not given for the opinions levied against our case, and to this day, I could not say exactly of what we were accused. To understand the grievances of the prominent panel of Muslim scholars represented by those who spoke out against us, some context is required.

Dr. Mohammad[1] stood in downtown Baghdad, just two blocks west of the Tigris, before the palace near the curlicue bend where Uday Hussein kept his collection of lions. Across the street, the National Museum of Iraq was being looted of its five-thousand-year-old history without much ado. At his feet, his people's greatest heart hospital was reduced to rubble. Plaster and concrete clouds filled the sky as remnants of Saddam Hussein's best heart hospital settled onto the soiled lab coats and street clothes of those who made it out alive.

Nations don't fall in one fell swoop. War victories typically come through a systematic dismantling of resources and hope. So in spite of international conventions that made bombing hospitals illegal, claims of such acts happening in Iraq dated back to the Persian Gulf War under President George H. W. Bush, the late nineties under President Bill Clinton, and now also during the invasion of Iraq in multiple places, from Baghdad to Rutbah, under President George W. Bush. Some, on the other hand, say Dr. Mohammad's hospital was merely the victim of nearby bombings and not destroyed by a direct hit.

The doctor scolded himself for not fighting harder to stop the burning and the looting. His entire adult life had been devoted to saving lives, not fighting or taking lives.

What could I do? I'm just a heart surgeon, he thought, trying to console himself.

Much was made about the madness of Iraqis destroying their own country as American soldiers were alleged to have stood by smugly: "It's not our job to protect them from themselves." But war brings impossible decisions for all sides. With limited troops, there was no way the guys on the ground could reasonably protect everything that genuinely needed protecting. The fact that hospitals and museums were robbed does not say anything definitive about the character of the U.S. troops. Conversely, not every Iraqi who participated in the famed "looting of Baghdad" did so maliciously or retributively. After thirteen years of economic embargoes, many fathers had experienced firsthand the anguish of losing children to malnutrition, cholera, or tuberculosis. Untold thousands of men in Baghdad were without jobs. If Saddam was really being ousted from power and his government was no more, many reasoned that it was only fair for them to take back the proverbial "pound of flesh" he had extracted from them, having enriched himself on the backs of cheap labor and fear in the highly centralized Ba'athist government.

Who can say how many of those who stooped to stealing baby incubators and anesthesia machines were calculating profiteers, how many were disaffected youth, and how many were just loving fathers who hoped a single sale on the black market might finally be God's way of delivering them out of destitution and poverty and back to a place of security and dignity? In any case, it was a violent scene, so Dr. Moham-mad just stood by as millions of dollars in heart and lung simulators and costly imaging equipment were manhandled, broken, scavenged for parts, and ultimately hauled off to the souk, where professional underground dealers auctioned off the wares to smugglers who moved the gear out of the country through any number of holes along the neighbors' fence lines.

As the good doctor watched everything he had worked to build for the people of Iraq burn around his feet, he contemplated the wrinkly grandmas waiting for bypass surgeries and their wrinkly grandbabies whose hearts were full of holes and bad plumbing. He had been their senior surgeon, and this had been the one place in Iraq where young and old could come for care.

Where will they go now?

An American tank rolled over the cinder blocks and rebar sticking out of the hospital's outermost wall. What had once been a waiting room or the accounting department was now strewn across the parking lot from the massive explosion and the adjacent buildings that had fallen on top of it. The tank stopped beside him. Mohammad began screaming at the commanding officer, and out came thirteen years of deep-seated hatred and frustration at the United States, the United Nations, and Sad-dam Hussein himself.

Surprisingly, the commanding officer did not pull his pistol and shoot him like any number of Saddam's Republican Guard would have done just days prior. After years of forced disappearances, unspeakable torture campaigns, and an institutionalized neurosis that still defines many Iraqi people to this day, Mohammad had spoken his mind and lived to tell about it. Perhaps a foretaste of the promised liberation had indeed arrived.

Tears began to flow as he watched his hospital burn.

"Sir! Sir! Don't cry, sir! We will rebuild it better than anything Saddam ever had," the officer said reassuringly to Dr. Mohammad as he pounded on the roof of his tank and told his driver to move along.

But the CO had no authority to make such a promise, and he certainly did not have the skill to assess the extent of the damage or make an estimation about the cost of repairing or rebuilding the country's only heart hospital. Seventy-five percent of the hospital was destroyed, including the ICU, the children's unit, four surgery theaters, and all the equipment that was needed to make them run properly. Within weeks the military's medical mission concluded that the hospital was beyond repair.

"Let it go. Walk away. It's not worth it," they said.

There was a lot of talk throughout the war of Iraqis waiting around for handouts. The stories and images of looting led many of us throughout America to conclude that Iraqis were savages who would ultimately destroy anything of value they had in their hands. A mythic, simplistic narrative took hold—a story of American patronage and lazy Iraqis just waiting around for another opportunity to score a free lunch from some gullible soldier who was asked to play social worker for the day. To whatever degree these stories and stereotypes were based in reality, they were *not* talking about Dr. Mohammad or his friends.

Ten days later, four hundred staff from the bombed-out hospital met to discuss the next steps. In the previous week, some had grabbed their own pistols and AK-47s and stood guard to protect the site from further pillage. But the time had come to decide whether or not the fight to protect and rehabilitate the center was worth continuing. Overwhelmingly, and without the patronage of a functioning government, they voted to undertake whatever was necessary to rebuild their hospital.

There was not a person in the surrounding neighborhoods or the back alleys of the Baghdad black-market bazaars who knew the value of the looted medical equipment better than the men who had originally procured them and used them to save lives each day. So these doctors ventured into Baghdad's seedy underbelly to reclaim their hospital. For weeks they perused unsavory shops, describing machines and instruments that were nothing more than widgets to the "Ali Babas" who would one day soon land in a hospital with shards of exploded Mercedes through their chests and wish to God the place was better equipped. Combing through one alley after another, ducking under corrugated metal roll-up doors, Mohammad and his colleagues deftly tracked down and bought back a significant amount of that which had been stolen.

Grassroots campaigns were organized among mosques and churches throughout Baghdad to raise the money they would need to buy back their equipment before it left the country entirely, to rebuild walls, and to get back to the work of saving lives. Week after week they passed the proverbial plate (or skullcap) and collected money for further renovations and buybacks in an effort to get the hospital functioning again.

When they couldn't ultimately find all the supplies and furniture that once filled the hospital, they held demonstrations and peace marches throughout the surrounding neighborhoods to encourage those who had opportunistically enriched themselves to give back what they had stolen so that the hospital could get back to work.

Against all odds and in the almost complete absence of a functioning government, the doctors and their ridiculous scavenger hunt earned the attention of a top-of-the-line medical firm, which provided new medical equipment. As the summer drew to a close, Mohammad and his colleagues were back to functioning at 50 percent capacity, performing a couple of operations each day and learning how to marshal their skills to care for the spate of car-bombing victims whose blood was just beginning to stain the streets, as it would for years to come.

The fact that this was the only hospital now in the entire country that was capable of performing even the simplest heart surgeries—and none of those for children—meant that thousands of boys and girls every month were still waiting in line, dying, with parents blaming the ill-equipped doctors for inaccurate diagnoses, bad administration, and their inability to refer each family to a free or relatively low-cost solution outside the war-ravaged country.

Mohammad was furious that neighboring Arab states could not be found among those working diligently to rebuild Iraq. Why didn't Lebanon and Saudi Arabia show their true solidarity as Muslims by throwing open their doors to welcome and treat the sick children of Iraq? But the real firestorm came when Dr. Mohammad learned about a group of Americans who were seeking out children from all over Iraq and providing them with free heart surgery in the land of Iraq's longtime enemy, Israel.

From his corner of Baghdad just outside the Green Zone—that beer-and-whiskey-soaked "city inside a city" along the Tigris River—Dr. Mohammad opened the lid of his laptop computer and began typing, letting the visceral impulses of his humanitarian and nationalistic outrage steer him to religious counselors who would eventually manipulate his empathy and turn it against the very children he was desperately seeking to serve and save.

He addressed his open letter to the most important and powerful of the hard-line political groups in post-Saddam Iraq: an alliance of illustrious scholars who were known for rejecting participation in the political process, denouncing cooperation and engagement with Americans, and covertly supporting al-Qaeda and other terrorist networks across Iraq as long as they fought and killed Americans. The group aimed to be the supreme Islamic authority for all those focused on fighting for Iraqi nationalism.

Dr. Mohammad described his experiences with the bombing and looting of his hospital and the staff's collective efforts to rebuild and serve as many Iraqi adults and children as they could. And his questions for the mullahs were fairly simple and straightforward: 1) Was it permissible for good Muslims to allow their children to be sent to and treated by their enemies in Israel through the help of Christian Americans, and 2) why were none of their fellow Muslims from across the Arab League coming to their aid? Why did they abandon them to this humiliating position?

Who would not be sympathetic to all Dr. Mohammad had been through, including the destruction of his hospital, the loss of so much of his career and pride, and the personal assassination attempts and threats that he and so many colleagues constantly endured? I try to hold out the benefit of the doubt that perhaps he did not know with whom he had lodged his complaints. Maybe the fog of war had blinded him to the identity and ideological bent of the spiritualists he asked for guidance. Or maybe he had reached a point of desperation and felt like it was time to turn to new channels he had never considered before. Or maybe he knew exactly what he was doing. Like a starving lion with a bloody steak waved in front of his face, this clerical council had an insatiable appetite for anything that could undermine "The Occupation." Their struggle was not always strictly Muslim versus infidel, but more often citizen versus occupier—a distinction that neurotically engulfed even those of us who were working as hard as they were (and often with better resources) to save kids' lives.

Aspiring to attain the prominence of the Shia ayatollahs—brokering power, moving the nation to their will—they strongly promoted resistance and violent action against Americans, saying that taking up arms was a duty that took precedence over fasting and even prayer. Given the thrust of their sermons, fatwas, and public policy, it seemed prescient that they gathered each week in the memorial mosque in Baghdad that was built to commemorate Saddam Hussein's "victory" in the "Mother of All Battles"—the Persian Gulf War, in which he was routed and chased, tail tucked, out of Kuwait, Basra, and southern Iraq. Saddam's megalomaniacal claim to victory was based, in part, on his successful bombing campaign against Israel. And so, from inside the Mother of All Battles, in the shadows of the mosque's minarets (which were deliberately fashioned after the barrels of Kalashnikov rifles and the Scud missiles Saddam fired at Israel), this clerical coalition met each week to promote Iraqi unity through subterfuge against Americans and the nascent Iraqi government, claiming they were each puppets in a Zionist plot.

Given the council's heritage and trajectory, Dr. Mohammad certainly did not have to worry about his impassioned letter decrying the American-Israeli plot to "save children" landing on deaf ears. But it was not enough for the council to tell Dr. Mohammad that he and his patients should stay away from the Americans and the option in Israel. Nor was it enough to stoke his national pride and denounce Israel entirely. Instead, the grand sheikh invoked the greatest kind of fear—the fear of apostasy—by saying that anyone who allowed a patient to go to Israel would ultimately be responsible for any child or parent who turned away from Islam as a result of Christian or Jewish help. The assurance that they were doing their religious duty was meant to console parents as they consigned their children to death by refusing help from Americans and Jews.

The grand sheikh's most poignant argument was this: "We must stop this treatment lest it lead our children and their parents to love their enemies, leading to apostasy!"

I was overcome by his unwittingly life-changing insight, and it was probably in that moment, more than any single other, that I committed myself to a life of preemptive love.

It was immediately obvious that the impact of the fatwa would probably fall more on the families who had been suddenly forced (by their own leaders) to choose between faith and family. The statement was littered with warnings to nations and parents who would "sell their children cheaply" to the enemy, with innuendo, conspiracy, and a shot across the bow that said, "God will not accept humiliation in front of the enemies of Islam."

The message ultimately concluded that those of us who were responsible for all this lifesaving (they called it "phantom deception") must be brought to justice—it said we were deserving of death. Although none of us was named in the edict itself, Iraqi news agencies began tracking us down and blithely added fuel to the fire by broadcasting and printing names and the places where we lived and worked for the first time.[2]

I'm pretty even-keeled. (I have a flair for drama and hyperbole when I'm trying to be entertaining or it serves my personal interests somehow, but I don't typically overreact in the face of crisis. Especially when others around me are already doing that.) Still, when the word *fatwa* entered my life through the phone that spring morning—shaped as I was by the lore surrounding Rushdie versus Khomeini—I was fearful. Fearful for Jessica, fearful for the kids.

I knew plenty of widows who were raising their kids alone. Could Jessica handle it? Would she resent me? Would her parents forgive me?

What would it be like for my son to grow up without a dad? Would he honor God, treat women well, and become a good husband if I wasn't around to show him how? Who would take Emma on her first date and show her what she's really worth? No one could do that like me! Would she miss me if I wasn't there to walk her down the aisle?

Oh, God! Would Jessica remarry? Wouldn't I want that for her and the kids?

Would I?

When I said, "Love first; ask questions later," I did not know this was what it would mean. But we were already in this mess, and there was no turning back.

I knew this cleric's harmful words were being pushed across websites and networks that all had unmediated connections to al-Qaeda. So, in between putting on a brave face for my family and my team, I was fearful. Death does not frighten me apart from the way it affects my family. But torture? Torture frightens me for my own sake. I literally lay awake wondering, if kidnapped, what I might endure and what I might have to do to make it stop. Would I pay? Would I read prepared statements denouncing my government? Would I sell out my friends? Would I denounce my life's conviction that God, the creator of the world, sent out a Word from his very heart and named him Jesus, and that the well-being of everyone who ever lived is inextricably tied to his life, his death, and his resurrection? Would I deny that to keep my fingers intact or to protect someone else?

The fear of torture . . . that's my kryptonite.

In spite of my fear, however, I remember being genuinely overjoyed by the mullah's conclusion: "this treatment may lead our children and their parents to love their enemies!"[3] He might have gotten 99 percent of his response exactly wrong (and utterly failed to provide an Islamic justification for his fatwa), but he saw what we saw: that preemptive love had the capacity to overrun his hatred and unmake violence. When he looked across Iraq at the thousands of families in need, he knew intuitively that preemptive love would work. And *that* scared him more than the tanks and bombs, because every act of violence can be spun one way or another to increase fear and ensconce the powerful, but only mercy, through a constant campaign of giving itself away, can undermine hate.

The grand sheikh had created a world around him in which people hung on his words and did his bidding in an effort to save their souls, regardless of the fact that he was sending them headlong into death with their own children in tow. Within a very short time a major Muslim relief organization succumbed to the fear and withdrew their support, leaving us without the local expertise we all needed to obtain entry into Israel.

The Israeli prime minister Golda Meir famously said, "Peace will come when the Arabs will love their children more than they hate us."[4] While there are many more requirements for an abiding peace than this, few things do greater damage to the claims and aspirations of moderate Muslims and Arabs around the world than wildfire stories of a religious or nationalistic zeal that sentences children to death. Sadly, this mullah did not love the Muslim children of Iraq more than he loved himself, and Iraq fell further from peace because of it.

Meanwhile, the threats of death and punishment were manifestly real.

A couple of weeks after the news coverage reached its height and petered out, a white Nissan Patrol skidded to a halt on the main street down from our office and tried to abduct one of our friends—one of those named in the news coverage of the fatwa. As he did all he could to physically resist the kidnapping, he reached around and lifted the back of his jacket to reach into his pants. His attackers panicked and fled the scene. He was reaching for his phone in a last-ditch effort to initiate a call for help—to open up a line like they do in all those Hollywood movies he had watched to learn English, so that he might at least shout out what was happening to him and someone would come to his rescue. We can only guess that his would-be kidnappers thought he was reaching for a gun and assumed he would get it faster than they could get theirs. In any case, we were relieved that they were ill-prepared amateurs who gave up easily. Still, it was the children and their families who endured the greatest backlash.

A group of seven Iraqi children and their parents (mostly mothers) were en route to our surgical partners in Israel when they stopped over at the organization's guesthouse in Jordan for the night. A number of agents acting on behalf of the sheikh and the association appeared at the residence and, posing as doctors, made specious offers about alternate arrangements that had been made for their children to receive the necessary treatment—two thousand miles away in Algeria.

The fundamentalists easily cowed three of the mothers into walking out on the hospitality of their Christian hosts, thereby rejecting a sure thing in Israel on the mere speculation of a more Arab or Muslim solution down the road.

By the end of the month the political uproar over our fatwa reached all the way to the Iraqi parliament. Although the fatwa itself was never referenced or featured in any of the coverage or their public justifications of the furor, this opaque religious association was the obvious ghost in the machine. We received no word of parliament denouncing the imams' extrajudicial calls for our death (which would have only served to acknowledge the fatwa and its source as the influential root of the uproar). What parliament did instead—just like Khomeini and so many after him—was argue ex cathedra that our work was seditious and harmful to the people and the government of Iraq by creating grassroots diplomatic relations with Israel in circumvention of the Arab League's boycott. One lady on the health committee said (with a straight face, no less), "No one

is allowed to leave the country for medical treatment without our knowledge." The Muslim scholars had further poisoned the well with spurious
claims that Israeli hospitals were known to be illegally harvesting the
organs of Arab children and conducting experimental research. "Why
else would they be destroying our children with one hand and spending
money to save them with the other?"

It takes so long for those who have been ruled by dictators to understand the freedom of movement and expression that a group of charitable
organizations could have, quite separate from our respective governments, just as it takes so long for those in highly democratic countries to
understand the fear and neurosis that can eventually define a people and
systematically strip them of their freedom of thought, not merely their
freedom of expression.

Accomplishing exactly what it was designed to do, the fatwa created
fear and a powerful public outcry that would serve to further stoke the
flames of Iraqi nationalism and undermine any sense of cooperation
with Americans, whether soldier or civilian. Now families who accepted
our offer for treatment in Israel were not only at risk of being branded
as apostates, but they were, in any case, traitors to the Iraqi state and the
Arab street.

Thankfully, four of the families had the courage to stand their
ground in the face of intimidation and moved forward with their scheduled surgeries in Israel. Like those who had gone before them, they
found the doctors and nurses and social workers in Israel to be wonderful people who were full of kindness and love, absolutely nothing like
the horror stories they had heard. The mullah's nightmare—and that
of his friends in parliament—had just come true: of these thousands of
children whose lives we would save, some would one day carry the scars
on their chest to law school and on to the halls of parliament, where a
new story of preemptive love would be told and the people of Iraq would
turn over a new page with the people of Israel, in circumvention of the
Arab League's boycott.

Days later we learned that the mullah's Algeria option failed to materialize, and the three children and their vulnerable mothers who were pressured into changing course were stuck without surgery.

I was passing through Istanbul and stayed in a grubby sidewalk motel for the night. Flipping through the Turkish TV channels in my musty room, a jangly guitar hook and a male falsetto caught my attention. I settled back into the pillows on my oversized bed as the melody washed over me:

Always love . . .
Hate will get you every time!

The music video featured people from every walk of life mindlessly watching their TVs—elderly people holding their coffee, families having dinner, children in isolation as they nodded off to sleep. All of a sudden a boy lunged forward and unplugged the set, took it in his arms, and marched outside, where he was joined by hundreds of others who had spontaneously unplugged themselves, opening up space and air and energy for other messages to come in, as if for the first time.

The chorus came back around:

Always love . . .
Hate will get you every time!

One by one they laid their consoles to rest, creating a veritable TV graveyard in an open field as the band played on. Lying in that bed, having just touched down from Iraq, where men were literally slaughtering each other in the streets over ethnic identity and political power struggles, the words hit me with tremendous force. Somewhere in the third verse I got lost in thought, wondering if it really was that simple. Were we really poisoning our minds with the things we watched on TV—with our imbalanced news reporting; with our prime-time action shows that desperately seek to remind us that we must retain our right to kill and torture others in order to be safe in this world; and with our religious leaders, many of whom have monolithic visions of a paradise that sounds nothing like the scriptures from which they were culled?

Suddenly, all of the unplugged televisions resurrected with a single song:

Always love . . .
Even when you want to fight!

When the fatwa came out, I sent an e-mail to our team inviting them to our house that night for prayer:

> Let's pray for the aggressors. Let's hope to engage them in dialogue and love. Let's hope to serve their children and their families. We should long to give them more than good news; we should give them our own lives as well.
>
> And let's not back down. Above all, this is our time to follow Jesus. I've talked a lot about preemptive love, loving our enemies, not resisting an evil person, feeding our hungry/thirsty enemies, and being at peace with everyone as far as it depends on us. But it is not just rhetoric. This is our way of life.
>
> We love others because God first loved us in Christ. We should not be cowed into submission or fear by a bunch of thugs who want to harm us.
>
> We have nothing to lose and everything to gain.[5]

That night, while everyone finished eating dinner and served up tea, I slipped upstairs to put Emma and Micah to bed—one of the most cherished, soul-soothing routines in my life. I lay down in their room to read a few books, sing a few songs, and pray.

In our family, we don't practice any of the standard "God, protect me!" prayers. Not because we are flippant about our kids and their well-being, but because our compass got recalibrated somewhere along the way. We look up sometimes to find we are using a completely different road map than almost everyone around us. So we use that precious time before bed to tell stories of sacrifice, not safety. In our stories, the heroes do not always come out alive when all is said and done. And when they do, they pass through death to get there.

Since the day our kids were born I've been asking God to shape them into people of peace—at peace with God and at peace with the world around them, a world where families are sentenced to death for simply showing love. That night, with the threat of the fatwa still looming overhead and all of its drama yet to unfurl, I sang a new song to my kids:

Always love . . .
Hate will get you every time!

CHAPTER 6

The Sheikh

The doors to the hotel conference room swung open, and out into the atrium poured a stream of turbaned clerics, a mosaic of Sunnis in gilded gowns, red felt fezzes, and trapezoidal turbans mixed among a sea of Shias in black ankle-length parachute robes along with headdresses that variously designated who could (and could not) claim to be a scion of the Prophet Muhammad. The older men with mostly white in their beards moved slowly, hanging back while spry understudies and young men in blazers and aviator sunglasses scrambled to cut an imposing perimeter to ward off any would-be attackers. It was a rare ecumenical gathering in the heightened civil conflict of 2006–07. There were even a few representatives from the historic Christian congregations mixed in among them, equally regal with robes and beards, their priestly collars or huge metal crosses their only distinguishing features.

I was huddled in a corner of the hotel lobby near the front lawn with a notebook and a dictionary practicing a new set of words for the day, trying my best to be a respectful guest in my new host country. There was only a single empty teacup beside my blue shoulder satchel on the coffee table in front of me, a clear indication that I had not been sitting there long. (A typical language study session for me would normally re-

quire a combination of three or four bags of tea and three-in-one powdered coffee drinks.)

Studying in a hotel lobby is generally a bad idea for a people-watcher
like me. While it gives you a sense of being among the people and might
allow you to soak in a bit of the culture and language as you work, there
are plenty of distractions to take you away from actually studying.

I couldn't help but look up, transfixed, as the conference-room doors
swung open and the lobby filled with the men who were, by many accounts, to blame for the sectarian conflict across Iraq. These men, to
a person, were the men who stood each Friday throughout the eight-
year war and guided their congregants with scriptural advice as to how
they should respond to one another, to the Iraqi government, and to
the American soldiers, diplomats, and civilians who were now at work
among them.

Like most people, I regard myself as more than a little enlightened.
And when it comes to Islam, in particular, I had no doubt that I had a
better grasp of the Qur'an, variations in Muslim belief and practice, etc.,
than most people around me. Still, begin filling a well-known hotel with
senior Iraqi clerics from both sides of an ever-widening conflict, and all
my well-groomed enlightenment suddenly went out the window. In my
heart and mind, I might as well have been back home with Bubba talking about "rag heads" and how all Muslims are terrorists. I was overcome
with fear.

My eyes began darting around as I gathered my things and tried to
stuff them into my bag to leave, throwing a few thousand Iraqi dinars on
the table to cover my tea and leave before one of these guys pulled back
his robe to reveal a vest of C-4 that would avenge the losses from which-
ever side had struck the other more recently. To write such a confession
of my inner fears today seems a little silly, but this was Iraq in 2007.
Daily suicide bombings at checkpoints, restaurants, hotels, and local bazaars were as normal as anything else in Iraq at that time. And targeted
attacks on political and religious gatherings were especially effective in

instigating retaliations and ensuring a general level of chaos and fear continued to reign.

I was still cramming books in my bag as one of the delegations peeled off and began looking for a place to sit in the overstuffed couches around me. I stood to leave, far from the model peacemaker I thought I would be in a situation like this.

I was woefully underdressed for the occasion. I was still new in Iraq at the time, and I had not yet acquired a gentlemanly comportment or learned that most of America has lost its sense of occasion. All around us nowadays, men and women alike dress as though they could not be bothered to care. The people of Iraq, however, whom I once regarded as uncivilized and in need of my help, taught me that the way I dress says a great deal about my father and my grandfather before him; about my regard for my wife and kids and their standing in society; and about what I think of the company I keep, its value, and the effort it is worth to me.

Being a very typical American, I figured I was free to wear whatever I wanted and do whatever I wanted. T-shirt and jeans? Sneakers and baseball cap? Combat boots and safari hat? Why not? In addition to my crumpled clothes, I had recently had a run-in with Ebo and a set of electric shears, so I was very self-conscious about my shiny, domelike pate. I sure did not feel free when surrounded by well-dressed, starched and pressed Muslim leaders from across the country.

One of the guys with a finely trimmed black beard cut through the couches, whipped his robe over the coffee table, and claimed the alcove and its surrounding seats for his delegation. As he stood, waiting for the elder statesmen in his group to arrive, I grabbed the last of my things and tried to leave unnoticed.

"No, no, no, my friend!" he said in an immediately winsome accent, with a genuine smile that could have charmed the most ardent of enemies. "You stay with us!"

In an instant, I was disarmed. My fear was gone. If you could have stood ten feet away and looked inside me as these guys approached, you would have seen my fists up, ready for a fight. As the warmth of his words entered the room—"My friend . . . you stay with us!"—my fists came down—involuntarily. Such is the power of preemptive love.

I've never been one to turn down an invitation; I just needed a little help this time. In fact, we have a general principle that we try to use in acclimating to the various cultures of Iraq in which we live and work. For the first six months, we say yes to everything.

"Do you want to go eat sheep brains and intestines with me at four A.M.?" a friend might ask.

"Yes! Yes, I do!"

"Do you want to go with me to my fire-eating, sword-thrusting Sufi worship gathering?"

"Yes! Yes, I do!"

Saying yes to the innumerable invitations around us is an incomparable way to learn and another way to love first and ask questions later.

After six months and a lot of experiences that we might have otherwise avoided, we enter a period of asking, "Why?" By this point we have learned some of the language, we have a greater cultural context in which to interpret and place each experience and invitation, and we have witnessed and experienced certain things for ourselves, rather than relying solely on the testimony of others.

An old lady might say in her colloquial dialect, "Repeat after me, 'There is no God but God and Muhammad is his messenger.'"

When we ask why in response to such a well-meaning (but possibly manipulative) directive, we get a conversation in return, rather than give the erroneous impression that we intend to convert to Islam, and rather than shut down a relationship with an immediate no that gives no room for discussion or understanding of one another.

After seasons of *yes* and *why,* we pass, as it were, into a cultural adolescence, having learned from our hosts why things are the way they are *in their own words.* We are free to make informed adult decisions about cultural values and practices and determine if and where they depart from the things that we ourselves hold to be most valuable. Of course, our road map is not for the faint of heart. There is plenty of risk with loving first   saying yes   and asking questions later. Indeed, even we use it more as a guideline to urge one another deeper into preemptive love than we do as a set of commandments against which to grade each other. But there is something beautiful about entrusting yourself as an individual and as a community to the people around you and saying yes as a way of showing honor and love.

And so, I sat back down with my new friend and the five imams, sheikhs, and muftis in the delegation who carried out their religious duties and lived in Baghdad, Kirkuk, and Mosul—the three most ethnically and religiously diverse, divided, and violent cities in the country.

My new friend introduced himself in broken English: "*As-salaamu alaykum,* peace be upon you. I am Sheikh Hussein from Baghdad. We are conference of Muslim scholars. We are against the terrorists."

He was effervescent and magnetic. If the worldwide Muslim community wanted a convincing spokesperson to denounce terrorism and make the case for a moderate Islam that was truly a religion of peace and love, they could do no better than a bearded Arab leader like Sheikh Hussein.

Seven small *fenjan* cups full of Arab coffee were placed on saucers in front of us as the smell of cardamom signaled that the time for friendship and conversation had officially arrived. I leaned forward as Sheikh Hussein regaled me with stories of the war, politics, the present Sunni-Shia conflict, and the numerous acts of terrorism he and his friends had endured over the preceding four years since the toppling of Saddam's regime.

Every time he stood in front of Iraqi TV crews and denounced Sunni al-Qaeda and Shia militias, reprisals were sure to follow. In response to his public calls for Sunni and Shia Arabs to pray together in an effort to stanch the bloodletting around the country, his Baghdad mosque where he led prayers each day was bombed. He barely escaped a high-speed chase in which men with automatic weapons tried to abduct and kill him.

And, to cap it all off, his seven-year-old boy's best friend was murdered in front of Sheikh Hussein's house while a soccer ball rolled past his son, who stood frozen, shocked to see his playmate bleeding out on the street.

I would later learn that I was the first American he had ever met. He saw the camera strap sticking out of my bag.

"I want to send a message to the people of America." He certainly wasn't camera shy.

I pulled out my camera, set it on video mode, and began recording.

"Good evening, lady and gentleman . . . ," he began with his signature smile. "We are against the terrorists and terrorism. We are with the love to all people: Muslim, Christian, Jewish. We are *against*"—his voice became really impassioned—"the killing of any people. We love the God . . . We are with peace from the heart. We will work with any people, any country, any religion in service to all the people. We love the people of America, France, Germany, Australia. This is our message: We want peace. Only."

The red recording light turned off, and the other men from the delegation clamored to be heard. "Send that to all the people of America!" they shouted, as though changing the minds of all Americans was as simple as reaching into their living rooms through a quick phone call to Big Brother. Their message and desires were spot-on, but they clearly did not understand the rising tide of Islamophobia and what it would take to really reverse the trend in the middle of a conflict that was largely understood as a war on Islam itself, in spite of the many attempts by the presidential administration and commentators to convince us otherwise.

The imam from Kirkuk asked me what we were doing in our organization to help his city. I hated to admit that we were doing nothing. I had some friends who lived and worked in Kirkuk. A number of my Iraqi friends were from there and still had family there. To hear them talk about it, the city was completely off-limits, especially for a new guy like me. No one who wanted to live should even consider working there. The clerics were visibly disappointed in my answer. I asked what we could do to help.

"The children," one guy said. "The children need so much. They are sick. They need surgery. They need education. Food. Clean water. If you come to my city, I will put an umbrella of protection around you. You can live and work from my mosque. No one will be able to touch you."

I take those invitations very seriously. But everything was so new to me, I did not know what to say. The conversation slipped away, but I never forgot the way he threw the doors wide open and offered to put his reputation on the line for me and the children in his community. These guys were one of two things: charlatans who would say anything to net a foreigner or the polar opposite of our fatwa-flinging enemies who denied children the right to be helped by Americans and treated by Israeli doctors.

Hours had passed, and we were quickly exhausting all of our shared language. When I didn't know a word in Arabic, I turned to Turkish. Modern Turkish has many Arabic words built in, and it was the only language other than English in which I was truly conversational at the time. The guys from Mosul and Kirkuk turned out to be Turkmen, and they translated between my Turkish, the South Azeri Turkmen language of their heart, and the Arabic trade language to keep conversation going. When Turkish failed, we fumbled around in Kurdish, before throwing up our hands and returning to English and Arabic. It was sloppy and beautiful. It was love in motion.

The coffee was long gone and the time had clearly come to say goodbye, but before I left, one of the men asked me to pray.

"You are a man of God," he said. I could barely see his lips moving behind his beard. "Please pray that I will find a wife." He was so affable, I did not even notice the pain in his request. Blinded again by my own assumptions of Arab male misogyny—and ignoring my principle of saying yes as a way of extending love to others—I assumed he was joking, aiming to get a second or third wife for purely pleasurable purposes. I made an off-color remark about how difficult it was for any man to make one wife happy and questioned how he could possibly care for another.

His countenance changed. His one and only wife had been killed recently in a suicide bombing, and though he missed her greatly, it was too difficult to raise their children alone amidst daily car bombings, assassination attempts on his life, and his pastoral efforts to mitigate violence and shape the city of Kirkuk as it teetered on the brink of all-out civil war.

I was humbled by all that these men had been through, by my own presumptuousness, and by their peaceful postures and requests for spiritual intervention and help from someone outside of their ranks. I held out my hands in supplication, as though something tangible were going to immediately fall from God, and began my prayer in Turkish: "Oh, God, you know the concerns of my new friend Hussein. You are the creator of the world and the provider of all good things. Please bring a wife to Hussein to love him, his children, and to create a new life together. In the name of Jesus Christ, amen."

When I looked up, he had a sparkle in his eye. He seemed pleased enough. And although all spiritual common sense would say that prayer is directed to God and *not* to be uttered for the approval of others, I must admit, I was relieved to have his approval. Then I recognized the deviousness of his smirk.

"You forgot to pray that she would be an *American* woman!"

The room erupted in laughter. And there it was. The ultimate declaration of peace.

"Who am I to presume to tell God *whom* he should provide for you?" I joked. "It is enough that we let him decide."

We stood for ten minutes of man-kisses and good-byes as all the cell phones were passed around for photos and the obligatory exchange of numbers.

As I returned home and relayed the stories to Jessica, the look in her eyes made me wonder if I had let my guard down way too much. I had just given away my full name and phone number and allowed myself to be repeatedly videoed and photographed in an environment where various tribal sheikhs and religious clerics were in league with the Ministry of Interior, tracking phone calls, intercepting e-mails, and staging kidnappings for politics and profit. I pursued the fear in her eyes and asked if I had gone too far or shared too much of our information with these new guys who were only a degree or two (at most) removed from the insurgency and state-sponsored terror. Her response tells you everything you need to know about my amazing wife:

"We didn't move here so you could play it safe. Nothing is going to change that way."

I left the country on a fund-raising tour, spreading the message of preemptive love. While all my other American friends in Iraq seemed to stand at a distance, fearful of engaging Muslim leadership directly, we were being uniquely welcomed into Muslim communities in Baghdad, Kirkuk, and Mosul through the sheikhs, imams, and muftis, who, by all accounts, seemed to be significant gatekeepers for their people. To be fair, a few months prior I had tried to run away as well. I was no exemplar of courage or self-sacrifice. In fact, if it was not for the love of Sheikh Hussein and the way he overcame my fear, I would have fled the hotel and missed out on an amazing set of friendships altogether. Even so, I had this nagging fear that I was stumbling into something that was far more complex and layered than I'd bargained for.

However, one of the great things about building a movement that tells people we are committed to loving first is that every time I step onstage, I blackmail myself. I publicly declare myself to be someone I'm not, in hopes of forcing the true me (the cowardly recluse) to act in a way that is consistent with the image I keep painting of the man I aspire to be.

When I returned from abroad, I had new money in hand, a refined vision for providing heart surgery to children across Iraq, and thousands of new contacts across the country in front of whom I had committed myself to continuing to love boldly in a place where no one else wanted to go.

My phone rang once or twice a day for the next few weeks.

"Mr. Jeremy, *habibi* . . . are you well?" It was always Sheikh Hussein. If speaking another's language is hard when you are face-to-face, we seem to lose half of our speaking ability when forced to speak over the phone without the body language and the light in our eyes to communicate what our words fail to do.

"I miss you . . . I see you soon, God willing?"

The next day, Cody and I met Sheikh Hussein at the hotel for coffee. (When you share so few words, you can't get too complicated about your meeting requirements.) As I walked into the hotel, I walked right by the sheikh without so much as a word. His turban was gone; his outer robe was gone. Even his inner gown had been replaced, and there he stood, in a suit and tie, grinning from ear to ear.

"Hello?! Mr. Jeremy . . ."

I whipped around, surprised—then embarrassed—by my oversight.

"Do I look nice? I am like a businessman!" He let out his magnetic belly laugh.

Cody and I were underdressed again. As twentysomethings, the only people we knew who wore slacks—let alone suits—worked in department stores. Sheikh Hussein had dressed up to show us respect, but he also had another reason for losing the robe and donning new duds.

"I am a man of God," he said, "and that is a matter of the heart, not of outward appearance. I am not holy because of my clothes. I can dress Western like you, or I can dress like the other clerics from around here. God looks on the heart."

As we talked over tea and coffee with Sheikh Hussein and his friends, I revisited the invitation to help the sick children of Kirkuk. Were we still invited? Would they still do everything they could to ensure our well-being? They wanted more from us than we could offer. They found it hard to understand that we would focus so narrowly on children who needed heart surgery.

"What about our children who have cancer? What about the children with cerebral palsy? What about the families who live in neighborhoods without clean water?"

We were so green it was extremely difficult to hold our ground. We had come to Iraq to help, and finding sponsors like these men who could open doors across the country during these difficult days of the insurgency was no small thing. We waffled back and forth from time to time in the early days as we seriously considered expanding our services to address human trafficking in Iraq, poverty alleviation, and other pediatric health concerns. Ultimately, however, we felt intuitively that our impact would be minimized if we tried to be experts in more than one field too quickly.

We told the men that we had one service to offer: if they had children in need of heart surgery, we would do all we could to help.

While Cody sat across the table from me and made conversation with the rest of the delegation, I leaned over to Sheikh Hussein and tried to make a casual inquiry about the top-ranking mullah who had just issued the fatwa.

"Do you know the grand sheikh?" I asked.

"Oh, yes! Very good man! He is my friend," the sheikh said as he pulled out his phone. He went to the photo album and swiped through a few screens. "See, here I am in his house just last week."

Really? The guy who just called for our death and is actively preventing children from receiving the treatment they need is a "very good man"? What is going on? Did I pronounce his name correctly? Are we talking about the same guy? How could a man who is vehemently opposed to cooperation host this guy in front of me who maintains that all he wants is peace? The xenophobe is mentoring an understudy who openly says that he loves Christians and Jews?

My mind went racing again. Was this all a setup? Like the men who acted upon the grand sheikh's fatwa and posed as doctors to deceive some of our families into accepting their solutions in Algeria, perhaps Sheikh Hussein was posing as an ecumenical peacemaker in an effort to entrap me and score one for the home team through kidnapping, blackmail, etc.

News stations and plenty of friends had warned us before we moved to Iraq of the Qur'anic provision (*al-taqiyyah*) that allegedly allows Muslims to lie and maintain secret agendas among non-Muslims. So was he really cut from the same cloth as the grand sheikh? Were they really friends, or was he boasting of connections that were far beyond his reach?

I didn't ask any follow-up questions. I just smiled and moved on.

One afternoon Sheikh Hussein called me for lunch. "Please come, Mr. Jeremy. I have the grand mufti of Iraq and the king's grandson for lunch today. We want to hear about how you help children."

I flew down the stairs from my office to the street, where I hailed a taxi and headed home. Rifling through my closet, I laid hold of my one and only suit. The one-inch shoulder pads and the pleated front and cuffed pant legs screamed, "Welcome to your junior high dance, 1992!" but I knew this was one time I couldn't afford to be underdressed.

When I arrived at the sheikh's modest home, he met me in the street with a retinue of his boys and brothers in tow. We embraced like true friends as he grabbed my hand, interlocked our fingers, and led me from the street through his front gate into a tree-covered courtyard. As we ascended the concrete stairs I caught a glimpse of the meeting room to my left—ten or fifteen men were in the process of standing up to receive me as I slipped off my shoes and entered.

Ducking into the clouds of smoke in the men-only meeting room, the wisp of a black scarf disappeared behind a corner at the back of the hallway ahead of us—probably a wife, sister, or mom trying to get a glimpse of the first American to ever enter their home without a gun, a dog, or an exit strategy. Unlike the homes of my many Kurdish and my more worldly Arab friends, there were no signs of women anywhere in the sheikh's home. The boys served the tea, coffee, and fruit in between emptying ashtrays, fetching notebooks, and answering the door and phone calls.

A quick survey across the room revealed Kurds in cummerbunds, *jamanas,* and baggy *sharwals*; Shia-Arab politicians and business types in suits; and Sunni clerics in robes and headdresses, including the grand mufti of Iraq. Having introduced myself briefly to everyone in the room, I received their welcome and blessing, and we took our seats in a semicircle on the ground around a plastic tablecloth so lunch could be served.

Wherever Sheikh Hussein was, it was sure to be the most diverse gathering around. He was like parliament on wheels, only everyone was smiling and getting along instead of bickering and boycotting one another.

The two younger boys—no more than seven years old—placed bowls of apricot soup, hot flat bread, and various pickled fare before us as Sheikh Hussein's younger brother entered the room with his arms spread nearly as wide as they could go around a massive four-foot-diameter pewter serving bowl filled with biryani rice, almonds, and raisins beneath a full roasted lamb unlike anything I had ever seen. Lunch was served.

An hour later men began rising to wash their hands in a basin by the door as the younger boys poured fresh hot water for rinsing, brushing, and grooming after one of the first meals I'd ever had that could truly be called a feast. As tea was served and the room lit with the glowing orange flecks of cigarettes at nearly every seat, the big moment had finally arrived. Sheikh Hussein looked at me and said, "We all represent thousands of constituents, tribesmen, and worshippers. We have too many children who are dying from heart problems. Can you help us?"

Until now, there had never been a good reason for me to tell the sheikh that our partnerships required us to send children to Israel for heart surgery. As far as he was concerned, we were sending children to world-class facilities in America, or at least to nearby neighbors in Iran and Turkey. This was one of my early classrooms where I learned that the things I deem to be good news are often not received as good news by those who have a different framework for reality than I do. The poor sheikh was not at all prepared for our lifesaving solution.

Unaccustomed to speaking in such a high-stakes environment, I merely opened my mouth, and words seemed to pour forth. I led with the least controversial part of my proposal. "Sheikh . . . respected gentlemen . . . Praise God that we can save the lives of your children by sending them outside the country for surgery! We have already had much success with this among Kurdish and Arab—Muslim and Christian—children across the country. If you will send your children to us, endorse our work, and provide us with the authority we need to do our work among you, God willing, we will be successful, lives will be saved, and peace will be achieved between us."

The room was abuzz with affirmations and a general sense that something significant was happening among us. One of the elders had the wherewithal to interject and ask a critical follow-up question: "Where will the children go?"

"We take them from here to Jordan, where they meet with a cardiologist and we determine their suitability for surgery."

I don't think I was trying to be deceptive. But in light of the recent fatwa, maybe I was. I was trying to move us down the road as far as we could go together, building as much goodwill as possible, before unveiling the shakiest part of our proposal.

"So the surgeries will occur in Jordan?" It was one part statement, two parts question. He was onto me.

Earlier in life I'd had a dear friend who spun lies about nearly everything. Nothing was ever as it seemed with him. And somewhere along the way the lies always came crashing down on each other. As a result of that friendship and countless hours in Sunday school, I have a strict no-lying policy. I'm not above delaying, sidestepping, or obfuscating, and if I was abducted and tortured I would surely lie to save the lives of my family and friends, but generally speaking, I don't lie to get ahead. Neither the fatwa's promises, the grand mufti's suspicious glare, nor the conspicuous Glock in the waistband of the president's personal adviser made this Israel point worth lying about.

"No, sir . . ." I'm not sure if my voice cracked on the outside, but my confidence was quickly diminishing in the face of his calculated skepticism. "After the doctor sees the children in Jordan, we send the urgent children to Israel for treatment."

The room erupted. Through the din of voices I heard charges of espionage, subterfuge, and hypothetical questions that, honestly, I had never had to really consider—let alone answer—before a panel of elders.

There's a reason you don't question the monkey when the organ grinder is in the room.

In the face of such dissent, our host, Sheikh Hussein, acted quickly to silence any concerns that he himself was colluding with me in an effort to undermine the state and prop up the occupying forces across Iraq.

"It is impossible for our children to go to Israel for surgery," the sheikh said.

I wondered if he was aware of the fatwa and its promises of punishment for those who walked down this risky path toward wholeness.

"Their neighbors at the street level and our peers in leadership across the country will surely say that we have become agents of Israel. There must be another way."

One by one these influential men weighed in with cautionary tales, proverbs, and predictions about what would happen if we continued down this path. I had clearly lost the room. There was no chance that anyone in this group would ever acquiesce in their personal convictions on this point, let alone commend us to families under their care as a viable solution for their children.

I was deeply saddened and disappointed by the ways these men put such a primacy on preserving their personal reputations at the very real cost of children's lives. Where had all the talk of love and acceptance gone? Having lost the room, I figured I had nothing left to lose. (It occurs to me that I had lost focus on the grand mufti, the fatwa, and the number of guns within reach.)

"Dear Sheikh, which is a greater sin in the eyes of God: to let a child suffer and die to preserve your reputation, or to become friends with your enemy?" I countered, harkening back to my nono's sermons, which, ironically, featured Jewish prophets challenging their kinsmen to do justly and love mercy.

On cue, man after man spoke up to defend their friend and host. Surely it was right and just to help the children. That was, after all, why we had gathered together. But we must be practical, they insisted. Someone mentioned the government hospital in Baghdad and asked if we could work there instead.

Like all good capitalists who came of age in the denouement of the Cold War, I was vehemently opposed to government solutions. "You have no idea when our governments will be able to serve these children. How much longer should we wait for them?" I countered. "We *know* your children will die without surgery. We *don't know* what the death squads will do. Let's take a risk for our children!"

This deep-seated fear of Jewry was another holdover of Saddam's Ba'athist regime. In the late 1960s Saddam orchestrated a dramatic public trial and hanging of a number of Jews, declaring them to be spies of the relatively newly formed Israel, which had recently earned the white-hot hatred of the Arab world in their surprising Six-Day War victory (with the attendant land gains that came with it). In the years that followed, the Iraqi Jewish community, once vibrant and numerous, endured massive state-sponsored persecution and attrition. The narratives promulgated by Ba'athism ensured that the country was reared on a steady diet of anti-Semitic propaganda, fear, and, ultimately, the willingness to kill brother, sister, mother, and father in service of the party, the state, and pan-Arabism.

In a last-ditch effort, I told the sheikh and his guests stories of Iraqi Muslim children whom we had sent to surgery—families who had actually met Jewish doctors, nurses, administrators, taxi drivers, rabbis, and host families. There was real change taking place in these families *and* in their neighborhoods as they returned to Iraq and shared a story that defied all they had ever heard about Israel and the Jewish people.

"Let the governments pursue their cease-fires and treaties. But true peace is more than the absence of conflict. True peace happens in the heart when nemesis neighbors prioritize each other's well-being over their own."

I might as well have been speaking a different language. I had veered off the topic of the world we actually lived in. I was speaking of that faraway country again, with its constitution. I was speaking as though it was already among us, but there was no place like Iraq to remind me of the myriad ways in which it was not yet here in its fullness.

"We are waiting on a leader who will stand up and do the risky thing rather than the certain thing. It's certain that these children will die if they are not treated. You are all right: it would be risky to send them to Israel. Your neighbors in the militia might retaliate if they find out. But there are other families who have chosen the uncertainty of terror squads over the certain death of their child from heart disease. And those children are running in parks playing football and going to school today while your children are sick at home. If you are the men of peace you claim to be, we're ready to walk forward with you into things that are risky."

The smoke had cleared as the politicians, plutocrats, and clergy filed out of the sheikh's house with their cigarettes and salaams. I began buttoning the cuffs of my shirt and had grabbed my jacket to leave when Sheikh Hussein took hold of my hand and asked me to stay behind for a few minutes. Our interlocked fingers told me this was going to be serious.

In that unsettling quiet that occurs only after a storm, the sheikh gave me one of the greatest gifts I'd ever received.

"One of the families in my Baghdad mosque has a little baby girl who is going to die soon if she does not get her heart surgery. I could not admit it in front of all the other men—they are not like me and will not understand—but I will send this baby to Israel. We have to save her life. I'm at your service. How do we make this happen?"

I asked Hussein if he was aware of what his friend the grand sheikh had been up to recently in issuing a fatwa denouncing our work and calling for the punishment and death of those who dealt "falsely" by sending children to Israel. This was the first time we had actually acknowledged the huge elephant in the room between us.

The caught look on his face made it immediately apparent that he was aware of the fatwa and had been throughout all of our recent meetings. He affirmed his friendship with the grand sheikh. Although we were in the privacy of his home with just the two of us there, he did not throw his mentor under the proverbial bus. He did not seek to save his own reputation by defaming another. Even at the time I took great solace in that fact, hoping that if we ever crossed a similar threshold together in the future he might extend the same character defense of me in the face of real opposition. But he also made it clear that he believed the grand sheikh had made an egregious mistake. Sheikh Hussein said he would stand by us and work with us to save this one child's life, with one proviso:

"Mr. Jeremy, we must be very careful; do it in secret."

I agreed.

I asked if he could arrange a way for me to meet with the grand sheikh to personally appeal to him, in light of Sheikh Hussein's endorsement, to overturn the fatwa and make it permissible for children to cooperate with well-meaning civilian Americans and Israelis who wanted nothing more than to save the lives of Iraqi children and to pursue peace between our communities, which had so long been at odds. I always work off the assumption that it is harder to hate (and, therefore, kill) the enemy you know and with whom you've shared a cup of tea than it is to kill the enemy you've never met.

Sheikh Hussein agreed to talk to his friend.

A few days later, I was invited to dinner in the home of the sixty-year-old chieftain-grandson of Sheikh Mahmud—the 1920s-era king who fought the British in Iraq in the wake of the collapsed Ottoman Empire. The king's grandsons—the chieftain and his brother—had been present in the previous meeting when I made my initial overture, and although they were not at all in favor of my Israel proposal, they were keen to establish a relationship and explore other opportunities together. Over the course of five hours of food, tea, and tobacco, we discussed history and the mythic conflicts their family had fought in against the British, against Iraq, and against the Ottoman Turks. As the head of his tribe, the chief shared with me the weight of his burden to find treatment and care for some ten thousand people who looked to him as arbiter, protector, and patron.

Again, the meeting in Sheikh Hussein's house that seemed to be such a failure had given birth to a new set of friendships, as the chief and I began a year of meetings, travel, and exploration together in an effort to heal the hearts of his tribe's children before it was too late.

In Baghdad, as the impact of loving first in these seemingly intractable situations continued to gain an irrefutable momentum on the testimony of more and more lives that had been saved across the country, Sheikh Hussein reached out to the grand mufti and was able to get his assurances that he would do whatever he could to ensure that any child seeking surgery would be left unharmed insofar as it was in his control. He also assured Sheikh Hussein that he would not do anything to further promote or support the fatwa.

When a tribal chief called from Ramadi—the capital of Anbar province, where al-Qaeda and the insurgency raged on—I knew we were beginning to make some real progress. He had kids who needed help. Was there anything we could do discreetly to help these families who looked to him for options?

Word spread so far and fast in the course of two months that the Grand Ayatollah invited us to Baghdad and Najaf to negotiate a solution for the countless children in his personal backlog who waited in need of surgery. Astutely, Sheikh Hussein broached the topic of race and place in a culturally appropriate way that I could not have managed alone. He inquired how much of an obstacle (indeed, how much of a political risk) it would pose for the cleric to send the children to Israel. The ayatollah's deputies spoke up and assured us that his priority was saving lives, helping their people, and working for peace—not playing geopolitical games.

In spite of our tenuous beginning, it seemed a new day was dawning in Iraq . . .

Sheikh Hussein and I continued to move from one depth of friendship to another. Each time he called me to his house to meet some new delegation I expected to finally get *the* call: "The grand sheikh will see you now." This was to be my time to actually take all my idealism about peacemaking and loving first into a head-to-head conversation with someone who was not only philosophically and theologically aligned against me but had actually called for our deaths and actively tried to sabotage our work. Edward Said,[1] the inimitable (and highly controversial) Palestinian scholar and writer, said something that affected me deeply in my feeble efforts to love into situations where I found myself in far over my head. He said, "It is up to us to provide the answer that power and paranoia cannot. It isn't enough to speak generally of peace. One must provide the concrete grounds for it, and those can only come from moral vision, and neither from 'pragmatism' nor 'practicality.' If we are all to live—this is our imperative—we must capture the imagination not just of our people, but that of our oppressors."[2]

Over the months, Sheikh Hussein and I met countless times, and the fatwa and its concerns featured prominently in the bulk of our conversations. But each time I thought I was to meet the grand sheikh himself, I was forced to settle for acquaintances and those deputized to do reconnaissance and speak on his behalf. I was still naive enough at that time to believe that such a meeting was not only possible (in fact, I still believe and work under those assumptions today) but actually likely to happen simply because I asked for it.

One day over coffee in the sheikh's parlor, the sheikh said, "I've called the family with the sick baby and told them about the option in Israel. They are all in. I am all in."

It was a stunning development. Not only had Sheikh Hussein, our visionary local leader, embraced our call to preemptive love, but his moral vision had proven to be aligned with a very needy family who lived so near to the hard-liners in Baghdad that it would be seemingly impossible for them to embark on such a journey without being surrounded by threats to their lives and happiness if they chose to risk it with us in Israel in the face of the fatwa.

With the momentum of this great news, I was finally let in on a collective secret as to why my pending meeting with the grand sheikh had been so delayed—in fact, why it was an utter impossibility, in spite of our overtures, requests, and high tolerance for risk. Sheikh Hussein leaned in to whisper, indicating that what was coming was a touchy thing to say, in spite of the fact that we appeared to be all alone. It would still be a few years before Jessica and I would experience the angst of living under constant surveillance with the acute awareness that our lives had been videotaped, our living room bugged, and our closest friendships infiltrated. Sheikh Hussein seemed to live it intuitively after so many years of Saddam's tyranny.

"I have to tell you something about the grand sheikh that you do not know," he began. "The grand sheikh no longer lives in Iraq. He fled the country some time ago and now lives in the safety of a compound outside the country where he drives luxury cars, has a militia of bodyguards, and cannot possibly understand, let alone share in, the sufferings of the Iraqi people as he calls upon us to oppose the occupation and fight against people like you."

It was alarming to learn that we had been caught up in yet another proxy war, where a man in a different world held his finger over a button that had the capacity to trigger punishment and death for Americans across the country and, ultimately, for our Iraqi neighbors and their little children. Not only did his acts of violence originate from a sterile environment where all truth and perception were mediated to him through intelligence reports and computer screens, but his religious edicts, which were meant to make sense of the turmoil and somehow comfort those in need, did not originate from a place of shared suffering and experience. Since I had grown up seeing my nono sitting at the side of a marriage in crisis or with a child on his or her deathbed, it was a deeply held truth for me that the most lasting change comes from a place of mutuality. Clearly Sheikh Hussein had come to believe the same thing, disgusted as he was with the grand sheikh's charlatanry.

I dared to offer my perspective on a different way by relaying a story of some friends—a community of Iraqi Christians—whose archbishop had been kidnapped by al-Qaeda. Running low on support and even lower on cash, the terrorist group reached big and demanded $3,000,000 for his release. From captivity, however, the archbishop managed to deliver a message to his church, prohibiting them from paying, knowing that the money would be used for evil. His body was found in a shallow grave about a month later.

"The government is talking about retaliation and capital punishment for those who kidnapped and murdered the archbishop," I explained to Sheikh Hussein. "But his church is opposing any kind of eye-for-an-eye approach because they say it would be so unlike Jesus Christ, who gave away his life to his enemies."

Sheikh Hussein jumped to his feet—I'm not even sure if my story was finished—and began clapping, kissing my hands and head, and praising God that anyone would live this way in defiance of all reason and nature. I just laughed and cheered with him! I did not know what lay ahead for the grand sheikh and his fatwas from abroad, but with men like Sheikh Hussein at my side, it seemed he had already lost.

We made haste to get Hussein's gutsy initiative to send baby Noor to surgery under way. A group in Baghdad helped with logistics; a church in South Carolina gave generously. The day of her departure, we spoke one last time with her family by phone. Sheikh Hussein was intoning words of comfort in Arabic as they sat in the airport waiting for their flight to take them out of the country; they would be the first in the history of their entire family to leave Iraq. I'm certain the sheikh's smile was felt as much as it was heard on the receiving end of the line. Suddenly, he said, "Okay, one second . . . ," as he passed the phone to me.

Putting the phone to my ear in the home of this cleric where I had never seen a woman, I felt like I was breaking some taboo as I heard Noor's mother on the other end whispering something to the person beside her in Arabic. Turning her face back to the mouthpiece, she took a leap across the Great Gulf of Language in an effort to get to me and convey her gratitude:

"Mister . . . my child," she said haltingly, "good . . . is good. You save my child."

Her daughter's name, Noor, means "light," and is often construed to mean "God's light" or "light that guides." And here she was, this fifteen-month-old little baby girl in the Baghdad airport, illuminating the way into a future where God's light, unlike all the other luminaries by which we live, does not cast a dark shadow across our ethnicity, geography, or history. Light was driving back darkness. The obviousness of it all only made it more profound, as though someone had planned it that way so we would all get the message.

I handed the phone back to Sheikh Hussein, where he received a final barrage of blessings for the both of us and hung up, fearful of what still lay ahead, but overjoyed that we had risked it and all taken the plunge together. With the fatwa still looming in the distance, it seemed like the history of a people hanged in the balance.

And who's to say it didn't? How many hearts were really healed that day?

Years later, with the daily fighting behind us and most of the country making meaningful forward progress, Noor is still alive and well, preparing for her first year of school, because of her parents' willingness to step out into the unknown and because of Sheikh Hussein's boldness in confronting the system that was handed to him in pursuit of a world remade, where adopting Jesus' model of dying to love and serve those who oppose you and hate you is normal, and where being a Jew—or not being a Jew—does not determine whether you ultimately live or die.

CHAPTER 7

Serving His Enemies

It was an inauspicious autumn day in Iraq when I visited my shoemaking friends in the Soap Makers' Quarter to discuss a new round of production. Sheikh Hussein had provided a significant influx of interest in our work from cities and communities around Iraq to which we had little access apart from him. Baby Noor had successfully returned from surgery and was growing into a healthy little girl back at home. My weekly meetings with tribal sheikhs, Sunni muftis, and Shia mullahs to discuss helping children in their communities were creating more opportunities than we could possibly accept.

Standing on the corner across from the neighborhood bathhouse, I looked up to see a man waving at me. He cupped his left hand out in front of him and pinched three fingers together with his right hand and made that little swirling hand motion that is so ubiquitous across the Middle East, stirring sugar into an imaginary cup of tea, inviting me to join him for conversation and tea in his shop.

That is how I met Mr. Mahdi.

Like many other sections of the bazaar, the Soap Makers' Quarter is primarily known for one thing: its cobblers. Against intuition, tradesmen and -women gather together so that when you want to go to buy car parts, you only need to visit one street, rather than running all over town visiting isolated neighborhood shops. When you need clothes, you go to one street. Technology? One street. And it's nothing for your shopkeeper to walk to his friendly competition across the way, procure the item for you, and then sell it to you in one smooth motion. Better luck next time hitting up the right guy off the bat!

The Soap Makers' Quarter, as its name suggests, was historically the place to go for soap, but globalization had long since caused the bankruptcy of the local soap industry and made room for the Hawrami *klash*-makers to settle in and sell their wares. All the *klash* shops on the street—some twenty or thirty of them—proudly displayed the magnificently colored soles and the pristine white of their shoes in huge glass display windows for all to see. Over the previous year and a half, I had frequently darted in and out of the various shops looking for shoes worthy of our customers in America. But the essence of our model relied on partnerships with four men whom we had asked to buy into our vision, forgoing some of their financial profits up front in order to create a social profit for their community and the children who needed heart surgery. The model was new and exciting for all involved. To the best of local recollection, no one had ever talked about using business for social good before. At best, most business profits that were given charitably were used to build mosques, to help nearby family members in need, or to give handouts to beggars passing by each day. Local and national news began praising the shoemakers for their vision and their selflessness. Local artists, actors, musicians, and real estate developers joined in.

In the quarter, other shoemakers couldn't help but notice the unseemly Americans who showed up each week to cart off boxes and boxes full of shoes, each one representing a season's worth of sales and thousands of dollars of revenue. In this small subculture spanning the mountains of Iraq and Iran, shoemaking was quickly becoming a lost trade. Our promise to save lives with every shoe purchase held out the hope to these other shoemakers of new markets in Europe and America, potentially reviving a shoe that most local youth were beginning to see as quaint and antiquated. Naturally, I thought Mr. Mahdi was trying to find a way to get in on the action. Not only were some of the shoemakers unhappy about the unscientific way we had settled upon a few key partners without testing the waters or asking for bids on the work, but one guy—the self-proclaimed don of shoemaking—came just shy of making us a Mafia-like offer we couldn't refuse when he claimed to control numerous production chains across the region and employed threatening language to induce us to abandon our other partners and sign an exclusive deal with him.

To my relief, Mr. Mahdi had not called me over to discuss shoes at all. In fact, Mahdi and his family were cousins of many of the guys we were already using. Many of the shoes we had already sold were shoes that his family had worked on at some point in the production process. Over tea the family said many kind things about our efforts for the children of Halabja and Iraq and noted some of the news articles that had recently covered a huge celebration banquet we hosted for all of the children whose lives had been saved in the last year.

Then, out of nowhere, came a plea I'll never forget, in part because it is so deeply disconcerting in such a patriarchal society to have retired war veterans supplicating before novices like me in search of help.

"Mr. Jeremy, you've worked for so long selling our shoes—*my family's shoes*—to save the lives of other children. Will you help us save our *own* daughter now?"

You might not expect a man with thirteen children to even remember all their names, let alone weep with the passion and sensitivity of a man who is about to lose his only child, but that was Mahdi, as tender a father as I had ever come across in Iraq, reminding me how dangerous our profiles, generalizations, and stereotypes of each other can be, often erasing our shared humanity and laying the foundations for theories and philosophies that allow us to disparage and disregard one another.

Mahdi and his family lived on the Iranian border, where so much of Saddam's fighting against Iranian forces took place throughout the

1980s. Like Nasreen, Bakhtiar, and Arazoo, Mahdi, his wife, and his eight sons had fled the chronic violence and Halabja chemical massacre by heading east toward Iran, where they settled with tens of thousands of others in refugee camps and ultimately managed to establish a sense of normalcy among the wider Kurdish diaspora in Iran. When his daughter Khadeeja was born years later, she had a life-threatening heart condition. Scientific research[1] was beginning to suggest that paternal exposure to sulfur mustard gas, such as that used by Saddam Hussein, could create a considerable increase in heart and other birth defects among the children of those exposed. How many tens of thousands of men had been exposed to mustard gas throughout the war and Saddam's internal campaigns under "Chemical" Ali? No one could say for sure. But every father in the northeastern part of the country with a dying child had reason to wonder whether or not their baby should be counted among the casualties these twenty years hence.

Khadeeja was sixteen years old by the time Jessica and I banged on the painted metal gate outside Mahdi's house on the northeastern outskirts of the city. It was lunchtime. She should have been in school like all the other kids, but walking uphill to class each day with an oversized, perforated heart proved more difficult for Khadeeja than she could bear some days. Her heart problem caused her to become exhausted easily. And between the years of running from Saddam and displacement inside Iran and Iraq, some of her older sisters had never finished school anyway. Some days—like the day we met her—it was just easier to stay home than fight back as her body failed her.

She was by far the oldest child Jessica and I had ever heard about in Iraq who was still living with a life-threatening heart defect. In our limited experience, the backlog of children waiting for surgery was remarkably skewed toward babies and toddlers. An eight- or ten-year-old was rare. But a sixteen-year-old? Most of these broken hearts had a short window of time within which they could be repaired. Outside of that sweet spot, surgeries became more complicated, risky, and expensive as doctors were forced to grapple with the heart defect itself *and* the collateral damage caused by the heart as it overworked itself to compensate for its own deficiencies.

Children with heart problems are often cold from poor circulation. How is she not cold in this icebox?

Her brother must have seen me shivering as he grabbed the idle kerosene heater and fired it up, drawing it in close where I could warm my hands and face.

Khadeeja had been rejected from every other avenue available. Since her diagnosis at four years old in Iran, Mahdi's family had moved from hope to despair time and time again. She had long been on the list of children registered with the First Lady of Iraq's charitable foundation, but their program partners in England and Austria wouldn't touch her case. A combination of medical ethics about the real lifesaving value of these kinds of late-stage surgeries and a cold calculus that many hospitals' charitable programs used in selecting poster children from abroad to receive first-class medical care had come together time and time again to keep Khadeeja in a perpetual holding pattern, waiting in line for a surgery whose success rate became less viable every day. And so she waited and worsened with time, making it even harder for us to try to save her life by the time I eventually met Mahdi and he asked us to help.

Mahdi and the family had almost given up hope. At sixteen, she was quickly approaching the normal marrying age, and everyone in the family had an acute awareness that marriage before heart surgery would be a virtual death sentence in and of itself, with the expectation that she would get pregnant immediately and put more stress on her failing heart than anything she had experienced to date. No one was dreaming about college for Khadeeja. She managed to squeeze in private viewings of popular American television shows and ogled the heartthrobs just like any other girl, but was anyone in her family truly holding out hope for a wedding dress, a party to end all parties, or kids for Khadeeja?

Khadeeja's electric smile and personality made a deep impression on me the day I met her. She was not a passive girl, content with sulking in silence or whiling away her days at home as the rest of the world moved on without her. She expected, against all the odds, to get the surgery she needed and finish school. She had dreams. With an optimism that didn't seem to fade as the years of adulthood approached, she did not know that she was supposed to have given up by now.

I was convinced that Khadeeja was going to make her mark on the world. And we were going to help her.

Earlier that year our relationships in Israel had taken an unexpected turn for the worse. It was 120 degrees outside as the most grueling part of the summer refused to subside. Ramadan was in full swing, with its prohibition on food or drink during daylight hours. Jessica had just boarded a plane back to the States for an end-of-the-summer visit with family, and I was alone with Scott and Abby, old friends from college who had recently joined up with our work in Iraq.

The notification came in an e-mail. Our partners in Israel had decided they wanted unmediated access to our partners in Iraq, hoping to speed up the funding process, eliminate the waste that often comes through intermediaries like us, etc.

It was a punch in the gut. Cody, in particular, had invested countless hours into both sides of this partnership, and we had accomplished so much together. In our short year of partnership, we had quickly become one of the largest donors to the organization in Israel, due in part to a local arrangement we had created with a very high-profile official inside Iraq.[2] The representatives of our high-profile government contact had initially been vehemently opposed to working with Israel in any way whatsoever. They had been keen to partner with us to save lives—their backlog of children was over three thousand at that time, with one hundred and fifty new children being added to their roster each month. But the political risks to their patron, and the unknowns about the physical risks to the families we would help, seemed too great for them to accept. They had insisted that we begin a new partnership together in India.

Although we seriously considered it, we had a strong desire to be heart-menders in every sense of the word: to be peacemakers, healers, and to reconcile that which had been torn asunder, including the intense distrust between Jews and Muslims, Israelis and Iraqis.

Over the course of those early negotiations, Cody had traveled regularly to the head offices with plans and proposals and ultimately had won them over to the idea of working with us in Israel. Without him, it was nearly impossible to imagine our friends in Israel making any lasting inroads with this politician and the associated foundation.

Our naivety to the way of the world at that time blinded us to the fact that they were, in many ways, setting us up for the fall, allowing us to be *their* partner so that they could always maintain a real deniability about having any relationship with Israel themselves. With their functionaries and party players in increasingly open friendship with Iran, such escape hatches were par for the course. Cody's plan was an immediate boon for us in the early days—an agreement to help nearly fifty children per year together, with a cash contract worth $120,000 annually. These were numbers far greater than we could have dreamed of on our own as a three-month-old organization the day Cody reached out to them and dared to rope the moon.

We ultimately refused the premise of the e-mail from Israel and insisted that we were the main financing body with whom our partners in Israel should be concerned. But they saw a bigger kitty behind us and believed we were an obstruction to greater profitability for their organization. We tried to appeal to them on the grounds that our visas were actually maintained under the aegis of the very patron from whom they sought to estrange us, but none of our arguments availed.

I later learned that they had amicably absorbed another entity in Iraq, one of our early partners, which now gave them an official presence in the country and a new burden to fund salaries and office expenses and maintain a public profile worthy of such a footprint. Up until this point, the group in Israel had never even met a representative—let alone the leadership—of our key political and financial ally in Iraq. But the acquisition suddenly gave them local staff on the ground, and within weeks they were positioning themselves to change the fundamental agreement upon which we were established in Iraq.

That summer, while we were lining up a huge list of kids to help, they sent their new employee—a friend and close colleague of ours by all accounts—into a joint meeting to unilaterally declare an end to "the triangulation of partnership," a fancy phrase that primarily meant, "We want all the control."

In many ways, the group in Israel was right. Things had been triangulated and become complicated. But the spirit of brotherhood had suddenly been upended.

What were we doing? What were we offering to this world around us that was literally blowing up by the minute, if those of us in the know—those of us on the inside—couldn't figure out how to dwell in unity?

Our team was blindsided . . . devastated. Everything we had built to that point was suddenly crashing down around us. Not because of a fatwa. Not because of an unproven idea, a poor model, or a lack of funding. Rather, because our closest ally stood holding the sledgehammer.

The guy who engineered the squeeze-out asked me to keep sending money and funding children through their agency, but they had simultaneously ripped the rug out from beneath our feet, undercutting our relationship with our sponsor and host, throwing us onto rocky ground with regard to our residency and work visas, and violating the very nature of our agreement and the plausible deniability our high-profile partner had come to rely upon in order to save lives.

The final e-mail on the matter had all the gloss and gall of a southern pat on the back, landing squarely atop the protruding knife handle. The thrust of it said, "Don't stress too much about this; there are greater things on the horizon if you'll just accept this as a gift from God. But God is sort of bound up and cannot do too much for us until we let go of our small vision."

It struck me as odd that I was the only one being asked to let go of my small vision. In all our discussions, he never responded to my concern that he was the one acting erratically. I call it the "God card," the permit that sanctions bloodshed, genocide, and lesser power grabs like this, born from the myopic conviction that God is on our side, so we cannot be wrong.

Everything changed that blistering Ramadan day. But you know what? He was right about one thing: it was a gift from God.

It was not uncommon for Jess and me to take Emma and Micah with us to visit patients and their families. Jessica's maternal instincts and her knee-jerk inclination to give everything she owns to help others were some of the earliest hallmarks of our work and indisputably catapulted us through our early impact and beyond. Naturally, mothers and fathers loved her presence and her friendship. There's certainly a place for a stoic doctor in a lab coat or an administrator in a suit when your child's life is on the line, but nothing puts a parent at ease like knowing that a real live mother is going to be there every step of the way, holding your hand, whispering in your ear, offering you a hug, and fighting your battles for you.

Mahdi and his family invited us to join them for dinner one winter evening so we could discuss next steps for Khadeeja and her surgery. With the new developments in Israel, we were actively seeking alternatives. Moreover, the doctors in Israel had just declared Khadeeja inoperable.

Over dinner, Mr. Mahdi packed white bean and tomato soup into patties with oily short-grained rice, balanced one on his fingers, and shoveled it into his mouth, licking his hands clean with each scoop. Mahdi had grandkids who were older than his youngest son, so he was a natural at making sure all the mouths at the table stayed filled. When our son, Micah—then one year old—looked to be struggling with his bread or drink, Mr. Mahdi kindly slopped some soup and rice together and shoved his fingers into Micah's mouth. No one was going hungry at this table!

We had come over that night with a very clear sense that we were there to help them, but it seemed as though Mahdi and his family were helping us just as much. It had been a hard season for our family, with the Israel group forcing the hand of our local patron and our visas, banking, office space, and housing all hanging by a thread. I had missed our family's Thanksgiving for the first time earlier that year. It wasn't only our first holiday apart, but it was Jessica's first holiday in Iraq, and she had been left preparing a feast and celebrating with friends in the cold, intermittent darkness of a city without electricity.

I never realized how important Thanksgiving was for me, officially announcing Christmastime, ushering in the promise of new life and joy while all around is dead or dying. Thanksgiving always opened the door for hope. Without being around to celebrate Thanksgiving that year, the hope and the renewal never came, and I was left with ice on my heart that wouldn't seem to melt.

Until dinner with Mahdi. His family made us feel warm, normal, and loved—even as we sought to do the same for them. In Mahdi, Khadeeja, and her twelve siblings, Jessica, Emma, Micah, and I found a family that cozied up to us and a place that was something like a home away from home. They were brothers who called me to the bazaar to drink tea while they hammered out a new pair of shoes; sisters who taught Jessica how to stuff rice into properly hollowed-out eggplant skins and told us we were missed; and gray-haired forebears who fed our kids with their fingers, challenged our parenting, and nagged us when we weren't doing things the right way.

With our Israel partnership on the skids and their declaration that Khadeeja was inoperable, we were back to the start in our effort to save Khadeeja's life. I reached out to my friend the chieftain from that first debacle of a luncheon at Sheikh Hussein's and devised a plan to travel with him to Turkey to search for a hospital that would partner with us to save the lives of the children in his tribe and young women like Khadeeja.

We traveled to Turkey with a few Turkish businessmen who promised to be the vanguard for our efforts, curating a list of hospitals and meetings with top leadership to negotiate a charitable deal. Sadly, their motives for helping became increasingly suspect as the trip wore on. At the end of each meeting, after it had been well established that the hospital in which we were seated did not have the capacity to perform highly complex congenital heart surgeries, the conversation would turn to adults in need of bypass surgeries, cancer treatment, and elective procedures, like breast enlargement, Botox, and nose jobs.

The chief had unknowingly fallen in step with the bait-and-switch masters of medical tourism. Dejected, the chief and I ended our last night together in a tiny hotel room, rifling through legal documents and contracts, awkwardly pretending that neither of us was carnal enough to be amused by the screaming and the knocking of the bedposts against the wall next door.

I arrived back in Iraq empty-handed, but the trip had unlocked a vision that we had never entertained before. What if we could do it all ourselves—door-to-door? What if we had direct access to the medical experts and did not require an intermediary like the one we had recently lost in Israel? What if we were more than a financier, funneling money to other organizations to carry out the work?

In the previous arrangements, we were never left holding the bag for excess medical bills or logistics gone wrong. We did not know what it was like to repatriate the body of a child who had died in the operating room. In fact, we barely knew anything about the children we were helping, as most of them had been mere recipients of our money, not recipients of our time and attention.

What if Khadeeja could mark a significant turning point, where the relationship and trust we nurtured were as important as the resources and time we spent?

Throughout our tour of Istanbul with the Turkish snake-oil sales-men, the names of two different medical institutions kept coming up. We needed to research, regroup, and make an independent trip back to Istanbul.

I imagine it was somewhere between the fifth and sixth bites of his Big Mac, as Scott was sopping up a few dollops of Thousand Island dressing, that he noticed the paper advertisement on his red plastic tray celebrating the twenty children from Iraq who had recently received life-altering eye surgery at the Anadolu Medical Center in Istanbul, Turkey.

With suicide bombings as one of the hallmarks of the country's sec-tarian conflict—to say nothing of the earliest days of heavy bombard-ment by coalition forces—Iraqis incurred innumerable eye injuries from the high-pressure blasts of air and shrapnel that often became embedded in and around the eye. While military personnel adapted routines and protocols to reduce their injuries by wearing ballistic eye armor, civilian families simply going out to shop for the day's food remained highly vul-nerable to such injuries—or death.

Scott and Abby were in Istanbul on a mission to find us a new surgi-cal partner. My previous efforts with the chieftain had not been a total waste of time. At least now we knew there were a few hospitals in Tur-key worth pursuing—and now Scott and Abby could add one more to the list, a hospital that had already shown an interest in providing chari-table surgeries to children in their own backyard.

In between meetings with a few regional centers and the massive Harvard affiliate that we really wanted to land, Scott tracked down the website for the hospital he saw in McDonald's and fired off an e-mail to the top decision maker, introducing our work and attempting to make a case as to why their state-of-the-art hospital should help us save the lives of thousands of children, many of whom were Kurdish—the sworn enemy of many Turkish nationalists—and why they should do it at a loss.

Scott and I were shooting text messages back and forth between Istanbul and Iraq. To our collective surprise, he got an immediate response from the head of cardiac surgery:

Can you see me today?
—Professor Sertaç Çiçek, MD

Dr. Çiçek (CHEE-check) had recently left the Harvard group that we were so pining after, and he'd become the top heart guy at Anadolu, a new nonprofit hospital funded by the profits of the holding company that owned the domestic production and/or distribution rights to scores of brands, including Miller, Efes Pilsener, Fanta, Coca-Cola, and Mc-Donald's. The cradle-to-grave strategy apparently included bringing you safely into the world, then consistently robbing your health through years of terrible food and drink on the promise that it could all be given back to you through a world-class medical center that offered coronary-artery bypass grafts and liposuction. Nevertheless, the medical center was full of great people who approached their work with tremendous excellence, were at the top of their fields all around, and were given the freedom to operate independently of the holding group and its charitable foundation.

And, not to be outdone by the Harvard program down the road, Anadolu had retained the world-renowned Johns Hopkins Medicine—one of the great pioneering institutions in pediatric heart surgery—to certify their programs and monitor their protocols.

Like the stereotypical heart surgeon, when Dr. Çiçek walks through a door, he doesn't enter a room as much as he fills it. His close-cropped silver hair would look fatherly on your average Turkish shopkeeper or newspaper salesman. On Çiçek, however, for all his size and stature, his silver hair evokes the feelings you might have around the shiny barrel of a stainless steel Smith & Wesson . . . or an arctic wolf. After meeting him the first time you'd swear he was ten feet tall and probably bulletproof. In fact, he cut his teeth as a soldier in the Turkish military. At the exact time Saddam Hussein was beginning his chemical weapons campaign against Iranian troops and Kurdish dissidents, Dr. Çiçek was soldiering among the Kurds in southeastern Turkey.

To say anything further at this point will undoubtedly offend my friends on one side of this mountain range or another. Objective reporting about southeastern Turkey that seeks to acknowledge both the sins and merits of each side's argument is often demonized as undue sympathy to the "oppressors" or the "terrorists." The Kurds claim the land they call Kurdistan was arbitrarily (or, perhaps, strategically) hacked up and taken from them in the aftermath of World War I when the defeated Ottoman Empire was reimagined by Western powers as a jigsaw puzzle of weaker, ethnically incongruent states. The Turks, in a clear revision of history, long claimed there was no such thing as a Kurd, only "mountain Turks," and they made all manner of Kurdishness illegal. Naming children—let alone educating them—in the Kurdish language was illegal. Kurdish flags were obviously banned, but the neurosis sometimes went so far as to prohibit "Kurdish colors" from appearing adjacent to one another in public. Contemporary reports of mass graves continue to surface,[3] and suspicions exist among human rights groups that more atrocities would be discovered if the Turkish government didn't treat the Kurdish enclave as such a restricted area.

While Kurdish rebellions and guerrilla warfare have existed for decades, the modern Turkish state has had great cause to be anxious about Kurdish nationalism and the development of Kurdish political momentum since the late 1970s and the rise of the Kurdistan Workers' Party, a Kurdish terrorist group that has variously conducted kidnappings, assassinations, and suicide bombings on government buildings, buses, malls, and tourist sites across Turkey, Iraq, and Europe.

In the mideighties, amidst a peak of anti-Kurdish sentiment in Ankara and across the country, Kurds from northern Iraq began seeking refuge across the border in Turkey, doing their best to outrun what would soon become Saddam Hussein's genocidal Anfal campaign and the attendant chemical attacks. A young army medic named Sertaç Çiçek was among the Turkish troops tasked with attending to the safety of the early refugees, the establishment of camps, and the security of nearby Turkish civilians and institutions.

Perspectives on Kurdish life in Turkish refugee camps differ tremendously, with an average Turk believing they magnanimously opened their arms and coffers to extend a warm welcome to their Muslim neighbors to the south, while an average Kurd might highlight stories on the politicization and obstruction of international aid, Turkish feuds with Iran over responsibilities for refugees, and the occasional claim of state-sponsored food poisoning carried out by Turks against Kurds in exile.[4]

By the time international news coverage on Anfal and Halabja hit its peak, Dr. Çiçek had become physician in chief of the Turkish Presidential Guard Regiment Infirmary. Tens of thousands of Kurds remained exiled in Turkey into the 1990s, in grave distrust of Saddam Hussein's disingenuous calls of "Olly, olly, oxen free."

Fourteen years forward, and Dr. Çiçek was in the lead role in the new Hopkins affiliate, predicated largely on the condition that he be afforded the chance to develop a charitable pocket inside the program and allowed to travel the world contributing directly to the advancement of heart surgery for children in underdeveloped countries.

Coming from Iraq, entering the thirty-foot-tall vestibule of Anadolu's main campus for the first time is a bit like walking into one of Saddam Hussein's heyday palaces for all its veined marble floors, spaciousness, accoutrements, and indulgences of comfort and style. Scott was prepared to sell the surgeon, CFO, and CEO on the merits of helping us eradicate the backlog of children in need of heart surgery. Like with any business proposal, he expected a tough sell. What he found, in fact, was even more surprising.

Like the vanguard infantrymen of his youth, Dr. Çiçek was steps ahead of us at every meeting, having researched our website before we arrived, greased the wheels with the admins, and put together financial figures and projections as to what they could offer us.

"I can work anywhere in this country . . . ," he said, a sampling of how he likely threw his weight around and not-so-subtly succeeded in convincing management to make good on their previous promises and sanction our program, lest he begin responding to the numerous offers on the table for employment elsewhere.

Within just a few hours, everything had fallen into place.

Our colleagues in Israel had remarked earlier that the one thing you absolutely must have to make a program like this work, amidst all the internal politics of helping indigent children from abroad, is a surgeon in the local system who is passionately committed to the cause. In Israel, the cause had as much to do with peace between Muslims and Jews, Arabs and Israelis, as it did with heart disease. In Turkey, this former soldier who had been witness to some of the worst of Turkish racism, Kurdish terrorism, and Ba'athist genocide, as well as the best of human kindness, was our man, committing himself as much to our platform of peacemaking as to the eradication of the backlog of Iraqi children in need of heart surgery.

We took to calling him our "Surgeon of Peace."

While the getting was good, Scott produced an incomplete medical report on Khadeeja Mahdi and asked Dr. Çiçek whether or not he thought she was still operable. And in that moment, we saw what would become the recurring theme of our lifesaving, peacemaking work with Dr. Çiçek.

"Bring her to me immediately. I will do it."

Although his commanding exterior often belied his deep compassion, his natural impulse to put his reputation and his well-being on the line to help those in need reminded me so much of Jessica and Abby— these best friends since college who were repeatedly pushing me (and the rest of our community) to put more skin in the game, to risk, and to genuinely put ourselves on the line for those around us in need. As a first-time or one-off decision, Dr. Çiçek's overture toward Khadeeja, a girl we obviously loved deeply, might have been dismissed as surgical arrogance—surgeons tend to have a penchant for cutting and a reputation for callousness. But the coming years would demonstrate again and again the ways he would put his own program's well-being and his personal finances on the line to help us save the lives of the most down-and-out kids, who had often been rejected from every other avenue available.

Scott and Abby returned to Iraq that Christmas with a signed contract to send twenty children to Turkey each month at a considerable savings over Israel, a gift for the tens of thousands of children in Iraq waiting in line.

CHAPTER 8

"Anyone but the Turks!"

"Mr. Jeremy, don't do this to me. You've got to work something out for us," Mahdi said.

This was not going as smoothly as I had planned. For weeks we had been finalizing the details of sending Khadeeja to our Turkish "Surgeon of Peace" in Istanbul for surgery. We had been selling Mahdi's shoes for months in the States and Europe to pay for our portion of the surgery. We had solicited additional donations on her behalf. He had been selling shoes locally and saving what he could to pay for the portion we required of him. One college student from Ohio, Emily Miller, tired of seeing Western antipathy toward Muslims in Iraq, persuaded her entire extended family to give up their Christmases to help save Khadeeja's life. When all was said and done, they'd given over four thousand dollars for Khadeeja.

Airline tickets were bought. Khadeeja's bags were even packed. It was the eleventh hour, on the night she was set to leave, and here in her family's living room her father was getting cold feet.

I have worked something out for you, I thought indignantly.

Jessica and I had been separated inside Mahdi's house for hours, me in the front room with the family and neighborhood men, she somewhere in a back alcove where no man outside the immediate family dared to tread. The brown, boxy kerosene heater was blazing in front of me as men in military fatigue jackets with Russian muskrat *ushankas* over their ears filed through one by one to pay their respects to Mahdi and wish him well and pray God's mercy for him as he crossed over into enemy territory and handed his beloved daughter over to the oppressor to save her life.

I had not bargained on this. What an impossible proposal I had come up with for our inaugural trip to Turkey! Sure, I knew the macro-history of the Turks and the Kurds, but I never thought a father with his child in need would plead with me to let this cup pass. We were back to the same kind of impasse we had only recently overcome when we quit sending Arab Muslim children to Israel for surgery. The Arabs of Iraq were thrilled with our Turkish solution; there was no grave narrative of plotting and oppression like in the stories they had grown up hearing about Israel and Zionism. If anything, the Ottoman antecedent to modern-day Turkey represented the glory days of the caliphate and Muslim rule across the globe. Now, however, we were asking the Kurds to thrust themselves on the mercy of their nemesis neighbors in hopes of saving their children's lives.

"There has to be another way," he said. "Send me to Iran instead. I won't go to Turkey. We have friends in Iran. Khadeeja was even *born* in Iran. We can speak their language. They are kind, and they love us."

He was clearly suffering from a temporary bout of amnesia, brought on by the anxiety of leading his family into a harrowing situation that would be completely out of his control. In an instant, to protect his family from the thing he considered to be a far greater evil, he had done what few Kurds could, denying the despicable plight of Kurds in Iran, including political imprisonment and recent executions for "enmity against God."[1]

"The Iranians saved our lives when Saddam gassed us and sent us running from our homes. The Turks? They closed their borders and poisoned us in the refugee camps. And they flew their jets over our villages, even here in Iraq, to bomb our livestock, our homes, and our children."

If I was getting this among the men, with their pride and natural proclivity toward bravery and brinkmanship, who knew what Jessica was going through two rooms away with the women, who, once alone, frequently lost all sense of propriety and privacy.

I was not yet thirty years old, in a room of Kurdish giants who had not changed their clothing since the 1970s (before I was born), when they truly needed those military fatigues and trapper hats while fighting for freedom from the Ba'athists in the caves and mountains. I was to kiss their hands in respect when they entered the room. All my sage wisdom was stuck in the back of my cotton mouth, the tea glass, water glass, coffee glass, and powdered orange drink glass in front of me long empty. On what grounds could I advise these men, who had fought alongside the sitting president, on minority politics, parenting, or how to weigh the risk of a child dying against the risk of walking into the lion's den?

Sadly, I had no alternatives. Not only was I lacking any serious network in neighboring Iran, I wasn't entirely sure that the CIA compound on the hill near my house wouldn't empty out to arrest me and put me in jail for breaching America's thirty-year-long economic sanctions against Iran if I sent him to Tehran with money to pay for his daughter's surgery. In any case, it was against our policy, and the wheels were in motion. It was Turkey or nothing at this point.

Begrudgingly, through much trepidation, he agreed (again) to follow through with our arrangements for Turkey. As the elders lined the street and ushered the family into their caravan for the airport, Mahdi pulled Jessica aside.

"Make sure you come and check on my family while I'm away. You have become my daughter. You are welcome here, and I need you to care for my family."

When Khadeeja and her family landed in Istanbul six hours later, Dr. Çiçek had a car waiting for them. When you've lived the majority of your life in scantly populated mountain villages, morning rush hour in a city of thirteen million people can be a little unnerving. For two hours in stop-and-go traffic they were carried behind "enemy lines," in a black executive limousine van, through the grandeur of Istanbul, surrounded on every side by majestic mosques, Roman aqueducts, suspension bridges, and waterfront palaces. Khadeeja took particular interest in the upscale promenades, sidewalk dining, and articulated "slinky" buses.

Mahdi and the family did their best to speak in the airport (and even in the limo-van) in hushed tones, fearing what would happen to them if they were overheard speaking Kurdish.

Their introduction to Dr. Çiçek and the team was warm, and they were treated like distinguished guests. To our great joy, all the preoperative tests yielded results that made Dr. Çiçek eager to operate on Khadeeja, confident that he had the techniques necessary to repair her heart *and* overcome the chronically high blood pressure in her lungs that had resulted after so many years of compensation for her failing heart.

In addition to all of the medical reasons one might trot out to promote heart surgery in early childhood, the psychological impact of a high-risk surgery and all its attendant scars as an adolescent should not, in my opinion, ever be downplayed. I cannot imagine what sort of thoughts and fears went through Khadeeja's mind as she listened to Fatima, the Kurdish nurse from southeastern Turkey, do her best to translate the Turkish medical jargon into the southern, highlander dialect of Khadeeja's family. It's amazing what a sketchy translation can do to heighten fears and apprehension:

Very risky . . . death . . . 90 percent . . . God willing.

I've been the only familiar face around to scores of children as the red "Authorized Personnel Only" sign on a hospital's hermetic doors taunted us and the little one entrusted briefly to my care cried his or her way into the belly of the operating theater. Khadeeja was our oldest friend to ever pass through those doors, and while it's a heartbreaking scene to watch a toddler disappear behind that curtain, the silent resignation of a sixteen-year-old makes you speculate all the more about her state of mind as she passes out of sight.

I had two major knee surgeries when I was Khadeeja's age. Scary, but not life-threatening. I wouldn't wish my presurgery imaginations on anyone.

Upstairs, Mr. Mahdi and his wife fasted, fumbled their prayer beads, and read the Qur'an. Unlike some hospitals in the States, there were no staged updates (not that they expected any such extravagance). Instead they waited, without word, for hours on end. It seemed time had stood still. Or perhaps time was in fast-forward. *Has she been in there a full day already?*

Finally, a nurse appeared and made hand motions implying they should follow her. Down the corridor they stumbled, toward the elevator, where they were finally conveyed to the admitting desk of the intensive care unit. In the awkward, confined space of the elevator they each studied the nurse's face for a clue as to whether or not Khadeeja was alive.

There it was. That was a smile . . . she must be okay! Wait, she stopped. Maybe it was a nervous smile. She's trying to mask the fact that Khadeeja is dead. I knew we never should have come here . . .

The nurse swiped her special access card, the hallway opened to them, and they were seated in an austere postoperative consult room. Upon her arrival, Khadeeja had mistaken the hospital for a hotel, such was its beauty, the size of her private room, and the faux photo above her bed that concealed the built-in oxygen lines, electrical outlets, and gauges.

This must be the room where they tell you your kid is dead. There is nothing nice in here—just a table and chairs. They all told us we couldn't trust the Turks; probably just a plot to kick us when we're down, like Mardin all over again.

In burst Dr. Çiçek, Nurse Fatima at his side with her ever-present walkie-talkie phone.

Although the practice had long evaporated from contemporary Turkish culture, these elder Kurds jumped to stand in his presence, a show of honor and respect, instinctively reading his stoic face for signs of life, or . . .

"Khadeeja is well . . . ," he said without breaking a smile. "The surgery was uneventful. She will be in the ICU for a few days, where we will monitor her closely. You will be able to see her in a few hours." Fatima translated.

Khadeeja's mother almost fainted. Mahdi praised God, thanked the doctor, and lifted his hands in prayer for all involved.

Khadeeja recovered quickly, just as expected, and soon the family was using their interim days before her final checkup to visit friends and family throughout the diaspora in Istanbul.

Three weeks after Khadeeja's surgery, Jessica stood in the freezing midnight air, just past the blast walls, crow's-feet, and tire strippers at the exterior security gate to the regional airport near Khadeeja's home. Across the street, local security forces were evacuating a quarter-mile-long line of cars, deploying bomb-sniffing dogs, and manually searching anything that looked suspicious. With Turkish and Iranian fighter jets bombing the Qandil Mountains, the Kurdish-Arab conflict raging on the fault lines, and the Sunni-Shia strife throughout the south, these sorts of security precautions were entirely normal, even in the relatively humdrum cities, reminding everyone around that terrorism and ethnic violence were very real and that any hope of sustainable peace was still pockmarked and tenuous.

A small utility vehicle pulled up, and Khadeeja's red crocheted cap was quick to emerge from the backseat to greet her brothers and sisters, aunts and uncles, who had all gathered to welcome her home. They had sent her off for an impossible mission, many of them probably resigning themselves internally to the reality that they might not see her alive again. In spite of the cold, the scene was electric.

The next day, I joined the family for lunch at the house.

"Mr. Jeremy, I have to tell you, Dr. Çiçek is such a great man! By God, he is a real Muslim! A *real* Muslim, I tell you!"

The massive transformation of the heart expressed in that single statement was enough to fuel me for years to come. His outsized fear of "the other" was gone. A wall of divisiveness that said, "*Those* people—those *Turks*—are entirely different from *my* people," was gone. And that place in his heart that was once occupied by terror and caricature was replaced with one of the most profound things he could have possibly concluded:

"Dr. Çiçek is a *Muslim*. He's just like me, and I'm just like him! We are from the same group; we belong together in the same sentence, in the same people, in the same room!"

Months later, with Khadeeja back in school and all going well, I was on the Iranian border, visiting Mr. Mahdi's hometown village. As I left the main square (nothing more than a mosque and a few shops at the base of the mountains), I headed east, uphill toward the mud-brick residence of one of our elder shoemakers. I was doing my best by this point to dress appropriately for my context—suits for business meetings, village attire for village meetings, etc. In spite of my best efforts, I didn't stand a chance of blending in. I was spotted, singled out by a man from behind his thick-lensed glasses, hunched over a cane, walking in the middle of the dirt road.

"Hey, I know you! You are the bald American who gave Khadeeja her heart surgery! We know about you and the *Muslim* doctors in Istanbul who saved her life! You're a good boy! Thank you so much!"

It was not that surprising that Mahdi's heart followed Khadeeja's. I had spoken frequently about human-scale diplomacy and face-to-face peacemaking efforts, but I was altogether unprepared for the wildfire spread of Mahdi's good news, his passionate defense of the Turks who saved his daughter's life, and his ability to completely reimagine the history he had been handed in light of kindness and mercy. The operative word was no longer *Turk*. Or, at least, *Turk* didn't immediately evoke negative thoughts the way it once had. For a short time, in the life of at least one family and their village, *Turk* meant "lifesaver," our kind of people.

Khadeeja was now a part of our story, and together we had entered a much greater story. Preemptive love was remaking the world, setting wrongs to right.

CHAPTER 9

Facing Down Death

The rat-tat-tat on the office door startled me out of my midafternoon rice-and-beans carbo-crash. We had only been sending children to Turkey for a short time, and word was spreading across Iraq about a group of Americans and a Turkish surgeon who were helping a number of down-and-out, last-chance children who had been rejected by all the other organizations abroad. For better or worse, the rumors rang like an amnesty bell to parents everywhere whose children had been denied a chance at one of the coveted surgery spots. The politically connected families—the wealthy families—consistently found ways to leverage their family's lineage, their insider information, or their wealth to ensure their kids ended up on the invite-only government lists in Baghdad and Erbil. But your average family, with an official salary of a few hundred dollars a month and no cultural cachet on which to trade, might be left at the back of the line with an urgent child while the less acutely ill children of old-guard sheikhs, parliamentarians, and ministers easily cut their way to the front of the line for the treatment they needed to live. Iraq was rife with playground politics, where the strong survived and the weak were trampled underfoot.

The knocking and the doorbell sounded again as I approached the door and peered into the peephole. Through the fisheye lens I saw a single figure standing on the ten-foot-wide landing of our top-floor apartment office—a lone soldier. His jaw was cut from granite, and he had the shoulders of a Depression-era carnival strong man—the cartoon characters who wore unitards and lifted black spherical dumbbells of iron ore with mind-blowing kilogram numbers painted in white.

Even when we are on our best behavior, our hearts seem designed to sink when the rapping at our office door is a black-mustached man in a red beret and combat-ready military fatigues. Once the image is seared in your brain, the imagination finds clever ways of preparing for the worst.

His knocking was a little brusque, wasn't it? Is this guy about to bust the door down? Or, *Was that knocking . . . or shots fired?*

A hyperactive imagination is doubly rowdy when you live in Iraq, run around with gun-toting sheikhs, and have a fatwa calling for your team's death hanging over your head. It's like the lump that rises in your throat when the cop pulls up behind you (even though you know you are going the speed limit) or kids who instinctively tuck their toys away when Mom startles them, catching them imagining their way into far-off lands. From the ground up, we are taught to fear authority.

The real-life soldier was much smaller than the foreboding, broad-shouldered menace cut by the convex distortion in the peephole. Instead, the most humble of all the local soldiers I had ever met spoke peace to me and asked if he could sit.

Yusuf was my age, newly married, working at a military outpost in the storied city of Kirkuk. Kirkuk is Iraq's Jerusalem, restive and highly contested between the country's Turkmen, Kurds, and Arabs. It's rumored to sit on lakes of underground oil, and Saddam pursued an aggressive, violent Arabization process in Kirkuk, expelling Kurds who had lived there for generations, overwriting the headstones of Kurdish graves with Arab names, inducing Arabs to move in and marry Kurdish women, thereby diluting bloodlines and reducing Kurdish claims to the land. After the 2003 invasion, the Kurds were quick to reclaim power and embark on their own version of Kurdification, ostensibly reclaiming that which was historically theirs, but doing so inevitably at the expense of young Arab families who knew Kirkuk as home.

With U.S. military backing, the Kurds currently had the upper hand in Kirkuk, although threats from terrorists within and Baghdad's military posturing outside gave the residents of Kirkuk in every quarter reason to fear for their lives and their future. As though Yusuf's struggles weren't hard enough, he had just learned that his newborn baby daughter—"Hope"—was suffering from many life-threatening holes in her heart. She needed help, and she needed help quickly.

One of the little-confessed secrets of international development work is that people like me, who, by necessity, work with limited funds for outsized problems, often make our decisions about who we help and who we reject based on something more than hard-and-fast metrics about income, need, and prognosis. The truth is, some of the checks and balances that we put in place to help us make wise triage decisions also cut out the very humanity that drove us into these intractable problems in the first place. We want to make unbiased, non-discriminatory decisions that give all children an equal chance at life, but there are unknowns in our calculus that we often do not even realize until we have walked away from the decision and reflected on it after the fact.

Hope was a tiny baby with a big problem. She probably wasn't a very good gamble in the grand scheme of what we were trying to accomplish—especially not with a surgeon who was new to our work, who had put his neck on the line, and who needed a string of big wins in order to grease the wheels of the bureaucracy that we would inevitably need to keep our program running well. In retrospect, I did not choose to send Hope to surgery on the basis of her medical need alone. There was something intangible there: her father's smile; the chance to introduce preemptive love into a community of soldiers and possibly change the dominant conversation about good guys versus bad guys going on around the country; the threat and the promise of making good on my initial conversations with Sheikh Hussein in which he and his friends offered me every ounce of protection they could in order to establish a lifesaving coalition in the ravaged city of Kirkuk.

The Jewish prophet Daniel is said to be buried in Kirkuk—the same Daniel who was thrown into the den of voracious lions and presumed dead, the Daniel who came through unscathed by a miraculous deliverance at the bidding of the very God who created the lions and apparently controlled their appetites. Like flaunting the fatwa of the grand sheikh, meeting with the grand mufti to combat the fatwa, and our insistence on sending sick kids to their enemies in Israel and Turkey, working with a soldier to save the life of his baby in the explosive city of Kirkuk had a lions'-den quality to it. Our closest friends insisted that Kirkuk was a no-go zone. The only Americans we knew who ever traveled to Kirkuk did so covered in Kevlar, embedded in multicar caravans, under the watchful eye of numerous armed guards.

Kirkuk, however, was *not* just a thrilling risk for me. Our journey has never been about testing boundaries for testing's sake. The "love first" mantra does not spring from a self-aggrandizing desire to prove anything to anyone. In fact, having experienced Iraq, my inclination was very much to say, "Thanks, but no thanks!" In the end, however, love, once born in your heart, is a lot like the light of the sunrise, driving out darkness, overwhelming our senses, casting out fear. Love had been born in our hearts for the people of Iraq, and though the stakes were high, fear was on the run like so many shadows as the sun ascends its noonday throne.

The day had come to send baby Hope to surgery in Istanbul, along with seven other children who had pinned their dreams and greatest aspirations on us and a Turkish surgeon with a penchant for accepting some of the more dire cases around.

For the first few days, our nonmedical notes in Hope's file read like those for any other baby:

February 22—Hope and her mom arrived this morning. For some reason it took them two hours to get through the airport. . . . Hope seems to be doing ok—a little cough but no fever. We're waiting for the doctor to come now.

February 23—Hope is doing well. She is super sweet. All of the nurses love her. Her mom is really sweet also and seems to be calm.

Unlike our experience in Israel, where some of our children were forced to wait for weeks or months for the surgery they needed, Hope's surgery took place the day after she arrived, and her post-op prognosis continued to encourage us:

February 24—Hope is doing well but having some pressure problems that are normally expected in babies. She will likely stay in ICU the next few days. Her mom seems to be doing ok. She is a very smiley person, even when she's crying.

February 26—Hope is doing a little better! She has a ways to go, but her blood pressure is better, and she's breathing on her own now. Two great things.

The phone call came near the end of the trip. I was in Iraq; Scott and Abby were with the kids in Turkey, guiding the moms through the process. Seven of the "Great Eight" had already come through surgery successfully. Baby Hope was the last in line, and she was in the ICU. There are a lot of things I don't remember, but I remember sitting at the conference table with our team in the middle of a staff meeting when the phone rang. I remember pacing my top-floor apartment office—like I always do when I'm on the phone, but this time with more purpose. I remember looking out the window onto the streets below and wondering how many others had experienced something so tragic.

"Brother Jeremy, Hope is dead," Yusuf was crying, screaming, not from anger, but from anguish. She had died at six thirty, Sunday morning.

It was our practice at that time to send the mother with the child and require the father to stay back in Iraq. I'm not sure it was best, but it seemed essential at the time—a necessary evil of sorts. We had been doing this for a year and a half and had not experienced a death. We knew the mothers were scared, but the worst-case scenarios had never played out and we saved a lot of money by sending mothers alone. Saving money on airfare and accommodations meant saving more kids' lives. It seemed like a reasonable trade-off. Furthermore, the one time we made an exception, we did so at the cajoling of a few political players who induced us to let a certain father accompany his wife and child to surgery. Suffice it to say, it was a less than desirable experience. Fathering is not mothering, and most fathers are understandably unaccustomed to sitting by their child's bedside every waking moment. Moreover, bored fathers make very volatile houseguests, especially when the house is a hospital and a father's complaining and insubordination has the capacity to really rile up the other mothers, who are taught from birth to look to men for leadership, guidance, and problem solving.

Now we had a mother alone in Turkey with a deceased baby; a father in Iraq with an angry, advice-heavy extended family; and a ton of questions about how this happened, how we were going to get the body back home *immediately* for a proper Muslim burial.

I also had a lurking fear in my heart that somehow another misstep might result in a visitation from Yusuf and a platoon of friends in red berets. Perhaps it was time to call in that favor with Sheikh Hussein and secure some of his group's promised protection.

Abby did what Abby does best: she mothered this broken mother. She held her, she served her, and she sat quietly for hours on end. Presence is sometimes a greater expression of preemptive love than any bold action or program.

Hope's mom grieved differently than we might. She wailed, she screamed, she thrashed. But she also grieved in ways that were amazingly familiar. She gazed off into the distance; she lost her appetite, only to go out the next day and indulge in a new comfort food she had never heard of before: McDonald's.

In the most heartbreaking moments, she simply held Hope's baby blankets, clothes, and bottles in her hands and close to her face, trying to get that last smell or memory of her baby before it was gone forever.

Scott had the thankless task of working with officials in Turkey to repatriate baby Hope's body. It was exhausting, confusing, and a process that preyed on the vulnerable, who will do *anything* to see the affair through to the end. Promises were made and broken, and graft and extortion seemed a matter of course. On the other hand, we were new to the process, working in two foreign languages that were not our own, and were left holding the bag on an issue that we had only barely considered up until that point. Maybe all these revisions in contracts, prices, and the timing of delivery were just par for the course.

After days of uphill battle against the bureaucracy that exists between Turkey and Iraq, and after thousands of dollars had been expended in trying to expedite the process of repatriation, we had learned a lot of things we never wanted to learn about how to get a body from one country to another, how to put pressure on foreign ambassadors, and how to circumvent airline policies for charitable purposes.

Hope's body was laid in a little wooden box and placed in the hold of a cargo plane. Her tracking number was 610/IST/22000672.

Watching a family off-load a carton-coffin from the back of an ambulance and into the back of a pickup truck is an exceedingly harrowing experience. The soul cries out instinctively against tiny caskets. I've never known more intuitively that this is not the way the world is supposed to be than when I have stood beside a parent whose child is wrapped in white and ready to be lowered into the ground.

The range of blowback we've experienced from families whose children have died is as varied as the human heart: from anger and a sense that we lied and betrayed the family to a genuine feeling that we did all we could and did it honestly. But sometimes someone needs to be the scapegoat, and we have often been the best candidates. Other times, we've received gratitude, friendship, apologies for the turmoil, and an obvious acknowledgment that, defying stereotypes, we were people who had given ourselves fully to their families and that their losses were, in some very real way, our losses as well. This is how it was with Yusuf and his wife.

We gave the family some time to grieve, and though we longed to be present for them, we also had to admit that we were not truly friends—at least not in a conventional sense. At best, we were vendors of a service, and our contractual obligations were fulfilled. At worst, we were the people who killed their only daughter. Our need to be with them through the death of Hope seemed far greater than their need to be with us.

I met with Yusuf in our office about a week after Hope's arrival back in Iraq and her multiday funeral. Unlike all of my previous experiences of funerals in America, Hope's funeral in Iraq seemed to portray an upside-down set of values when compared to my own. In America, mourners heave food and flowers into the homes of those grieving. In Kirkuk, mourners showed up empty-handed, continually streaming into and out of the living room, while Hope's grieving twenty-year-old mother was expected to fulfill all of her normal wifely duties, hosting her guests, serving tea and biscuits, and exhausting herself in the service of those who ostensibly came to pay their respects.

When Yusuf and I met in the Westernized enclave that was the Preemptive Love office, he confided how angry he was with his culture and his family over the experience.

"They make my wife serve them when they should be serving her. She is tired. She has nothing left to give. And yet they all come and expect to be served and pretend that they are doing us a favor. Just let them stay home." His voice escalated. "You guys did more for us than them. We do not need this so-called consolation."

Weeks later we accepted Yusuf's invitation to lunch. This time, rather than darting through the streets of Kirkuk in an armored convoy, we took our humble hatchback. When it comes to personal security, I've always preferred the inconspicuous. When every other American in Kirkuk, Mosul, Baghdad, and Fallujah has protocols that require them to ride in SUV caravans with four-inch-thick bulletproof glass, driving through town in a lone car always seemed significantly safer to me, if only because it doesn't scream, "Look at me, I'm important and wealthy!"

Yusuf's living room was austere, both in its lack of furniture and in its lack of emotional color. In fact, it wasn't his living room at all. Yusuf and his wife lived with his dad, but the whiplash journey from pregnancy to birth to the diagnosis of Hope's life-threatening heart defect had taken a toll on all of the family and the relationships therein.

"We went around to all of our family members and asked them to help us with Hope's surgery," he said of the harried period of time between our saying yes to surgery and the deadline for him to present his family's portion of the money to purchase airline tickets and schedule the actual procedure. "Of course, we are young—we just got married two years ago—we did not have the two thousand dollars you asked for by ourselves. So we asked our parents, our cousins, and our aunts and uncles to help out. But they are selfish. They do not care about us. They think their problems are bigger than ours: their car broke, they are buying new furniture, whatever." Yusuf was so hurt. It was hard to tell if cultural norms had provided a venue for him to share these resentments or if he was somehow expected to just keep it all in and follow the decree of the elder men in his life.

"The guys in my unit actually gave more to help my little girl than my own family did. One of our aunties actually told us to let Hope die . . .

'You are young, you will have other babies,' she said. Now that we have come back here without Hope, they are blaming us. 'We told you not to waste your money on her . . . ' No one values little girls. If my child was a boy, I would have raised the money faster, but by God's decree I had a little girl. And she was my little girl. Shouldn't I do everything in my power to save her life? How can they tell me I should do nothing?

"Now they are telling us, 'Get over it. Your time has come. God willing, you will have other babies, and they will be more beautiful than that one.'" I stole a glance at Yusuf's wife, expecting her to be crying by this point. Sadly, she was not.

"I don't want another baby. I want *my* baby!"

CHAPTER 10

My Brother Rizgar

The taxi circled the block a few times, the driver carefully checking the rearview mirror for a tail. The drive had been long and dangerous from Kuwait through Iraq. Passing through Saddam Hussein's checkpoints was the scariest part. Especially when you were a wanted fugitive responsible for funding the Kurdish insurgency.

The Kurds had only recently become a factor in the global consciousness. The West was emerging from the Cold War era, and Iran had long been considered the most menacing threat in the Middle East. With that in view, U.S. foreign policy was said to tilt toward Iraq, with Saddam Hussein becoming an ally of sorts. Saddam had committed several horrific attacks with chemical weapons through the 1980s, but he had only recently ordered the attacks on Halabja that would garner worldwide attention and turn the Kurds into a convenient trump card to justify all future forays into Iraq.

In the pre–Persian Gulf War era, the Kurds still fought a bitter guerrilla war against Saddam Hussein's troops. Even today, many a Kurdish home across the country is adorned with photos of fathers, uncles, and brothers who turned their faces toward death and fought Saddam's forces in defense of their ancestral homeland. But not everyone who sought to bring Saddam to his knees took up arms or headed to the hills. Some, like the man I know simply as Khala—"Uncle"—supported the decades-long revolution through black-market trade, massive business initiatives, and the creation of kingly riches.

Khala's wife opened the steel gate as he backed his taxi into the narrow carport and switched off the headlights to avoid drawing attention. Like rats and cockroaches, Ba'athist apparatchiks crawled around the cities, sometimes flaunting their strength and identity in public, arresting or killing suspected dissidents on sight for reasons as arbitrary as the color of their socks; other times blending into the fabric of society, passing on the contents of inviolable conversations until one day brothers and friends simply disappeared into Saddam's dreaded Torture House, where faint screams heard late in the night told neighbors and cautious passersby all they ever needed to know about the headquarters of the Iraqi Mukhabarat.

Once he was safely inside the concrete carport, Khala's wife scuttled around the front of the car and pulled the gate down, lifting the metal latches to avoid unnecessary clatter that would alert the neighbors as to the exact time Khala had returned from one of his mysterious absences. In Saddam's republic of fear, one couldn't be too careful—not even among friends and neighbors. Gates shut, the kids were summoned to help unload the week's take.

Khala was a Kurdish nationalist, a devout patriot, and a revolutionary. But since his youth he'd had a unique knack for making money. While other young men dreamed of ambushing battalions of Ba'athists, Khala knew he was destined for greater—albeit strategically similar—things. As a young man, he would push his wooden handcart, piled high with village grapes and other fare, from his village in the flat Hotlands near oil-rich Kirkuk to the more metropolitan areas that crawled with Arab Ba'athists, where he would sell off what he could for a profit and turn his cart around to do it again the next day.

Over time, Khala was able to upgrade from a pushcart to a pickup and, with his own set of wheels, began pursuing opportunities to move other products that might produce wealth with which he could support his brothers in arms as they fought Saddam for a free Kurdistan. Soon grapes from the village gave way to gold from the gulf, and with every ounce of risk, the profits increased, resulting in more guns, more ammunition, more safe houses throughout the region, and, ultimately, more notoriety. Khala finally landed on Saddam Hussein's radar as one of the chief domestic engines behind the Kurds' indefatigable insurrection.

Khala's five girls and his only son handled the gold bricks and piles of cash adroitly; this was not their first exploit in trafficking. If anything, this was normal. So normal, in fact, that they may have never fully appreciated the value of what they had in their hands or the danger associated with financing the Kurdish uprising.

The middle one, the boy called Rizgar, stood over his father's shoulder as he moved furniture and opened the safe. How many times had he stood there and watched his dad stow away a stack of bills, a pistol, or a weathered Polaroid of Daddy's friend and national hero "Uncle" Jalal, the man who would one day become the country's president and peacemaker in chief?

With the gold bars and jewelry now unloaded, the spare tire was removed from the undercarriage. Khala shoved his key into the pin of the valve stem, releasing a stream of pressurized air that reeked of rubber and hot asphalt. Once the tire was totally deflated, the business end of a crowbar was jimmied beneath the rim until one whole side of the tire was off and stacks of cash wrapped in plastic bags began to poke through. With skill and persistence, fifty thousand dollars could be stored inside a spare tire without leaving a trace that would draw the watchful eyes of border guards or domestic Mukhabarat.

As the cash was loaded into the safe, young Rizgar stood by, admiring his dad, playing out various good-guy-versus-bad-guy scenarios in his mind's eye. Rizgar would have loved to dress up and play the Kurdish boy's equivalent of cops and robbers, but it was late and Khala was exhausted from hours on the road dodging checkpoints. Besides, tomorrow would be a big day converting the gold and the cash into weapons and supplies for his comrades in the mountains.

The rest of the house was fast asleep, content with the knowledge that Dad was home, so things were safe, at least for the night. But Rizgar had adventure in his soul, and it wouldn't be put to bed.

He crept from his pallet on the floor to the safe.

Maybe the furniture had not been put back in place properly. Perhaps it was only a single tea table or a small couch that concealed the strongbox in the first place. Whatever the case, Khala would soon wish it had been much more.

Like he had observed countless times before, the eight- or nine-year-old Rizgar turned the big black dial left, right, left, hitting each mark along the way, before pulling the latch that changed his family's life forever.

To this day, no one knows what got into him. He had not been an especially mischievous boy up to that point. The day he was born in a mountain tent with Saddam's troops too close for any mother's comfort, his parents named him Rizgar, which approximately translated to something like "free," an optimistic spin on the fact that he was born on the run from a tyrant, without shelter, without a home. And though Khala had lost his fortune and rebuilt his life a couple of times over by the time Rizgar broke into the family safe that fateful night, Rizgar's name had spoken some kind of restlessness into his young soul, telling him that he belonged in some far country. All we know for sure is that this single act—like Pandora's curiosity—unleashed all manner of chaos, sent a little boy on a harrowing journey, and plunged Khala's family into the depths of despair and guilt.

Rizgar grabbed a stack of bills—what probably seemed like an immeasurable fortune to a youngster—and snuck out the door unnoticed.

Climbing over the stucco walls was far preferable to opening the front gate, so up he went and off into the midnight air on the adventure of a lifetime.

He rounded the corner toward Saddam's Torture House, but every kid knew better than to brave that path—even the birds and the moon refused to fly overhead. No Arab Ba'athist in a rooftop watchtower would abide a Kurdish kid in baggy pants walking by in the middle of the night. Rizgar turned south toward the main drag, not yet aware of his trajectory or his intentions and how far they would lead him away from home.

"Take me to Zhako!" he said with authority to a taxi driver.

The driver looked dumbfounded. In a culture built on the social distance and expressions of propriety between the powerful and the weak, the elders and the young, this young boy was clearly lacking in manners to speak to an "uncle" in such an abrasive way. In fact, Rizgar's family was deeply rooted in manners, proper codes of conduct, and lives that were Godward in their orientation to all things. But Rizgar was living out a fantasy, not channeling his inner Emily Post.

"Do you know who my father is?" Rizgar said, dropping his father's full name.

The taxi driver most certainly did.

"I am on an errand for my father." It wasn't completely implausible. Saddam had been on a genocidal campaign against all battle-age males, and young boys like Rizgar were increasingly fatherless, uncleless, and brotherless. To fill the void left, boys were called upon to do extraordinary tasks for their mothers and their families. In some ways Saddam sought to nurture dependence on and reverence for the state and the party. In other ways, babies grew up fast under Saddam.

"And you have money to pay?"

I imagine Rizgar shot him another one of those "Do you know who my father is?" looks.

"I have to deliver this money for him." He flapped a pile of cash into view for good measure. "Do you think I would have this much of my dad's money on my own without him knowing about it?" Kevin McCallister could not have been more cunning.

The truth was, this little kid did not even know what—let alone *where*—Zhako was. It was just a word he had heard bandied about by the grown-ups. He had barely ever left his neighborhood; the driver probably could have taken a trip around the city, collected his fare, and saved everyone a whole lot of hassle. Rizgar certainly did not know that Zhako was the border village to the north with the enemy Turks. But little boys around the world know that once you've put on your cape and donned your mask, you absolutely *must* jump and prove you can fly, gravity be cursed.

But the driver believed the bit about Khala sending his son on a mission, and every self-respecting Kurd wanted to be found serving the national cause of overthrowing Saddam Hussein; warding off the international predators in Turkey, Syria, and Iran; and ultimately creating a homogenous homeland for Kurds worldwide.

He lit a cigarette, rolled up the window, and put his foot on the gas, headed north for the border. Rizgar's adventure was finally under way, and he couldn't help allowing the taxi to rock him to sleep as they zipped back and forth through the mountains of northern Iraq.

"All right, kid, Zhako." The sun was well into the sky. What would have been a four-hour drive as the crow flies could easily become an eight- or ten-hour drive through the broken-down mountain passes the Kurds were required to take in order to circumvent Saddam's checkpoints and known strongholds in Mosul.

Rizgar paid the driver and jumped out of the car, tumbling forth into a garage full of taxis and lorries, smugglers and soldiers. Like at most border crossings, no one thought twice about a child with no luggage wandering around alone. There were orphaned street children everywhere trying to scrape by, washing windows, selling gum, running chai to taxi stalls and bus stands. But Rizgar knew he was in over his head, vulnerably out of place, feeling naked and exposed. In his mind, everyone was looking for him, eyeing him, accusing him of abandoning his father, breaking his mother's heart, and making off with the family's fortune. He knew instinctively that he had to get out of sight before he was caught by the authorities and dragged back to the Torture House.

Scores of eighteen-wheelers stood in line, waiting for inspections, stamps in their passports, or the release of some portion of their goods from customs so they could cross the border into Silopi, where they would disperse to the Kurdish regional "capital" of Diyarbakir, to Ankara, or a thousand miles away to Istanbul, where East meets West.

Rizgar turned around. His taxi was gone, back to his hometown, no doubt. He wondered if the taxi driver would tell his dad what he had done or where he had gone.

Why would he? I already told him my dad sent me, he thought to himself, just now reckoning with what he had landed in. A sadness set in. Not even the heroic *peshmerga* fighters would know where to find him.

Ahead a Turkish driver speaking Kurdish climbed down from his canvas-covered lorry to attend to business. Or maybe he was a Kurdish driver speaking Turkish? The languages in Zhako did not sound like anything back home. The Kurdish was completely different, like everyone had woken up really tired and just needed a little more time to pronounce each word. And the Turkish, save the occasional word on loan from Arabic, might as well have been Chinese.

Rizgar threw one foot on the bumper, lifted up the canvas tarp, and darted behind the boxes of chai, completely out of sight as long as further inspections didn't off-load his cover. He was safe—and hidden—again. From here he could plot his next move.

But the nose is a great betrayer of childhood adventures. Bubble baths call princes from their palaces. The smell of dinner beckons pirates from their ships to wash up. And pillows of Ceylon tea can cut through the fog of any fantasy to bring a boy back to Mom's living room, where charred teapots atop kerosene burners and tulip tea glasses with bellies full of sugar are all it takes to feel safe and loved.

Rizgar was 250 miles away from home, separated by mountains and rivers and plains. There was also his vague awareness of Saddam's troops running somewhere through the hills in search of treasonous Kurdish boys like him. Unlike his fairy-tale counterparts, Rizgar had not left a trail of pebbles or bread to lead him home.

As he contemplated the long journey back the way he came against the vast unknown ahead, the truck's engine roared, and Rizgar fell asleep, the great Kurdish pirate of lore setting sail on a sea of tea to the end of the world.

There is a direct correlation between the length of the drive to Istanbul and the amount of Nescafé three-in-one coffee, cream, and sugar packets in a trucker's cab. A professional can go the distance from the Iraqi border, across the Syrian border through Urfa and Adana, northward, skirting the western edge of the nation's capital, and on to Istanbul's Büyük Otogar in just twenty-four hours. When you are nine years old, however, in the bed of a truck with nothing but dry, crumbled leaves in tea bags and cigarette wrappers, *just twenty-four hours* seem like eternity.

The first thing Rizgar noticed on the streets of Istanbul was the complete absence of anything closely resembling home. Where his hometown had a huge, open blue sky, Istanbul had smog clouds and forests of concrete where old women hung their carpets from balconies that kissed the sky and blocked the sun. In the alleys below, a motorcycle whined, a shopkeeper scrubbed the area around his storefront with soap and water, and a boy his age lowered a wicker picnic basket on a rope from the sixth floor above.

The basket landed at the base of the mosaic-tiled apartment building on the cobblestone sidewalk with the grace of a hot air balloon's gondola, and with it, Rizgar's eyes lit upon the unmistakable sign and scent of a curbside baker.

He made a beeline for the bread.

Shimmying up to the counter, he boldly asked for bread. Unfortunately, no one around him understood a word he was saying. With Turkish-Kurdish relations being what they were at the time, it had probably been many years since the average Turk on the street had heard any form of Kurdish spoken freely around them, despite the fact that the Kurds allegedly comprised the most numerous and densely populated minority group in the country. Rizgar tried again, hoping decibels would suffice in the absence of a Kurdish-Turkish Rosetta stone to reconnect their estranged peoples and land him the lunch he so desperately needed.

An old man took inventory of the small kid cutting in line immediately: his disheveled *sharwal* baggy pants, his especially flat head, and his obnoxious flaunting of the Turkish proscription on the public usage of the Kurdish language. The old man pegged him immediately as one of Saddam's legendary Anfal orphans, a refugee from Iraq who had, by the grace of God, made it to Istanbul, where he clearly lived on the streets, surviving day-to-day on the kindness of strangers.

"Are you alone?" the man asked quietly in Kurdish, pulling him out of line to talk more discreetly on the street.

"Yes," Rizgar answered, already seeing his ticket out of this loathsome situation.

"Where are you from?"

"Kurdistan!" Rizgar said, loud and proud, invoking a word that screamed sedition, separatism, and—most assumed—loyalty to the Kurdish terrorist networks that had led the word *Kurd* to become ensconced in official Turkish dictionaries as a pejorative, disparaging word.

"Chhhht!" he chided. "Come with me."

He dragged Rizgar to a nearby door, pressed the buzzer for the apartment upstairs, and told his wife, "I've got company coming up with me."

She was waiting at the door when the elevator rattled to a stop and the two emerged on the landing.

A kid . . . a Kurd! she must have thought, ushering them both inside, praying to God the neighbors hadn't been snooping through their keyhole like they often did. *Why do they need to make it their business what time my husband leaves the house or where he buys our groceries?*

The neighbors across the alley could see straight into the dining nook when the drapes weren't pulled. She remedied that immediately.

Over breakfast, Rizgar consumed copious amounts of bread, butter, cream, preserves, olives, tomatoes, cucumbers, cheese, and chai. If he had scavenged food in the last two days on the road, he didn't remember it a bit. Between bites, he gave cryptic answers about his family in Iraq, Saddam Hussein, the war, and spun his tale to make himself the ultimate victim, an orphan on the run from the evil Butcher of Baghdad.

Being free from his mom and dad was something like a dream come true (until the lights went out each night). Being completely self-absorbed and myopic, he had no concept of the pain and suffering he was causing back home. You might expect a family that had evaded numerous execution orders signed by Saddam Hussein himself to be war-hardened and callous, but the tragic, mysterious disappearance of their only son revealed a fragile humanity that nearly did them in. The most notorious dictator in the world couldn't stop Khala's black-market financing of the Kurdish rebellion. But then again, he ultimately did not need to: one boy and his late-night excursion nearly did that all by himself.

The savvy young Rizgar milked the generous family in Turkey for all he could: a less conspicuous tracksuit and sneakers to replace his Kurdish *sharwal,* a few good nights of sleep, three square meals per day (plus snacks), and a little bit of pocket money for walking around. For all he knew, he could have settled in with this family for the long haul and started a new life in Turkey. But something called him forth. He had not yet reached the far country for which he initially left home, and though this continual feast seemed to be set and replenished each day by the decree of God himself, the comfort of the table also threatened the song and the adventure in his heart. He knew he could sail farther still.

One day, not long after arriving, Rizgar left his Turkish hosts and never came back. Days turned to weeks and weeks to months as he boarded trains and buses and stowed away through the Balkans, Germany, and France.

Was it a bus first out of Istanbul and then a boat? Or did a boat cut across the Sea of Marmara through the Dardanelles and into the Aegean Sea?

Rizgar could not tell you. He was nine years old; brushing up on world geography was not an especially favorite pastime for him. Bulgaria, Bosnia, Belgium . . . they might as well have been the same contiguous country, except that the signs differed and every time he learned a few words of survival—*food, money, orphan*—he found himself in a new locale that wouldn't trade on his linguistic currency.

Throughout the ordeal he slept in countless train stations, learned to spot a persnickety traveler who discarded street food without finishing it, and became a scammer supreme.

One evening, on the banks of the English Channel in northern France, near the end of the workday, he boarded a ferry and hid in the cabin of a truck in the hull of the boat headed to what he assumed would be just another stop along the way.

After rolling off the ferry in England, he coughed or sneezed or otherwise startled his gracious unwitting host. This time, instead of evading the system, he was picked up by the police and handed over to a British social worker who worked his case like the future of the world depended on it.

The months of travel had changed him. He was seasoned now, suspicious of adults, and genuinely believed himself to prefer his own company to the supervision of grown-ups. He looked like any other street kid, no definitive clothing, thousands of miles and an implausible number of countries away from home. The caseworkers tried to identify his language.

They sent an Arabic speaker into the interview room.

Nothing.

Next a Persian, then a Turk.

Albanian?

No.

Somehow, after hours of exhaustive failed interviews and flash cards, they stumbled upon a few Kurdish words, and they were off to the races. Favors were called in, and a translator was eventually scared up to help navigate the young boy's fraying nerves and determine how he came to be in England apart from his parents.

A serpentine system of checks and balances, legal paperwork, disclaimers, social workers, and lawyers ultimately landed Rizgar in a children's home, from which he attended a local school and befriended a boy his age named Bobby.

Bobby took a liking to Rizgar, showed him the ropes, and helped him get into (and sometimes out of) trouble. One day Bobby went home and told his mom, "I want Rizgar to live with us."

And that was it.

For the next ten years or so, Bobby and Sharon were Rizgar's "home" in the fullest sense. Bobby and Rizgar came of age together, smoking cigarettes behind the bleachers, passing notes during worship at the nearby church until Sharon boxed their ears or thumped them on the head, and sending outrageous stacks of made-to-order pizza to their neighbors' doorsteps as they watched with amusement from Bobby's upstairs window.

Rizgar was old enough to know that he was a Muslim, which meant he was also old enough to know that Sharon and her family were Christians. And so, these experiences took on grander proportions than any typical childhood antics. Instead, they became an inoculation against the bigotry, hatred, and intolerance that sometimes surface when England's "curry capitals," "Little Pakistans," and "East Enders" are discussed. Rizgar was a Muslim living in a loving Christian home in one of England's most stereotypically divided cities, too Christian-loving for his hard-line Muslim friends and never willing to dishonor his father by renouncing Islam and joining the ranks of his new family.

Years later, back in Iraq, when Kurdish nationalists would suggest it was wrong to save the lives of Arab children whose parents had killed

Kurds or closed-minded Muslim hard-liners would chide him and question his faith for working with Christians, Rizgar would not only be immune to their disease, he would readily volunteer his own blood as an antidote to their fear.

Rizgar eventually dropped out of school and bounced around factory jobs making greeting cards and fiberboard before joining the British police in the Criminal Investigation Department as a translator. By this point as a young man, he had become proficient in Albanian (which he learned from Kosovar guys his age who had fled their imminent conscription into the Yugoslav army) and Urdu (which soaked into his subconscious during countless late-night meals in the halal dining establishments of West Yorkshire). To boot, he had improved upon all the dialects of his native Kurdish and picked up considerable Arabic through the time he spent among the anti-Ba'athists and Kurdish intelligentsia who labored for the eventual overthrow of Saddam Hussein and the creation of a free nation. It was among this stratum that a new friend recognized his family name and inquired whether he was Khala's long-lost (and presumed dead) only son.

More than ten years had passed, and Rizgar was old enough to understand the trauma his family had likely gone through when he ran away. So he was understandably nervous to pick up the phone and dial the number on the crumpled paper in his pocket. It was no mystery why he had not found a way back to his father and mother sooner. The shame of running away, the assumptions of all the pain and horror that he had caused, was insurmountable.

The phone was ringing now.

"Mama?" The words barely scratched out, like water from a rusty pipe on a hot summer's day. "It's me, Rizgar, your son." The voice was deeper than the Rizgar of her memories, the Rizgar frozen in time in his gray *sharwal,* the Rizgar she'd call for dinner from the park across the street, the Rizgar she'd tucked into bed more than ten years ago, the

Rizgar she had expected to wake up beside her the next day, the Rizgar she had lost. The innocent alto had become a battle-scarred baritone. But her baby wasn't altogether gone. She heard her son in there, across the line, across oceans.

Rizgar heard panicked cries and a crash on the other end of the phone.

"Hello? Mama? Hello?" But she wasn't there—at least, not consciously. Harried voices in the background were indiscernible, until the clanking and fumbling over the receiver ushered in a new interlocutor.

"Hello? Who is this?"

Rizgar recognized the voice immediately.

Tom Waits reading Flannery O'Connor had nothing on the sober sorrow in his father's voice.

"Baba, it's me, Rizgar, your son."

The rest reads like the second half of Jesus' parable of the prodigal son. Saddam Hussein had been toppled and found hiding in a pit near his hometown of Tikrit. President George W. Bush and Secretary of Defense Donald Rumsfeld could have walked unarmed through the streets of the Kurdish enclave. And Khala enjoyed the distinction of having helped his friends attain some of the highest positions of power in the land. All was coming up roses for the Kurds and Kurdistan, with many figuring it would be only a matter of time before federalism or secession allowed for the creation of an independent Kurdistan.

Having reunited with his father and mother, Rizgar decided it was time to leave his adoptive home in England; his brother, Bobby; and his mom, Sharon, and set sail again for the adventure set before him: marriage and the pursuit of peace for his people and their homeland.

With the boldness that you would expect of a little boy who ran away from home in the middle of a war, scamming and surviving his way across the world, the twentysomething Rizgar marched into the immigration office in England and gave an impassioned speech about the coalition victory in Iraq, the overthrow of Saddam Hussein ("God bless Tony Blair!"), and the self-determination of the Kurdish people. Many of the refugees in the waiting hall behind him longed for this to be their story, if only their backwater geography or geopolitical insignificance had not rendered their despot rulers and their collective sufferings invisible.

"I won't be needing this anymore!" Rizgar plopped his red British passport down on the counter. "I'm going home!"

And with that, in what had to be one of the most befuddling plot twists in the history of refugees and immigrants in England, Rizgar got himself legally deported back to Iraq, giving up his golden ticket to any country in the world and walking back into the lion's den as the world increasingly shut its doors to the people of Iraq due to a burgeoning refugee crisis and al-Qaeda's terror exports.

Khala was waiting on the tarmac with armed guards, uncles, and cousins aplenty when Rizgar's plane touched down. Whether it was the heat, the smell, or the obvious fact that he wasn't in London, Rizgar's immediate, visceral reaction was *What have I done?*

If there hadn't been fifty guys waiting at the bottom of those stairs, one of which must have been his dad, and if it weren't for that whole passport oversight, he probably would have turned around and headed back to England.

Down the stairs he went, into his father's arms and into a months-long homecoming, complete with the slaughter of the fatted calf (along with scores of sheep), rings and robes, and a party to end all parties. But all those things were expected in the "know no stranger" ecosystem of Middle Eastern shame-and-honor culture, with its conventions on hospitality, celebration, mourning, and relational reconciliation.

What Rizgar did not expect were the lessons he would be forced to learn about individualism versus collectivism and the suppression of his personal freedoms in deference to the preservation and burnishing of his father's good name. For Rizgar and his perennial restlessness, the freedoms of childhood under an autocrat were far preferable to the tyranny of adulthood under a benevolent father with a reputation to maintain.

From the critique of his clothes (too baggy, too black) to his hair (too long with too much product), to his tattoos (that they *existed* at all), to the manner in which he lolled about with no regard for the orientation of the soles of his feet—Rizgar could not do anything right.

His dad and mom were thrilled to have him home. And they showed their joy through tears, through words of great affection, and through apologies for whatever unspoken crimes of parenting drove Rizgar away from home. They also showed their love through lavish attempts to provide material benefits like cars, clothes, and cash. But Rizgar's early years in Iraq had not been marked by privilege, and he was a stranger to the silver spoon. He was pronounced "free" the day he was born in the mountains, on the run from a tyrant. But words work wonders, and our names are more than the handles by which we are pulled from one place to another. Names are creative, productive, and constructive in the most literal sense, bringing to life what might not otherwise be.

So, the promise of a home and all its trappings held no sway. They were like a cage for Rizgar, the "free." His soul had never known a home. Every day the Kurds around him were trading in the ancient dream of a unified country called Kurdistan for personal cell phones, sport utility vehicles, and Chinese electronics. But Rizgar wasn't wired that way. He longed for peace with his Arab neighbors to the south—he had met and befriended so many defected Arabs in London who wanted the same things he and his family did. And he longed for peace with his Turkish neighbors to the north, who had given him safe passage and shelter on his adventure of a lifetime. He longed for a greater country. So he joined the Preemptive Love Coalition.

Every successful Western company or development organization I know in Iraq has some variation of a driver, translator, or runner: a guy who knows the bureaucratic ropes for obtaining visas, making major capital purchases, and keeping the team out of court and out of jail. This guy is usually someone who can talk his way into or out of nearly anything and respects both cultures enough to lie on behalf of each in order to keep things moving forward. Rizgar was all that and so much more.

He came in unassumingly, casually offering to help us in the same way he had donated his time and money back in England to homeless shelters or for children in Darfur.

Initially Rizgar was just looking for a way to give back. The privilege of being Khala's son was stifling, in spite of all its perks. But Rizgar's casual volunteerism took on a more permanent character when I called him in one day to help me translate for a father and his little boy, Mustafa. Mustafa was eight years old, about the age of Rizgar's youngest nephew, only Mustafa was frail and looked as though he would break any minute, while Rizgar's nephew played on the street throwing rocks, terrorizing cats with bottle rockets, and pretending to be the world's next soccer star.

After Mustafa's father carried him in his arms to school each day because his heart was too weak for him to walk, his mom sat beside his desk in the middle of the classroom to help keep him focused and awake, refusing to allow his heart defect to become an excuse for indolence. Mustafa and his family captured our hearts, and Rizgar joined us in our passionate pursuit of helping children with life-threatening heart defects.

When we later discovered Mustafa's father had ties to the Islamist movement, we could have easily walked away from the obvious risks of entangling ourselves with "the enemy." No one would have blamed us. But that wasn't the way of preemptive love. So we took a risk on Mustafa and gave him the lifesaving surgery he needed. When we invested money and time into Mustafa that no one else in their community would, Mustafa's life was changed forever. Mustafa went from frail to feisty, in spite of the long course of his disease and the multiple surgeries he would likely require in the coming years.

We decided to keep helping Mustafa anyway, in spite of our concrete conclusions about the family and their ideologies, and we devoted ourselves to spending as much time with them in their home as we could.

The first time we visited Mustafa after surgery, we gave him a brand-new soccer ball, although honestly, it seemed like it was insulting to imply that a kid so weak would ever be able to hang with the boys on the street in a pickup game. Months later, over tea and cake, Mustafa's mom suggested he head into the other room and retrieve the surprise he had for us.

Mustafa returned with a tattered mess of a soccer ball: fuzzy, muddy, disgusting. The hexagonal pieces of leather were molting like a reptile as death gave way to life.

Mustafa held the ball high over his head as if to say, "You did not think I could do it, but I dominated this ball!"

When Rizgar saw what leading with love had done to overcome our fears and suspicions of one another, he made it his life's ambition to bridge the gulf between Muslims like Mustafa's dad and people like us whom they so deeply misunderstood.

As Mustafa described his most recent game-winning goal, his mom and dad sat on the couch beaming with pride and appreciation. I had seen it more than enough times by then to be thoroughly convinced that loving the ones we are supposed to hate—running *toward* instead of running away—was among the most revolutionary ideas in the world. But some scenes are more indelible than others, and this family, with her highly conservative dress, his bushy beard, and their smiles shining brightly against the backdrop of the Islamic doomsday poster on the wall behind them, forever left a mark on my Muslim brother Rizgar and us all.

CHAPTER 11

One Father Decides to Kill Us All

Some husbands forbid their wives from shopping in certain parts of town for fear of surprise credit card statements that will break the bank. Some forbid their wives from picking up stray animals, and others forbid their wives from grocery shopping on an empty stomach. By the time we had celebrated our second anniversary as the Preemptive Love Coalition in Iraq, I was regularly forbidding my beloved wife from visiting the local cardiologist's office—one of her favorite hangouts, the place where she met mothers in despair and extended hope to those in need.

Jessica's capacity for compassion and empathy is orders of magnitude greater than mine. Where I can be calculating and deliberate, Jessica will throw her weight behind something simply because her heart tells her to. Jessica always roots for the underdog. She doesn't want anyone to lose. She'll root for the dark horse in any competition, until the dark horse takes the lead, and then she'll become a turncoat and pull for the back of the pack. But that which makes her a terrible sports fan and bad at board games makes her the best friend imaginable, especially when you are the one who is down-and-out.

Jessica is the most justice-driven person I know. She frames conversations in terms of fairness and rightness. But Jessica is also a deep well of mercy from which many have drawn a soul-quenching second chance, in spite of what justice might otherwise demand. And so it was, with all her unique passions, that she entered the office of our colleague Dr. Abdullah—a local cardiologist with whom we worked regularly.

Sending Jessica into a hospital of sick children and expecting her to stay her hand was like sending a drunk into a bar and telling him to behave himself. Jessica is addicted to mercy. And that was a lifeline of tremendous proportions for Ali and his family.

Ali had just undergone a minor surgery related to the package of abnormalities that was delivered with him at birth and was now in the cardiologist's office for another checkup before climbing back on the bus for a daylong ride home to Kirkuk. He was young, but he looked and acted much older in some ways.

Ali slouched like an old man, standing off to the side, as Dr. Abdullah and his mom went through the robotic greeting ritual. He pushed his shoulders forward and tucked both hands into the pockets of his jeans when he was nervous, which he often was, between the constant visits to doctors with needles, knives, and cold stethoscopes and the chronic sounds of explosions and gunfire in and around his city. It's hard to imagine that Ali and his siblings experienced the laughter and the excitement that other children enjoyed at all.

Mom heaved Ali onto the examination table as Jessica stood over Dr. Abdullah's shoulder and listened to him explain what was going on with Ali's heart.

Unlike some of the other doctors and politically aligned local organizations, Dr. Abdullah treated every child the same, Kurd, Turkmen, or Arab; this political party or that; Muslim or Christian. He spoke all their languages fluently and always did his work with a smile, which is no small feat given the refrain he had to repeat each day to countless mothers and fathers from around the country: "I'm sorry, your child is going to die if you don't get them outside the country for surgery."

Of late, he had been referring children to us with increasing frequency, especially on the heels of Dr. Çiçek's successes with some of the children who had been long considered too far gone.

Ali gripped the gray bedsheet with his left hand as the doctor grabbed the white bottle of ultrasound gel and squirted a blob of jelly on the center of his chest. His muscles pulled, his skin tightened, and soon goose bumps covered his body as Dr. Abdullah pressed the wand of the sonogram machine into his rib cage in an effort to visualize what was going on with Ali's heart. High-frequency sound waves left the probe, bounced off the walls of his beating heart, and gathered on a nearby monitor, where Dr. Abdullah tried to interpret the various hues of red and blue blood flow, the magnitude of the hole in his heart, and ultimately whether or not his heart was worsening or holding steady.

Surprisingly, the government hospital had supplied Dr. Abdullah with a clerical assistant for a few hours. She planted her right foot behind her and drove her left knee and shoulder into the examination room door, closing out the moblike mothers and fathers who had been waiting for hours to be seen by the only pediatric cardiologist in the region and one of just a few in the entire country of some thirty million. America generally enjoys two or three of these doctors for every one million people. Iraq operates at about one-tenth of that capacity, with much of the diagnostic burden for thousands of sick children falling on Dr. Abdullah.

America's top heart hospitals warn parents that the ultrasound test could take up to an hour. They often excuse the sonographer from sharing any results directly with the patient and family, leaving that potentially difficult conversation to the actual physician. In Iraq, this division of labor does not exist. Dr. Abdullah spends about five to ten minutes looking at most kids, knowing that a more thorough investigation would deny even the most rudimentary exam or checkup for many of the others who are waiting in line. He is pediatrician, echocardiographer, cardiologist, receptionist, and general bearer of bad news to all. He occasionally has the chance to tell parents that their child *does not* have a heart defect—or that their child's heart defect does not warrant immediate intervention—but more often than not he has the ignoble task of telling parents what they most fear: not only that their child is facing down a life-threatening heart defect, but that there is almost nothing they can do about it.

We look to our doctors for solutions—not just diagnoses. Sadly, Saddam's wars against the north, decades of international sanctions against the south, and the various international bombings on Baghdad, Basra, and beyond had conspired to ensure that Iraq was still years away from providing any significant infrastructure for the hundreds of children who gathered each week in Dr. Abdullah's office, many of them coming a day's journey just to see him.

Dr. Abdullah handed a few paper towels to Ali's mom to wipe the gel off his chest.

"Look . . . Ali needs surgery. He's getting older. Things are getting worse. There is nothing I can do for him." He was generally very mindful of not presuming with us, but Jessica has a demeanor that says, "I'm here to help," and he knew full well that she had not merely come to shoot the breeze.

Jessica quickly intervened and let Dr. Abdullah off the hook.

"Here is the address to our office. Let's go straight there, and we'll talk about whether or not we can help Ali."

"And my little girl, too?" his mom replied hopefully. Dr. Abdullah had not yet said so, but the little girl tugging on Ali's shirttail and following him around like a puppy was also suffering from a similar heart defect. She would also need a drastic intervention in the coming months, and the mom immediately realized she had hit the jackpot in this West Texas girl.

Ali was one of those early kids who captured the heart of our team. At four years old, he was an old soul. At times he was just a normal kid, running around barefoot, punching his older brother in the chest like a champion boxer. But sometimes you could look at Ali and see what appeared to be the weight of the world on his shoulders, like he knew what he was up against, like he had calculated the odds and knew things weren't likely to come out in his favor but he would indulge everyone's best efforts and go along for the ride.

Our team had seen a major shakeup in personnel by that point. Scott and Abby were gone. Rizgar, our first full-time local staffer, was at our side for almost every major event. And a guy named Caleb had jumped out of the pages of a Nautica catalog to dive headlong into our peace-making, lifesaving work all over Iraq. Caleb was one of the first among us to consider himself a visual peacemaker—a painter of light, a shaper of images and imagination. Caleb actually believed that the way we took photos of children and told their stories would change the way the world saw Iraq and might actually help usher in a sustainable peace between all these little groups that seemed so bent on destroying one another, often for lack of anything other than a shabby caricature of a real Muslim or a real Christian, a normal American or a normal Iraqi.

It was autumn—which is barely a season in Iraq—when Rizgar, Caleb, and I drove into Kirkuk, Ali's hometown. I had been to the city a number of times by then, with each trip making the entire ordeal seem a little more normal. I started recognizing landmarks, not as places where that bombing or that assassination occurred, but as signposts to point me to friends' houses and as monuments of significant conversations that demonstrated what we really meant when we said "love first" or "preemptive love." A city that I had once lumped in with the chaos and devastation of the Battle of Fallujah was becoming more and more a place I wanted to spend time in with guys like Sheikh Hussein, Yusuf, and now Ali's family. Of course, my new conclusions were challenged every time a fellow American called me naive and warned me against the city or every time a local Iraqi expressed shock at our regular forays into a city that many of them had vowed never to enter for fear of their lives.

There was a red, antique woven rug with a beige central medallion hanging haphazardly bottom-up over a cinder-block wall that had been

MacGyvered together to separate the courtyard of Ali's house from the decimated street outside. Daylight poked through the grooves of the breeze blocks where mortar might ordinarily have been. Grapevines hanging overhead provided a little shade as we entered the home, but Kirkuk's heat and the season ensured that most of the foliage was falling. Spring always seemed like a better time to save lives to me.

Even though many of the families we helped were very poor, it was unusual to have a meeting in their homes in which tea and some kind of fruit or dessert were not served. As often as not, full-blown meals were hosted as an expression of gratitude and, no doubt, in hopes of tilting the scales in their favor in the event that we were on the fence with regard to their child. Ali's family offered neither tea nor a meal. The trappings of their home, the toys that appeared to have been recycled two or three times, and the hand-me-down clothes begging to be put out to pasture all testified to the severity of the family's predicament.

"About two hundred and fifty dollars per month," Rizgar said, translating for Ali's father as we filled out our paperwork on salary, assets, and medical history. Our standard $2,500 rate that we asked families to contribute toward the $10,000–$20,000 surgery was clearly not possible for this family. Even if they suspended every other expense in their lives, their minority share alone would have required a ten-month installment plan. We were not even sure Ali would be alive by then. And, in any case, what family could suspend every other expense in their lives?

"I tried to apply to [a charitable trust associated with a major political party]. But even though they have [a nationalistic word] in their name, implying they exist for all of us, they rejected Ali outright when they learned that I work as a security guard at the hospital funded by their rival political party. Why should it be like this? What does my son have to do with politics? What does being a security guard have to do with politics? I'm a lowly worker. Why is my son punished for my employment? I'm not even a party functionary. And for this we are denied help? Is this the freedom for which we've struggled all these years?"

Rizgar could see my blood boiling. These claims were certainly not new to him, but neither had they hit so close to home before. As a member of the privileged class himself, he had not exactly spent significant amounts of time among the urban poor prior to leaving his family's business empire and nearly bankrupting himself to join our ranks. And far from standing against this kind of corruption, he had often spent his early years back from England being initiated into the circles of those who perpetrated it. But those who divulged their secrets and called in personal favors with Rizgar often found themselves in the midst of his campaigns to expose their corruption. Rizgar woke up each day with a singular mission: to serve God by saving kids' lives and protecting our family at the Preemptive Love Coalition.

Caleb spent the majority of his time at Ali's house under the grapevines with Ali and the other three kids, including the little sister whose heart condition was just as precarious as her brother's. Ali's older brother was an incredibly loving, friendly young man. He played with Ali and the younger girls with great intentionality and tenderness. He seemed to understand that the bombs, the guns, and the militias outside their little protectorate were not the greatest threat to his family. He sought to maximize his time with his brother and sisters, in spite of the eight or more years between him and Ali. With an eight-year age gap, one had to wonder how many other children had been born and lost during that time. I don't remember having the pluck to ask the question, even though our workup on the family probably required it. Some things are easier left unanswered.

Unfortunately, the meeting was not all positive. An open-ended follow-up question about salary or employment caught both Mom and Dad answering with wildly disparate answers. Just as Dad repeated his previous answer, Mom threw in another number altogether. The room became really awkward as we all shot each other knowing glances of the game we were apparently playing. As best as we could tell, there was a side job that neither had considered relevant to our previous discussions—not in our office with her, nor in their home.

"So, is it about five hundred dollars per month or two hundred fifty dollars per month? Is it one job or two?" I asked.

It was hard to discern who was telling the truth, and who was hiding information (and money) in hopes of further endearing their cause to us. Ali's dad, who had been very affable and kind to that point, shot his wife a look.

You are about to screw this whole thing up. Shut up and let me handle this!

He had a second job. I'm not sure he was ever trying to hide it. I interpreted him as being calculating by answering only what he was specifically asked. Ali's mom, on the other hand, came across as manipulative and conniving. They both lost our trust that day. In any other case, we probably would have walked away altogether, but Ali's dad seemed to have a knack for patching things together, for making things work against the odds. Somehow, through a smile and a big dose of subsequent transparency, he won us over and kept us moving forward.

We left the house within an hour of arriving, paperwork in hand, and had committed to send Ali to surgery after Christmas. As we were often wont to do, we spent the car ride back examining the conversation from every angle. Every stray look or delayed response, every document or toy, and every shelf with suspicious dust patterns (implying an article of value had just recently been sold or stowed away) was considered.

We had a lot of questions about what it would ultimately be like to work with this family toward their financial share of the surgery, but Ali himself was innocent. And he was enough to keep us pressing forward.

Months went by, and Ali was introduced to the world through the Preemptive Love website, our year-end direct-mail campaign, holiday cards, news articles, and media pieces. Junior high students at a church on the West Coast decided to renounce their privilege for a semester to help save Ali's life. Birthdays were suddenly packageless; pool parties became fund-raisers; and Halloween, that paean to the paranormal, became an occasion to stuff pumpkins with cash for Ali instead of candy for personal engorgement.

I went to the charitable trust Ali's father had told me about. We had a good relationship with them, and I thought it would be an easy thing to help bridge the gap that the family had been unable to on their own.

"I'm here to discuss a child who needs surgery," I said, which was obvious enough with the file in my hand. "The child is from Kirkuk and has a fairly urgent case according to our doctors in Turkey."

Our meeting had started late, after working hours, so I was surprised by the knock at the door. In walked a man, alone. It was not common in my experience for visits like this to take place so late in the day. Most families were eating dinner by this time. A flurry of words was exchanged, much of it flowery language that amounted to "your wish is my command" by the local health supervisor at the foundation. The man's headdress and clothing told me where he was from and to whom he was loyal.

The health director turned back to me.

"Why don't you help this man's child instead? We know him."

There was no child in sight. No file in hand. I inquired about his diagnosis.

He had a simple, small hole in the wall between the blood-collection chambers of the heart, but this was based on the father's word, not a medical file or doctor's report. In any case, if it was accurate, he could probably live with such a defect for a fairly long time before any serious harm befell him. Ali, on the other hand, would not be so lucky. I told the health director we would be happy to consider this man's child, but I would need to see the file, consult with our doctors in Turkey, and place him somewhere on our list commensurate with his actual need.

"For tonight," I continued, "I'm here to talk about Ali."

"We cannot help you, I'm sorry. We are not contributing money to children like Ali who are not urgent. We must use our money wisely to help those children most in need."

"But this child you've just suggested could not possibly be in greater need than Ali," I countered. "His diagnosis doesn't allow for that kind of conclusion!"

It seemed Ali's father was right—Ali was being excluded for reasons other than his actual medical condition. Moreover, my own encounter that night told me all I needed to know about the "good ol' boy" system that passed as using money wisely to help those children most in need.

By Christmas, all of our costs associated with Ali's surgery had been raised, and we informed the family that the only thing lacking was their portion, in keeping with our desire to partner with families and celebrate their role in saving their children's lives.

When Rizgar called Ali's father to share the news, his mother picked up the phone instead and began an eleventh-hour negotiation, thumbing her nose at the way we'd overlooked her previous deceit and the concessions we had already made to accommodate their situation. Perhaps it was a last-minute act of desperation. Perhaps there was something else at play. But she managed to undo much of what we had negotiated with her husband (who likely had a better handle on the financial situation of the family) and ultimately made herself persona non grata. Rizgar hung up the phone after telling her that the price was set and they would be taken off the list if they did not come up with the money immediately. The mom went from negotiation to extortion, with the life of her own child hanging in the balance.

"Even if you lower our price to nothing, we will never send our son with you."

I confessed before that I am not above extending or withholding services on the basis of personal affection or disaffection for a particular individual and my projection of what it might be like to partner together for success in the life of his or her child. In Ali's case, I had extended every act of goodwill that I was willing to extend. Inasmuch as Rizgar had endured their lies and drawn his own conclusions about their intentions, he had had enough. He insisted Ali's family had disqualified themselves from surgery.

"There are plenty of other children who are waiting in line for our help whose parents deal with us the right way. They tell the truth. They work hard to raise their money," he argued.

To walk forward with Ali would only extend hope for their little daughter as well—a desire we were especially keen to suppress given the difficulty of partnering together in Ali's case.

But this was Jessica's child, and detaching Jessica once her mercy-laden heart had hitched itself to another person or a cause can be especially dicey. The only staff in Iraq with any institutional memory were Jessica and me. Everyone else had left the organization (Scott and Abby), was working in the States (Cody and Michelle), or was new (Caleb, Rizgar, etc.). It was never advisable that the bulk of the triage decisions rest solely on Jessica and me. Not only was it a bad organizational policy, but it was especially bad for our marriage.

Jessica, with her unwavering commitment to the riskiest, most urgent children, has led us to say yes to more high-risk heart cases in Iraq than any other group. She is the vanguard of our staff of taker-inners, last-chancers, and underdog lovers. Jessica gravitates toward helping those in whom the light of hope is fading fast. There is something wired up inside her to lay herself on the line for those who cannot find solutions elsewhere.

I agree with Jessica so much on these children and feel her convictions deep inside my spirit. But it has been a constant source of conflict in our marriage when situations arise where her compassion and my calculations collide.

We could help two children for the price of this one.

We could play it safe and make our donors happy with a glowing report of another life saved.

In situations like the one we experienced with Ali, the life and death of another person's child actually took on a personal dimension for Jessica and me that was unhealthy and, in this case, dangerous for all involved.

Ali's dad must have sensed something deeply empathetic in Jessica. When he returned from the market to learn that his wife had answered his phone, he was furious. When he learned that she had threatened to walk away altogether in hopes of forcing our hand by preying upon our good intentions, he knew she had destroyed the entire relationship with us and all chances for Ali's surgery. He quickly dialed Jessica and asked for a chance to sit with her and explain the situation.

Whether it was miscommunication or an outright act of Jessica's revolutionary heart is still a matter of debate around our office. But Jessica took her translator, Kanar, and met privately with Ali's father, believing that Rizgar and I had been too quick to judge and not wanting to see Ali left behind to die because of his mother's act of desperation. "Love first; ask questions later" often means filing a lot of things into the "What's the worst that could happen?" folder. Unfortunately, we had not actually sat down to consider the question. But even if we had, we would have never come up with what happened next.

"Are you the guy who sends children to heart surgery?" The animated, angry voice on the other end of my cell phone told me clearly that this poor father had just learned about his child's imminent death.

"Yes . . . I'm the guy."

"How much to send a child to surgery?" my would-be client asked.

"Well, sir, why don't you come in to my office with all the reports, and we'll look at your child's situation and decide how we proceed from there."

"No!" He was yelling unlike anything I'd encountered before. Normally fathers, even in their time of grief, still understood that decorum and decency were wise tactics for landing their child on the coveted surgery list. "Just tell me how much it costs!"

"I'm sorry, sir. Our program doesn't work like that," I said, trying to maintain my composure so that I could carry on this heated discussion in his native tongue. "We don't offer a flat rate. Every child's surgery is different, and every family's situation is different. Just come on in, and we'll be happy to talk through it with you."

"Do you have a translator?" he finally asked—the ultimate insult to my years of trying to speak the elusive languages of the Middle East!

"Yes, let me give you the number for my colleague Rizgar. He'll be happy to explain our program to you."

I don't know if it was minutes or hours later—the next twenty-four hours were a blur—but Rizgar eventually called me, worked up beyond what was reasonable for a single encounter with a stranger over the phone.

"Did you get a phone call from a guy today?" he asked. "Do you know who that was? That was the secret police in Kirkuk. Ali's father has lodged a formal complaint against you for extortion. He says that he gave you four thousand dollars to send his son to surgery, but you are refusing and demanding more money. Brother Jeremy, you didn't take money from this man, did you?"

"Rizgar, come on!" I said, repeating Rizgar's favorite phrase in moments of incredulity. "You and I agreed together that we weren't sending this family to surgery. As much as we wanted to, we just cannot trust them. I never took money from them. That's your job anyway. Why would I do that behind your back?"

He calmed . . . a little.

"Let me call Jessica, though," I said nervously. Jessica had met with the father a few days prior against my will. I knew Rizgar would be livid, and I had managed to keep the secret from him until this moment. "Jessica and her translator met with him a few days ago. I am certain she didn't take money from him, but if there is an investigation against me, we should call her to be sure."

Rizgar called Jessica and took her statement. She had not taken any money, but other salient pieces began falling into place once Rizgar relayed her version of what had actually happened.

"We got to the office early to meet with him," Jessica said. "It was just Kanar and me. We were sitting on the leather couches in the reception area when there was a knock at the door. The door was cracked open— it wasn't latched or locked. So Ali's father let himself in. He was really sweet and humble. It seemed like he was really glad to see us, glad we had taken his call and agreed to meet one last time with him to discuss the fallout. He knew his wife had put everything at risk for Ali. He said a lot of dismissive things about her. He was trying to keep us moving forward together," Jessica explained, "but he insisted that he didn't have the money that we required of him. I remember being very frustrated with the gall in his statement, because he had clearly just returned from a shopping trip in the local bazaar. When he slipped his shoes off at the entryway and sat down on the couches, he set his black plastic bazaar bag on the floor beside him, and a brand-new DVD player poked out for us to see. Why does a guy in this kind of poverty with a dying child need a new DVD player?"

An outsider might say that Jessica's indignation at the family's inability to prioritize their spending to save Ali's life was about to get the best of her. I think Jessica's indignation and insistence that the world bend toward Ali and children like him *is* the best of her. She speculated on the cost of the DVD console, scolding Ali's father about the dent that amount of money would have put in their responsibility for saving their child's life.

Why should we be out begging for money on your behalf when you won't? Why should children in America forgo their own electronics and gifts when you won't?

Jessica agreed to advocate on Ali's behalf with Rizgar and me, but she made no secret of her disgust.

It is still unclear to me how many times Rizgar stuck his neck out for my family to keep us out of harm's way. But this was probably the first instance of which I was readily aware. Rizgar traveled to the offices of top security officials in multiple cities and lobbied on my behalf, laying out my track record and insisting that I would never do something like what this man was claiming. I imagine that Rizgar wasted no time with pleasantries about the plaintiff. Knowing Rizgar, he was sure to have detailed every little act of deceit, every errant word, and every breach of contract to date that would serve to keep me out of jail.

Rizgar spent much of the next day or two on the phone with the agent who had contacted me initially. He had been hoping to catch me off guard with his shenanigans on the phone about a child needing surgery, trying to catch me saying a number significantly lower or higher than the four thousand dollars I had allegedly taken from Ali's father.

Unfortunately for me, relief and development organizations like ours across Iraq were waning in usefulness. The costs of doing business and serving others in a war zone were exorbitant. Humanitarian workers were known to travel in convoys approximating those of their political counterparts. Offices would run noisy gasoline-powered generators to keep the electricity and services flowing while neighbors languished, cut off from the formal power grid. But it was the high-visibility scandals that really served to add so much fuel to the fire of my own indictment.

Once, near the northern city of Mosul, it was rumored that an organization was hosting a widespread application for American citizenship for all those who had in any way worked with or for or around American troops during the previous wars. This application process, suspiciously, was open to extended family, cousins, etc. All one needed to do was bring proper documentation and render an application fee of a few hundred dollars. Applicants were told that they would receive information within a few weeks. After hundreds—perhaps thousands—of applications rolled in, the organization just disappeared into the night, making off with untold riches, leaving behind hopeless neighbors and friends, many of whom had banked big on the opportunity and handed over what amounted to the last of their cash reserves.

Legends like this were myriad throughout the war. It seemed that every province nationwide intoned its own domestic equivalent. Were these real stories or cautionary war lore? I will probably never know for myself, but, in some ways, they served the people well, acting as a kind of antibody against people like me, when people like Ali's dad needed a plausible fall guy.

Days later, while Rizgar reviewed Jessica's statement with one of the investigators on the phone, random pieces began lining up serendipitously.

"Brother Jeremy's wife was really angry that the father was telling us he didn't have money, because he came to our office with a brand-new DVD player. She told him that he should have spent that money on his son's surgery—"

"Wait! What?" the agent said, interrupting Rizgar.

"Yeah, she said he should have spent the money on—"

"No, not that. What did he bring to the office?"

"A DVD player."

"Was it in the box?"

"Yeah, I think so. She said she saw the box in the bag," Rizgar replied, clueless as to where this line of inquiry was headed.

"Was the box red and black with a silver DVD player on the front?"

"Uh . . . I'm not sure. I would have to ask her," Rizgar said cautiously.

"Rizgar, we haven't told you everything yet. When can we meet?"

"Thanks for agreeing to meet," the agent said. "We've been monitoring the Courtneys for a while."

I imagine Rizgar's brow furrowed. Protective of us as he was, clandestine stakeouts were bound to rub him the wrong way.

"We stopped investigating the Courtneys after the first day or two. It's not that. We're not looking *into* them. We're looking *after* them, looking *out* for them." He continued "We conducted a raid on Ali's home in Kirkuk a few days ago. We seized everything and everyone. They are not a normal family. They are terrorists. They are al-Qaeda. We were not sure what their agenda was originally. We know they've been trafficking in weapons and drugs. We have connections from them to others.

"I first became suspicious of the family when Ali's dad approached me in the police station and asked me for money for his child to go to surgery. The other officers and I rallied around him and gave some money to help the old guy out. But a few weeks later he came around again, and his story was all different. He had a letter signed by an American with your organization's logo on it and Mr. Jeremy's business card. When we started asking him about the money we had already given him, he seemed surprised, like he had forgotten that he already hit us up once. As he began fixing his story, the details just seemed wrong. That's when he said that he had given you all four thousand dollars, and now you were demanding more. That's why I called initially. The deeper we went, the more we uncovered.

"We started following certain family members, especially the wife's brother. When you said the dad took a DVD player into your office, well, I felt I really needed to tell you. During our raid, we found that DVD box in their home. It was not a DVD player at all. It was a bomb packed inside a box. The packaging was just to mask the explosives. We think he probably intended to blow up your office and your team. We are still interrogating them. We are not sure what happened. When you and Jeremy were not in the office and it was just the girls, we think he decided to wait for another opportunity to get all of you together."

Why would he try to kill us—the only people who could actually save his son's life? Was it all a setup from the beginning? No, that's not possible. Jessica happened upon this family in the doctor's office, and she initiated the process for Ali's surgery.

Maybe the bomb was actually made after the visit in our office. But why was the mom so belligerent in the first place? Was she savvy to the father's plans? Perhaps she was trying to sever the relationship to protect us? And why did he forge documents in my name? Why was he out misrepresenting me on the streets of Kirkuk? Why was he claiming that I was holding his child hostage until I received more money?

Did his erroneous story about me attract the attention of al-Qaeda and make him an unwitting agent for their retribution? Or maybe he resorted to contract killing as a way of raising the money for Ali's surgery . . . No, what sense would that make? There would be no one left to send his son to surgery. Was he angered by our requirement that they participate financially in Ali's surgery and took things into his own hands rather than admit helplessness?

With families coming into and out of our office from Kirkuk, Baghdad, and Anbar every day, how would we ever trust another family? Al-Qaeda had an endless supply of people it could cow into submission, and not a few ideologues either.

There were so many questions now. Loving first had really complicated things. In light of all that had happened now, it seemed obvious that we should have parted ways with this troublesome family at the first sign of discord. Instead, preemptive love had landed us on al-Qaeda's radar . . . again. The principal actors were in custody. That was a huge relief. Whether or not that would be the end of the story was still yet to be seen.

"What are we going to do about Ali?" someone asked a few days later.

It was an e-mail or a phone call, maybe a staff meeting. I cannot remember who asked the question first. Thankfully, I'm surrounded by people who all lean into questions like this. We are not a community where questions like this are scoffed at, where the token bleeding heart asks the ridiculous question and everyone rolls their eyes while waiting for me to reason with the lunatic who actually thinks we should still send the terrorists' child to heart surgery. No, we all tend to be equally crazy in this regard. Whoever asked the question first was simply speaking what was on everybody else's heart. "What are we going to do about Ali?"

As best we understood it, Ali's dad, mom, and uncle were all in prison. It was not even clear to us where Ali and his siblings were. When we had visited their house and Caleb told the kids that Ali was going to get his heart surgery, they jumped up and down like Real Madrid had just won the World Cup. Caleb got the whole thing on video—their excitement was thick and precious. Now we had no idea where these dear ones were. Maybe Grandma and Grandpa were still alive and managed to avoid being caught up in the scandal. If so, the kids were likely with them. Otherwise, all four children might be in the custody of the state. It was murky, at best, as to whether or not we would ever see Ali again. But taking Ali outside the country to Turkey for surgery was entirely out of the question. At the very least, the government would probably never allow any of the immediate family members to leave the country for fear that they would export their terrorism and cause an international incident or for fear they would escape and never return.

We went back and forth in serious consideration of the ethics of helping terrorists. Would saving Ali's life constitute some kind of aiding and abetting? How would our friends in the American military feel? How would our donors feel? What about all those kids in California who raised money for Ali—should they be given a say in how their money is spent? Should they be consulted as to whether or not four-year-old Ali should be treated like a criminal or rescued like a victim?

On the other hand, what an opportunity! Ali truly needed heart surgery to live. So did his sister. After all they had been through, after all the horrible things about Americans, Christians, and other outsiders al-Qaeda had likely indoctrinated them with in their few years on this earth, we alone were poised to write a new story, to help them write a new future. If we turned them away now, who knew how the rest of their lives would play out? If they were staying with Grandma and Grandpa, or if Mom was ultimately released to raise the kids, how could we be sure that they would not continue to walk down the path of terrorism and retribution? How might their family spin this whole story to incite further anger or violence against people like us?

Like the fatwa before it, this moment was a great divergence. Would we play it safe and walk away from Ali? Or was that really safe at all? Might it hasten an inevitable retaliation? Or would we press in and find a way to help Ali and his family in their time of greatest need? Would preemptive love win, or would our best defenses and justifications have us turn away a child who had done nothing wrong?

We would always have another child with whom we could play it safe. That was a well-worn path. And knowing how way leads on to way, it seemed that we would not only end up in an entirely different place henceforth but become entirely different people.

We made a pact: we were not giving up on Ali! The logistics would be tough, the obstacles greater than anything we had faced to date. But if preemptive love meant anything at all, it had to mean something here and now for Ali. His parents' terrorism and their subsequent arrest had left yet another hole in his heart. If we were to be about heart-mending, now was clearly our time.

Months later we crossed a historic threshold when we brought the first heart surgery team into Iraq to perform complex heart surgeries. Ali was at the top of our list. We had blackmailed ourselves again, saying we were going to do something and forcing ourselves to stick to our word. We had become new people in the process, testing the limits of our love, finding our hearts expanding to accommodate the vision we had cast: that we love our enemies and their children, though they kill us.

In the end, sadly, we were unable to save Ali's life. But the long, hard walk toward our enemies—toward the ones who plotted to kill us— changed us all forever.

I'm reminded of Robert Frost's famous poem about the traveler in the woods who predicted that he would one day recall his choice between diverging paths with a sigh. Jessica and I cannot relate. And knowing Jess, she would gladly welcome Ali's father and mother to our office or home again today to say, "I forgive you." Courage, love, faith . . . these are all muscles that grow in strength each time we push them to their limits.

> *I took the one less traveled by,*
> *And that has made all the difference.*

CHAPTER 12

Betrayal

To spite the images of Iraq as a dusty wasteland, vast swaths of Iraq cover themselves in blankets of lush greenery for a few weeks every spring. As they do, Arabs and Kurds flee the heat and leave their cities packed in chartered buses, SUVs, and small sedans to camp and picnic anywhere they can find a free plot of land. It is commonplace to see scores of cars parked along the edge of a random highway, people lined up on blankets, dancing in the sun, music blaring from car speakers or generator-driven home entertainment systems. Along the rivers, women squat and wash out the dishes from magnificent picnic dining. Forget sandwiches and fruit in plastic Baggies; in Iraq "picnic" means cinnamon and pomegranate lamb biryani; peppers, eggplant, and grape leaves stuffed with mincemeat and rice; and full-on portable barbecues to roast veggies and skewers of meat or fresh fish, with oodles of hot cardamom chai.

Years prior, upon our arrival in Iraq, some of us were on one of these daylong excursions with a group of college students who relied on our team for tutoring in their spare time. Unfortunately, being organized by college guys who had never cooked a day in their lives, their picnic featured more potato chips and Pop Keks than it did the usual family feast. (Their smothering mothers would have shuddered at the sight.) As the sun beat down, melting the remaining snow on the nearby Iranian mountaintops, we met Ayad, a soft-spoken young man who always used the proper etiquette when addressing anyone of an age or stature higher than his own. He quickly became an indispensable part of our team as cultural guide, interpreter, dear friend, and close confidant.

Ayad was great about refusing to speak English unless it was urgent or important, knowing how vital it was for us to learn the local language in order to thrive in our new home.

Ayad's father had long since passed away, and his uncle was responsible for watching over the family (although Ayad technically lived alone with his mother and sisters). Ayad's mom welcomed us into their home regularly for dinner or tea with much warmth and hospitality. Their family was, in many ways, our first home away from home.

We were blessed to be able to hire Ayad. His personality and his status as a fatherless young man did not make him especially inclined toward hard negotiations over his hourly wage, which probably would have made it difficult for us to hire him, living hand-to-mouth as we were in those early days.

Ayad worked for us part-time for years, always available at a moment's notice and keeping dependable office hours. During long car rides to the disputed areas of the country, we would talk about hopes, dreams, and the challenges of dating (or, rather, not dating) in a conservative, rule-bound place like Iraq, and the similarities of our situations, being without our fathers in a very patriarchal society.

Once we began our summer internship program and began hosting banquets for all of our "surgery survivors," Ayad became a friend to a rotating cast of college students and volunteers from the States. When Caleb arrived, he and Ayad hit it off. But one of the earliest volunteers to join us in Iraq and befriend Ayad was our stateside do-it-all, Leigh Saxon.

Jessica and I had met Leigh and her husband, Terrill, over dinner in a friend's home in Texas seven years earlier and became fast friends. Jessica and I had joined their church and grown closer to them with each passing week. I remember being on the road when I got a phone call on one of the first cell phones that was small enough to fit in my pocket. It was Jessica on the other end; Leigh and Terrill had just found out that their youngest son, Whit, had been born with a life-threatening heart defect. Whit's older brother Paul was one of Jessica's favorite little kids in the class she taught. Jessica would hold Paul and pray for Whit ahead of his surgery.

Whit was the first child we ever knew who faced down death. Thankfully, the American health care system is extremely adept at handling crisis situations like this for parents all over the country, and Whit's case was no exception. He was quickly scheduled for the first of what would ultimately be two or three stages of surgery. As he grew, the doctors predicted a few points at which they would likely intervene again to provide him with a total correction, ushering him into the normal life that Paul and their eldest son, Jack, were enjoying.

The Saxons were our heroes. They took it all in stride, never whined, and taught us all what it meant to live with open hands, receiving from God and others, giving to all who had need, and refusing to cling too tightly to that which is on loan.

But if someone ever wanted to make a case for a capricious God, they'd have a good example in what happened to the Saxon family. Shortly after Whit's successful heart surgery, the Saxons learned that Paul had neuroblastoma, an aggressive form of childhood cancer. The nationwide statistics suggest that Paul might have sooner won the lottery. The following years would be fitful, as our friends watched their toddler deteriorate to the point where he was nearly living in his stroller.

Most suburban moms and dads where Leigh and Terrill lived had their soccer fields, baseball diamonds, or gyms where they raised their kids, socialized with other parents, and, if they were lucky, squeezed in a bit of exercise for themselves chasing kids or screaming at the umpires. But the Saxons had the hospital. That's where they hung out. That's where most of their best friends were. They wore grooves in the halls of the cancer ward while most of their peers from work and church were giving their lives over to the new vocation called "soccer mom."

Against all her redheaded proclivities, Leigh managed to save most of her fire and rebelliousness for her thirties and the campaign she waged against Paul's childhood cancer. Unlike many in the South, with our intuitive understanding of propriety and our manicured personas, Leigh shoots straighter than a cowboy metaphor. Once the Saxons declared war on cancer, Leigh and Terrill became one of the greatest gifts of faith for me, not because they grinned and bore it and not because they constantly peddled platitudes about how good God was. No, if the inner conversations of the Saxon household were made into a movie, children probably wouldn't have been allowed in without an adult chaperone. They did not trap it in or wither away in the face of a theocratic rule book that dictated their responses to suffering. They vented. They kicked the dog (calm down, I'm exaggerating). And they didn't make any bones about closing the door in your face (Terrill hates unannounced visitors in his best of moods), refusing to answer the phone, or taking Paul on the scariest roller coasters against doctor's orders.

"What are they going to threaten us with? 'Your son might get a blood clot and die up there'? What a way to go!"

Jess and I can be about as raw and real as it gets. The Saxons were our kind of people: broken, battered, and not afraid to speak their minds . . . the kind of people we could trust, if only because they allowed us to let our gut out a little bit and be a little less protective of our own marriage secrets, our doubts, and our fears about this entire faith journey to which we had all allegedly devoted ourselves.

In July 2007, the week the Preemptive Love Coalition was born in Iraq to help children like Whit, Paul was laid to rest.

There's a melody running through my head right now when I think about Paul's life. This song and all the emotion it evokes in me is the only way I know to describe his untimely death. Living in Iraq, Jess and I hadn't seen him in years. I really wish Paul was here so I could sing it to him. He would be so big these days.

Somewhere early on in the history of the world things got derailed. Like most everyone, I have a hard time believing that God originally designed a world in which parents bury their own babies.

Due to our friendship and their personal story, I hoped early on that Leigh and Terrill would join us in helping children in Iraq. While they had the dubious distinction of knowing the horror of losing a child, they also had the privilege of seeing one of their other boys' life completely transformed through a relatively simple heart surgery.

After Paul died, Whit did what kids do: he asked those dogging questions that stump our titan theologians and philosophers.

"What will happen to Paul's body down there in the ground?"

"Where did Paul actually go?"

"Why did Paul die?"

I don't know what it's like to go through this agony, but I imagine Leigh and Terrill were asking all these same questions, in spite of the religious guardrails that aimed to provide them with handles for times such as these.

One night, at the height of Leigh's frustration with these natural, yet confounding, questions, Whit caught Leigh unawares as she was tucking him into bed. Whether he had worked through the first round of questions, or whether he had simply concluded that Mom and Dad were as clueless as he was about forever, heaven, and God, no one really knows. But that night, the direction of Whit's questions took an important curve around the bend.

"Mommy, why are we still alive?"

(I'm not sure it went down this way, but I imagine Whit tracing the five-year-old scar on his little chest.)

"Excuse me?" Leigh said, feigning a hearing problem that all parents suddenly come down with when buying time to formulate a plausible response.

"Why are we still alive?"

It is generally not considered good parenting to let your five-year-old drive the car, but Whit had just taken the wheel and turned a corner.

Leigh internalized Whit's struggle on the edge of his bed that night. "Why am *I* not dead yet? Why am *I* still here?"

Agonizing over Paul's death, questioning the apparent capriciousness of the years of suffering . . . all that was a necessary leg of the journey. But there are better questions still.

Leigh and Ayad formed a fast friendship during Leigh's first trip to Iraq. Jessica, Leigh, and Ayad traveled hours to meet many of the families we had introduced to the world through our newsletters, website, and photos. From dinner in the home of sixteen-year-old Khadeeja, whose father begged us to choose anyone but the Turks, to helping Daryan's mother, Shno Khan, learn how to feed her baby with a bottle for the first time, Leigh's years in the trenches with sick children made her a lighthouse to moms and dads whose primary concern was the well-being of their kids.

Leigh was a professional heart-mender from the word *go*. She shared Whit's story far and wide, doling out hope for families nervously awaiting surgery. She bragged about Whit's growth and energy and inspired in others a vision that their own children could perform similar feats. Leigh and Whit were, for many, the first people any of our friends knew who had successfully been through a life-altering heart surgery.

But Leigh also had the patience of a mother, sitting quietly with those who mourned the loss of a child or received news that their children were deemed inoperable. She shared her own story of Paul's war with cancer, her own fears, and her own doubts. And in a religious culture that eschews any such doubt or questioning of Providence, Leigh's transparency, born from a place of obvious struggle and not theological acrobatics, was as refreshing as a cup of cold water to many of the mothers with whom she sat.

Through all Leigh's tears and vulnerability, Ayad enjoyed the honor and burden of translating and conveying Leigh's heart to those they met.

Shortly after Yusuf's daughter, Hope, died, we invited him and his wife to travel a few hours from his father's house to join us for dinner with Leigh, this American woman who had been through something similar and might make a good friend.

The cultural norms for experiencing grief and suffering across the majority of Iraq leave much to be desired for those in pain. Where moms and dads like Leigh and Terrill have support groups, personal therapists, celebrity spokesmen, and countless titles on pain and suffering within a very short drive to the bookstore, the current expression of grief across Iraq's various cultures amounts to little more than a hostage taking, trapping mothers and fathers in their pain, and denying them the chance to enter into a dialogue with their family, their community, and, least of all, with God.

With Leigh visiting Iraq from the States, we hoped that we might create an environment in which two grieving mothers could find space to believe that all they were feeling was somehow natural, and, more than that, acceptable. Leigh wasn't there to be a fixer, as though we knew how to muscle our way through this kind of stuff. If anything, we wanted to simply say, "Our cultures may be different, but our kids and our hearts and our dreams break just the same."

As we ate dinner together and the two ladies exchanged stories and tears, nothing really happened. There were no fireworks. Neither mom was miraculously healed of her wounds. Each mom left as she had come, an amputee scratching an itch on a missing limb.

But they had shared in each other's pain—and even shared a few laughs. And it was beautiful.

We were just hours away from escorting our very last group of kids to surgery in Turkey. Jessica and I celebrated our imminent vacation after a years-long stint in Iraq with a meal at our favorite hole in the wall with a local approximation of eggplant risotto and rapiers with char-grilled meat.

Though Jessica and I had been very lonely in Iraq for almost a year, we ended the summer with a flurry of activity, including a professional internship for college students from the United States and Europe and Iraq's only annual celebration banquet and carnival for children (in our case, those children who had successfully undergone heart surgeries in the previous year). A group of longtime friends and stateside volunteers had traveled across the ocean (and against their families' strong judgment, at times) to staff the event's face-painting booth and to lead the kids in fishing for rubber duckies, beanbag tosses, and balloon art.

Rizgar was a little squirrelly throughout the celebration. On the one hand, he was gregarious, hamming it up for the interns whom he so loved, in part because he was their host and protector, but perhaps, in part, for the ways they reminded him of days long gone when he was a Western youth coming of age just like them.

Decked out in our finest local wares, Jessica, Caleb, and I sat onstage in front of hundreds of screaming kids and bemused parents who had never seen such festivities. We were doing our best impression of one of the numerous wedding parties we had attended throughout the summer, dressed to the nines, sitting stoically and frowny-faced so as not to break decorum.

A voice came booming over the house sound system.

"Are we having a gooooood time?"

An awkward silence ensued. Iraq does not have an equivalent of the African-American church's call-and-response culture.

"I do!" Rizgar said, enthusiastically answering himself, seeing that no one else would, in his unmistakably British-Kurdish accent. His short-sleeved white dress shirt was unbuttoned at least two notches too far. Had it been America, the copious amounts of chest hair emanating from inside would have frightened the children. This being Iraq, they just called him Uncle Rizgar and gave numerous kisses whenever they saw him.

But he must have received a phone call during the celebration at some point, because the rest of the day was marked by secrecy and evasion.

Since he was an extremely generous, attentive, and tenderhearted person, it would have been easy to chalk his distance up to the fact that all of us were about to get on a plane and leave him behind, alone in Iraq for the first time since we began working together. Maybe he just needed some space to prepare for the inevitable. But I sensed something else was afoot. Unfortunately, I was right.

I was pacing back and forth beneath the grapevine arbor that covers my courtyard in Iraq. Rizgar was on the other end of the line being maddeningly cryptic about our immediate and future security.

"I know you are taking these new children to surgery in Turkey tonight with Leigh and all the interns, but we really have to talk before you leave."

"I'm leaving in a few hours," I protested, put out by his claims of the urgency of the situation.

"Yes, but we really need to talk. Trust me. Someone is spying on us. They are listening to everything we say. I've already been to the office and swept it for bugs. Don't go back to the office before you leave town."

I had seen him get a little anxious before. His influential father, friend and confidant to many of the top personalities in Baghdad and Erbil, had given Rizgar permission to work with us on the condition that Rizgar make an oath to him to always keep us safe, fight our fights, and protect the family name in the process. Rizgar took it seriously, no matter how much we protested and insisted that he could not possibly be held responsible for the decisions we made independently of him. But his dad saw it differently. In Khala's view, it was Rizgar's job to either persuade us or obstruct us, but he had to keep us safe. And in the face of a list of tasks I had yet to accomplish in order to get this last group of kids to surgery in Istanbul later that night, I wasn't acting on his efforts to persuade me as quickly as he had hoped.

"I've got proof. You will never guess who it is. Just come to my house."

I tried to play the twenty-questions game with him over the phone in hopes of ascertaining how grave the situation was.

"All I can tell you is that they have been listening in your home and in your office."

Well, that certainly narrowed the field down to but a few people whom I had received in both places.

"Someone gave me a transcript of things you said in your home last Christmas. Now people are investigating you and making claims that you are—I'm sorry to say this to you—a *missionary*." He said the word like I should have been ashamed, invoking the rumor I had heard numerous times (always behind my back, never directly) that our heart surgeries were a ruse, a foot in the door to get people to change their religion. Once I got a phone call from a friend who worked at a satellite news station broadcasting to the diaspora, warning me that we were being discussed in the newsroom and that people were being cautioned against us and our wily ways.

"Who is spying on us? Is it Sheikh Hussein?" I asked, trying to guess which of my Arab friends might pose the greatest threat to Rizgar, my closest Kurdish friend and brother. Sheikh Hussein had been in my home and in my office. I did not suspect anyone of spying, quite honestly, but I had to begin my "Guess who?" with someone. Playing to Rizgar's personal insecurities and local prejudices seemed as easy a place to start as any.

"No," he said.

I rattled off a few more names as perfunctorily as the first—a few families, a few friends, a few religious leaders and politicians.

"Is it you?" I asked, only half joking.

"Just come over to my house. I'll show you."

I gave Jessica some lame excuse about why I had to abandon her to the packing, last-minute housecleaning, and fifteen guests from America and England; grabbed Caleb; and ran over to Rizgar's house. Caleb did not have any pressing work or packing to do—it was the weekend, and he was staying behind in Iraq until Christmas to staff the office—but he was unimpressed with any conspiracy theory that would pull him away from our guests and his new intern friends in the final hours before they left.

I don't recall whether or not we were served tea at Rizgar's house. It may have been one of those incredibly rare times in his home in which hospitality took a backseat to security.

What I do remember is the sound of the voices on Rizgar's clunky laptop as he played file after file for us. The audio had that distinctive crackle that goes hand in hand with all good spy recordings. It was like listening in on Watergate or playing 007, except I couldn't enjoy the thrill of the hunt—let alone the promised capture—because I was one of the voices, none the wiser to the fact that I had been the subject of under-cover surveillance in my office and in my home with my wife and kids. Even my trips abroad had been violated, with calls I placed from overseas back to Iraq being monitored and recorded.

"A friend gave these to me when they landed on his desk and he learned that we were being investigated. He told me we have a shrew inside our organization." I was pretty sure he meant a mole.

"Mole, shrew, whatever it is. He told me that one of the security arms had apparently used low-ranking officers to plant the mole to spy on you. But because of his friendship and loyalty to my dad and my family, he doesn't want us wrapped up in this. When the intel arrived on his desk, he buried it and alerted me to the situation."

The whole thing was absurd.

"They are following you. He told me he also has photo surveillance of you, like you with your guitar singing at a hotel with some other people." He had my attention. Rizgar was talking about an event I had never told him about, something completely separate from our shared expe-riences and friendship. Months later, evidence would continue to sur-face, further elucidating how many people had infiltrated our friendship network, including video surveillance from inside our home and private bank records handed over to the secret police by the bank-manager fa-ther of one of our volunteer student translators.

"Do you recognize the other voice on the recording?" Rizgar said, waiting for me to solve the puzzle myself.

It was the voice I had, for years, identified with guilelessness: respectful, timid, demurring, obedient. It was Ayad.

Jessica and I were set to leave the country in just a few hours. We would be gone for five months and planned on leaving the office in Caleb's hands. Rizgar was also leaving the country for a short time. We would all board the same plane together to take our final group of children from across the country to surgery in Turkey. Rizgar would stay in Turkey with the families until the surgeries were complete, while Jessica and I—along with all our American guests—headed back to the States.

Rizgar was extremely levelheaded and reasonable in our final hours in the country together.

"Look, you're the boss. Nothing is going to happen to me either way. Whatever information Ayad is passing on, it's not about me—and even if it was, I'm sure I could get out of it because of my dad."

"Well, we haven't done anything wrong, and we have nothing to hide," I argued, priming myself for a fight. But he wasn't arguing back. He was rarely this calm or collected in times of chaos. But the stakes were high, and he knew I had to arrive at my own decision.

"If you want to keep him on staff, I understand. He has been here since the beginning. It is difficult. If you want to fire him, I understand that, too."

I was sure there had to be an explanation. After all we had been through, it seemed wrong not to extend the same "love first" philosophy to one of our own.

Rizgar continued. "But I want you to know that I cannot work with him any longer. I don't need to drag my family down in this. All these years I have been working to advance the cause of Preemptive Love. I have run into so many barriers. It has always seemed like certain political opponents were a few steps ahead of us. We have been sabotaged; lies have been spread. Now I understand that it was him all along. I cannot work like that. I wanted to work with him so that we could succeed together. Whatever his handler has him doing in spying on us makes it very difficult for us to succeed. We cannot win if the major political parties are against us."

Everything he was saying made sense. Rizgar had access to information, through a predictably anonymous source, that had been shared exclusively in confidence between Ayad and Jessica or Ayad and others on the team. To our knowledge, there was no way for much of that information to have ended up in Rizgar's hands *but* through some nefarious espionage plot against our team.

We had heard the whispers in the bazaar and on the streets—that we were CIA agents, undercover, using heart surgeries as a cover for covert operations, even medical experimentation. The same types of rumors were rife about the Israelis when we were taking kids there for surgery: organ harvesting, experimental drug regimens, child trafficking, etc. How else could an occupying Christianizing or Zionizing force offer charitable assistance to people in need?

"One of the reasons you hired me," Rizgar reasoned, "was to be your adviser on local matters and to guide you through these kinds of situations. My advice is that you release Ayad."

"I want to talk to him first. He deserves a chance to defend himself. We should count him innocent before we do anything," I countered.

"I'm sorry, but I really don't recommend that," he said firmly. "We have all the evidence we need. We know what is what. It's better that you let him go without making a big deal about it. He doesn't know we have this information. That is *good* for him. This way he will be able to go back to his handlers, or whatever they are, and tell them that he got fired. That will be the end of it. But if we out him—if we confront him—he will not be able to hold it together. You've seen him. He will ultimately tell his superiors that he failed, that we found him out. And these people, man . . . it will be just like the movies. They want to be like CIA. Once they think their whole operation on you guys is busted, they will make him disappear just like they have been making journalists and political opponents disappear."

Ayad was such a simple, guileless young guy. It seemed implausible that he would be offed for something as innocuous as getting found out by a group of humanitarians who, incontrovertibly, posed exactly zero threat to national security. At the same time, the outsized financial investments and aspirations of the various Iraqi militias, security forces, intel-gathering arms, investigative units, secret police, cyber and telecom monitors, and informant networks made the entire thing seem not only plausible but, as Rizgar said, completely inevitable.

"Look, we all have to get on that plane in a few hours," Rizgar reminded me. "And I have to come back to this situation and work with him while you are gone. I cannot do that. If you want me as your adviser, you need to fire him. Immediately. If you don't want to fire him, I understand. But it means you don't need me as an adviser. I don't mean anything personal by it—you are still my brother—but I will have to quit in that case. I cannot work with him under these circumstances."

I don't know the name of the street where Ayad lives; it's probably just a numerical designation buried in a book of city codes. The people just describe it by its proximity to the things around it: the hotel, the long street, the park, the triangle. But I could drive to his house with my eyes closed. It was like driving home. His was a home that had warmed us in the winter, cooled us in the summer, enveloped us as though we were its own.

I called ahead before pulling up outside. I had decided to lay him off indefinitely, citing the uncertain financial future of our organization. We had just lost a huge financial contract we had been counting on, and paying Ayad to do little more than sit idly at a desk throughout the fall suddenly seemed like a waste of donor resources. More than that, the threat of losing Rizgar—not to mention the trail of dead that I presciently saw in Ayad's wake—loomed large overhead.

In the sterility of my car, the decision to lay him off had come easily. But the truth is, Jessica and I were never upset with Ayad. Rizgar helped us a lot with that.

"Don't be upset with him," he urged. "He is a vulnerable boy without a father to protect him. Unfortunately, this is exactly the kind of person they can get to and force their way upon. I don't know if they got to him through money or threats—some of his siblings travel overseas . . . who knows what they are involved in?"

Ayad appeared at the gate in house clothes; he was clearly still upset from our phone call an hour earlier. He returned a few of our things, maintaining his respectful demeanor. I wanted to scream, "Keep the paper clips! Just give me my privacy back!" but I had committed to the path that I hoped would keep him safe.

I wished he would have punched me or yelled at me. If he would have just spilled the beans about the whole thing or been defensive, at least that would have given me something to hold on to. Instead, I walked away with nothing but doubt. It was the decision I had to make. There was too much on the line to take a risk with the lives of so many people. I made the decision in good faith, but there was nothing about it that felt good.

Rizgar consoled us with the idea that it was a victory, a preservation of our privacy, our security, and our future. I saw it as unnecessarily binary, as nothing less than the failure to love.

Leigh was uncharacteristically silent, peering out the window of our charter bus as we drove to the airport that night. Every streetlight we passed cast a shadow across her face and into my heart. I knew she was disappointed in me; I could see it in her eyes. *Turning a young man out on the streets like that.*

The way she had laughed at one of Rizgar's jokes while boarding the bus was forced, and she didn't joke or pick back at him like he would have expected in return. I read the lines on her face under the glow of each streetlight, but I couldn't interpret them fast enough before things fell dark again.

Does she think Rizgar manufactured the entire ordeal? Some sick, heavy-handed plot to displace a harmless young boy and secure for himself the exclusive role of adviser and friend in the life of our family? I was offended at the silent accusation that I could be so gullible.

I thought back to hours earlier when I had stood outside Ayad's house and made a conscious choice not to lift my gaze above the stucco fence line. I couldn't bear to know whether his mom or sisters were peering out over the kitchen sink brokenhearted.

"Just one thing, Brother Jeremy," Ayad had said before I got in my taxi to leave. "I'm too young to give you advice, and you are—uh, *were*— my boss. But be careful who you listen to. Things are not always what they seem."

His eyes had teared up, and he quickly excused himself and headed back inside, embarrassed.

It's so hard to see things for what they are. Ayad may have been misleading me. He may have known we were onto him and was using this one last chance to release a red herring for me to chase. For all I know, he may have even been telling the truth. To this day, I cannot be sure who was innocent and who was guilty. Ayad may have genuinely believed that Rizgar was setting him up while something even more complex was actually playing them both behind the scenes. In any case, his words were foreboding, and they would knock around in my head for many sleepless nights, for years to come.

CHAPTER 13

Running for Cover

The view from my sister-in-law's back porch is breathtaking—especially when retreating from an Iraqi summer. My favorite feature is the private lake at sunup, with a surface so smooth that when a dragonfly takes off from the center, it looks as though a giant pane of glass has shattered as ripples rush to the shoreline and awaken the dawn.

Jessica, the kids, and I had just arrived back in Texas after an emotionally exhausting couple of days. Between firing Ayad for violating our most sacred spaces and passing on personal information about us to unknown entities, and our deep personal investment in a group of five children who were receiving surgeries in Istanbul *at that moment,* some time on the lake was a much-needed reprieve. Little did we know, we were still in the twilight hours. We would not simply be gently disrupted by the mere flutter of dragonfly wings. We were about to get the emotional and organizational equivalent of a neutron bomb dropped into our laps. I had family commotion all about me when I took Rizgar's call on my computer. I was expecting one of his routine daily updates on our kids in surgery.

C. Arkan will have her surgery this afternoon; the doctors are expecting ninety-five percent chance of a total correction.

L. Ibrahim is still in the ICU, expecting discharge around one P.M.

N. Mohammed is still in the ICU; she has had an infection around the wound on her chest. We're hoping for discharge to the ward this evening.

V. Bahman has finally undergone all her tests and was deemed operable!

What I got instead was this:

"Brother Jeremy? Hi, it's me, Rizgar. You are never going to believe what just happened."

It was not an unusual phrase for Rizgar. Like me, he can be rather excitable. And depending on the tone in his voice, what comes next is often either a joke that is meant to "get you good," some good news about a businessman who ostensibly wants to donate tens of thousands of dollars to Preemptive Love (but never comes through), or something very, very bad.

I nosed his tone of voice like a wine connoisseur might a fine merlot. Since Rizgar was an avid prankster, his words could not always be trusted. His words may have appeared dark and strong, but if the tone didn't linger with complexity and at least a little astringency, it was probably safe to call his bluff. Unfortunately, his tone smelled like cat urine on a mulberry bush. He was really stressed.

"I just got the weirdest call from Iraq. Some guy said, 'You are expected in court tomorrow.'" He was getting more and more worked up with each word.

"'You must have made a mistake,' I told the guy. He said, 'Are you Rizgar?' I said, 'Yes.' 'Then we've got the right guy.'"

"What is this about?" Rizgar had asked the guy.

"You will learn more about that when you appear before the judge."

"I tried to tell him that I was in Turkey with a bunch of kids who were getting heart surgery. I told him I would come see him whenever my work here was done. He told me that I had to be in court tomorrow, or I would be arrested in the airport whenever I returned to Iraq.

"You should have heard how I yelled at him! *Do you know who my father is?!*'

"'We know exactly who your father is, and this time, it doesn't matter.'

"Man, I hung up on him and called my dad right away. I told him everything, how this guy talked, how disrespectful he was. My dad said, 'Wait a few minutes.' When my dad called me back, his tone was totally different. He just said, 'Son, I'm blocked on this one. I don't know what's going on. You need to get back home so we can sort this out.'

"Brother Jeremy, what can I do? I have never seen my dad blocked on anything. You know my dad. You know my family very well. You know how many times he has intervened and fixed things for you, for Preemptive Love. If he is blocked . . ." His voice trailed off. "I don't even know what to say or think right now. I know I have a job with these families. I know they need me here. But, at the same time, there is something huge going on . . . I'm sure it's about Ayad, and the investigation into you, and all this other stuff we've been going through."

There was no discussion to be had.

"Get on the next plane back home," I said. "And I will see if I can get on a flight in the next few days as well."

"No, no, no, Brother Jeremy, seriously. Seriously, don't do that. You cannot come back right now. I have to figure this out before you come back. I really don't want to see you or your wife or kids again until this is all over."

The next flight available from Istanbul was days away, after Rizgar's deadline to appear in court. If these threats were genuine, Rizgar would be arrested in the airport.

After years of sending children to surgery, we were flying in and out with extreme regularity. We seemed to know all the ticketing agents in both countries, and Rizgar seemed to know everybody else as well. And the people he didn't know personally at least knew his dad or other members of his prominent family by name and reputation.

What would it be like to be arrested in front of all these people who have trusted us because we were saving children? What will this do to Rizgar's reputation, to his dad's? What kind of arrest are we even talking about—a covert "Come with us" and no-cuffs kind of thing, or a big show with guns drawn and dogs to sniff his bags? Is this about secretly securing some kind of intel, or is it about sending a public message?

Rizgar's family made phone calls, inquiries, called in favors, but most of the case against us was one giant enigma cloaked in mystery.

Although Rizgar had five children he was walking through surgery and was tending to the needs of their parents, translating complicated medical data, and running errands at the pharmacy, he had plenty of downtime as he waited out the next few days envisioning all the worst-case scenarios that might come our way. He used his overactive imagination, his deep desire to protect us, and all that spare time to alert Caleb to the looming danger. I wasn't on those phone calls and there is plenty of discrepancy about what happened next, but I imagine it went something like: "Do not go back to the office. Stay at home. Do not go out. They are going to arrest me when I get back from Istanbul. I don't want them to find you and arrest you, too. So don't give them the chance. Just stay at home. I will be back soon, and we will sort all this out."

We had been working for months at that time on introducing a complete turnabout in our programming: rather than continuing to send children out to surgery, wasting hundreds of thousands of dollars without impacting or improving the local situation for doctors and nurses, we were weeks away from bringing in a history-making surgery team to perform all the same lifesaving surgeries we had become known for *inside Iraq*. What's more, we would begin training doctors and nurses from all over the country to do these surgeries and care for these children themselves, until they did not have to send them abroad anymore.

But with the recent chaos and unexplainable circumstances all around me, everything we had been working to accomplish for tens of thousands of Iraqi children was going up in flames.

How did the firing of one young Iraqi boy undo so much?

The summer midnight air can be surprisingly cold, especially when you know you are about to be arrested and feel like your whole city has turned against you.

Rizgar stepped off the plane at three A.M. to no great fanfare. He hit the tarmac just the same as all the grandmas from Germany who had not been home since Saddam was ousted, the same as the Turkish businessmen who had come to capitalize on the region's exploding growth, the same as the American oilmen who came in search of black gold. Unlike the rest of them, however, he was about to be arrested.

Thankfully, the objective of the entire ordeal proved *not* to be about making a public statement. No dogs, no handcuffs, no guns drawn. Just a little eye contact, a nod, an acknowledgment, a surrender, and Rizgar was ushered away. Although the arresting officers claimed the right to incarcerate Rizgar overnight, his father worked it out so that he was remanded to house arrest for the night.

When Rizgar awoke the next day, he was taken in a private car to see "a guy." Not the way your brother-in-law "knows a guy" when the dishwasher breaks down. It was more like the way all the spies in every spy movie "know a guy" on the inside of every terrorist network or corporate corruption scandal at every major plot juncture.

"Look, Rizgar, this is not about you. This is about Jeremy and Preemptive Love. We know how many things you and your family have fixed for them over the last few years. We know you are protecting them. You need to walk away now.

"If you renounce Jeremy and anything to do with Preemptive Love— if you leave Jeremy to his own devices—we will spare you and your family any further embarrassment or legal trouble. This will be between us and Jeremy."

"What is this about?" Rizgar asked.

"If you don't—if you insist on continuing to meddle in this situation—your name is all over this organization. If you don't walk away now, you will go down with them."

Rizgar still did not know the charges, but he was sure he knew who was behind the setup and what it was all about. In just a few short years, thanks in large part to Rizgar's family, our organization had gone from an upstart shoe company to the leading organization in the country for children in need of heart surgeries. Our success and prominence were predicated largely on the fact that we saw every surgery as a *partnership* with parents, both financially and logistically. This immediately put us in a bad light with parents who were looking for handouts, who thought that somehow we owed them something by virtue of the fact that we were Americans. It meant that parents were not universally in favor of us. Some of them—like Ali's father—went and spread malicious lies about us.

But it also meant that, when all was said and done, when children had received their surgeries and were alive and well, when we came through and did for them what no other organization could or would, they felt dignity and pride in the role they had played and they sang our praises to other families, to the press, to other organizations, to political parties, and to the government.

We also worked hard to develop a local culture of grassroots giving, of empowering locals to handle their own problems, to quit waiting for the politicians to solve things that they could handle on their own. We held public fund-raisers, cutting coarsely against the grain of local culture. We encouraged "give back" programs through local businesses. We used emerging digital technologies. We raised money from well-to-do CEOs, passed the hat in neighborhood mosques, and used old-fashioned donation boxes in local grocery stores.

The head of one of the many local security apparatuses called us in multiple times insisting we stop our grassroots fund-raising, claiming that we were complicit in the proliferation of terrorism. "What will happen if you are successful in raising money in grocery stores and mosques for heart surgery? Al-Qaeda will start putting their own boxes out, asking people for money. Where will it stop?"

The truth probably had much more to do with the fact that the man in military fatigues was a party functionary, and unsanctioned activity of any sort was often seen as a threat. Rizgar gave him a few suggestions as to where he could shove some of our donation boxes, but our March of Dimes in Iraq had clearly started off on the wrong foot.

Our methods undercut the system of patronage that ensured only certain children were selected for surgery. Our system was not flawless by any means. We made mistakes. But we were more beloved by many than the political parties whose divisive agendas and ossified organizations were so widely accused of buying loyalty through their programs and service offerings.

In the end, Rizgar's conclusion was that we were upending the apple cart of political patronage, taking away from the ruling class the levers they used to manipulate society and keep the proletariat supplicant and dependent.

Rizgar believed he knew the exact man who had set us up. He had been coming after us for years in other ways already, had repeatedly questioned why Rizgar was working for us and had tried multiple times to hire Rizgar away, hoping to buy some of the clout that came with Rizgar's family name. In one of my first encounters with this guy, he misappropriated over fifteen thousand dollars that was earmarked for our children to receive surgery. When we caught the error, he came to my office and begged Cody and me to bury the evidence and lie to all the people involved. Unfortunately for him, we have this strict no-lying policy. In a country awash in corruption, our unwillingness to lie did not start our relationship out well.

Having failed to cause Rizgar to switch teams through monetary inducements, he apparently upped the ante and went for a more direct form of intervention.

Back in the office of the guy who was holding Rizgar's "Get Out of Jail Free" card, Rizgar made his stand. From what followed, my guess is that it included a few monosyllabic expletives telling the guy what he could do to himself. Rizgar demanded to face our accuser. Instead, Rizgar went to prison.

Back in Texas, I was calling Caleb and Rizgar regularly, hoping to get through for an update.

When I told others about Rizgar's being in prison, their visions were probably formed primarily through the demonizing lenses of movies like *Midnight Express* or television characters like Jack Bauer. Unfortunately, the worst-case scenarios I was imagining for Rizgar were shaped by the things we had just experienced days earlier with Ayad, by the insider knowledge we had as to "how things work" through Rizgar's family, and by numerous off-the-record conversations we had shared with the heads of local military and security throughout the years.

Rizgar was jerked out of his cell after a few hours in the 120-degree August heat and offered a cigarette. A deal had been cut. He could go home, where he would find out more information in due time.

I got him on the phone a few hours later.

"Brother Jeremy, here's what we're going to do. I just need two thousand dollars."

"For what?" I vividly remember walking around my air-conditioned rental house in Texas as I prepared my lecture against corruption and bribery.

"Don't ask questions you don't want to know the answer to."

I never imagined myself entangled in a situation where someone would suggest that I should do everything I could to maintain some sort of plausible deniability.

"Look, Rizgar, I'm not doing this. The reason this stupid country is the way it is today is because of this kind of stuff. I'm not feeding into it.

I'm not paying our way out of this. If they want to arrest me, let them arrest me. I'll be on the plane with the doctors in a few days anyway. They can grab me at the airport and take me to court. I will gladly sit in jail with you. We've done nothing wrong. I'm not paying."

I think my monologue was probably much longer than that. Through it all, Rizgar only heard one thing: "You can go back to jail for all I care. I've got my principles, and you don't factor in."

"Who do you think you're dealing with?" he yelled. "Do you think they care about you? Do you think this is America, that you can go to court and get a fair trial? They can—and *will*—do whatever they want to you. You have no idea what's really going on here or who is really pulling the strings on all this. This is your shot. Let me have the money, and I'll take care of it. You don't have to know about it or do anything."

"Rizgar, this is where preemptive love wins. This is where Iraq changes. It's right here . . . this moment." Knowing me, my tone was unbearably sanctimonious.

"Fine. Keep your money. I'll take care of it myself."

"Rizgar—"

"I quit. You're on your own."

I turned to lick my wounds and to the comfort of my friends. Predictably, they joined me in my righteous stance against Iraqi corruption and the inevitable downward spiral of the country into which we had invested so many lives. I got gold stars and attaboys all around for my principled stand on patronage and bribery.

"That's how they're going to learn."

"You did the right thing, refusing to pay like that. What would keep them from making you pay up every time they had a hankering?"

"You pay once, you pay forever. Good job, son!"

"Maybe now they'll see that you can't be bought or bullied."

We were all so glad Jess, the kids, and I were safe. No one asked—least of all me—what the implications of my righteous stance would be for Rizgar. I don't think the thought ever crossed our minds.

The phone rang a few hours later. It was him.

"Don't worry about it. It's all over," he said dismissively. "My dad gave me the money. We made the problem go away . . . forever. But seriously, I quit. I can't work with you anymore. You obviously don't know what you're doing. You think this is some game. You're playing by American rules. You're dangerous, and you're naive."

Caleb did not see Rizgar return from prison, shaken up. He did not see him leave again to pay somebody or destroy something—whatever it was they did in the intervening hours before Rizgar returned home and told me it was all over. But Caleb did hear the intervening vitriol about me, my leadership, and how I had hung him out to dry after he denied himself the free pass and went to prison for me. Rizgar was furious, threatening, and aggressive. With Rizgar no longer working for Preemptive Love, suddenly all bets were off with regard to our residency visas, our work status, and our organizational status. The trip that was just days away with our first-ever Remedy Mission team of doctors and nurses from around the world was in jeopardy.

The next hours were brimming with threatening phone calls from Rizgar to Caleb about his visa; his sudden, alleged illegal status in the country; and the exorbitant fines (or even confinement) he would inevitably face when he tried to leave the country. Rizgar variously insinuated that Caleb was being pursued by the police and that our entire organization would not only fall through the cracks, but, because of all the favors he had apparently pulled behind the scenes over the years, we would not be able to get any kind of official recognition or status after he and his family walked away.

Suddenly, our closest friend and confidant, a man who called everyone "brother" and "sister," was throwing gasoline on everything we had built together and torching it to the ground, casting himself in the role of tyrannical overlord, scorned and seeking retribution on me and the staff I had left in his care.

For some reason, Rizgar continued to take my calls from the States, partly to yell at me and partly to offload on me all the culturally offensive things our team had done during our years together. And he wasn't entirely without reason to be upset.

When I refused to pay the bribe, I did so from an ivory tower. I made a tactical field decision from the safety of an air-conditioned office over seven thousand miles away. In touting a naive version of preemptive love, I was inadvertently throwing one of my best friends and biggest advocates under the bus.

I was sitting with my pastor when it all hit me. We had brought shame on Rizgar's family. I had violated the basic solidarity that he assumed in calling us family. I had never intended my stance on bribery to result in his further imprisonment. The mantle of leadership that required me to make rapid-fire decisions with lives hanging in the balance suddenly felt like a noose around my neck.

I called Rizgar back again. "You have done some ridiculous, horrible things in the last few hours. I entrusted people and other valuables to you. They are not yours to threaten and do with as you please. They are entrusted to you from God," I said, invoking an Islamic idea that I knew was very dear to his heart. "You have acted like a child who did not get his way, and now you are threatening my people? You called Cody in the States and bad-mouthed me? You told him that you would start a new organization together with him but you would never work with me again? How dare you? You don't even *know* Cody apart from me."

I'm sure I went on and on for some time.

"But look . . . this is not all your fault. This is *my* fault first."

(To this day, Rizgar tells me that this was the turning point. In his culture, men do not apologize. They might do a compulsory form of religious forgiveness-seeking, but they do not admit fault and they do not ask forgiveness for specifics.)

"I did not respect you the way I should have," I said, continuing. "I started preaching at you for something that was not even your doing. You were placed in an impossible situation. I know you could have given us up, walked away, and left me to get arrested on these trumped-up charges in a few days when I arrived at the airport with the doctors. But you didn't do that. You actually lived a lot more like Jesus than I did. You allowed yourself to be taken in and punished in my place. I've talked a lot about that, but when it came down to it, I totally missed it. I didn't recognize how much of a sacrifice you made for me so I could go free. I could have made a sacrifice for you—I could have paid the money—not because I wanted to bribe or buy my way out of an evil thing I had really done, but because I wanted to buy your freedom and keep you from paying the price for something that you truly *had not* done. Instead, my response made it sound like I didn't care if you were arrested again. It made it sound like I wasn't thinking about you. Please, believe me, I did not want you to go to prison again. I just was not thinking through all the implications of what it would mean if I did not give you the money to pay the bribe."

We finally had some space to breathe.

"I was wrong. Will you forgive me?"

There were a few proverbs my parents used regularly to raise me and rein in my argumentative, combative personality. One of them was "A soft answer turns away wrath." In an instant, a soft answer to all of Rizgar's questions about our friendship, loyalty, and future turned away his wrath. In an instant, we were put back together.

For his part, Rizgar overcame all his impulses, admitted his own wrongdoing, and apologized.

After more than two hours on the phone, I asked, "Where does that leave us now? You quit. So, now what?"

His next words dripped with humility and repentance. "Well, you probably shouldn't do this, but if you will have me back, I just want to say that I screwed up and I want to keep working together. You truly are my brother; I just let other people come between us. I will never let that happen again."

Caleb was furious.

"How dare you make peace with this madman?! He has done nothing but say hateful things about you for days, threaten you—and us—and talk about what a betrayer you are."

Jessica's take on things wasn't any easier.

"Are you so afraid to see Preemptive Love fail that you will risk our family over it?"

"Naive" was probably the least offensive thing those closest to me called me and my leadership during that time. I was doing my best to juggle my responsibilities to my family, my future teammates, and my staff in the field. But those responsibilities were complicated by hundreds of thousands of dollars of unspent donor money, untold thousands of kids needing surgery, and an international team of doctors and nurses who were en route to Iraq for a landmark medical mission. When I start something, I expect to finish it. So, yes, one of the most difficult things was the threat that we would not finish what we started—indeed, what we had promised—to the now expectant, hopeful parents of Iraq.

But what those closest to me seemed to miss was the fact that I was not simply working for the ideals of preemptive love. I was not merely trying to prove a theory. I was not living a certain way because I had blackmailed myself into it. And I was not merely trying to make history by keeping the Remedy Mission moving forward.

I knew that I would not be well *personally* unless I was at peace with Rizgar. This was not altruism. I was unapologetically pursuing my own well-being and my own joy. Somehow God had woven our hearts together, and his betrayal and backstabbing were far more offensive and painful than anything I had been through in Iraq up to that point—more than the fatwa, more than the attempted attack by Ali's father, and more than Ayad's disloyalty. I knew in my heart that this would be the moment that Iraq either ate me alive and left me a bitter shell of a person, or it would be the moment where I learned definitively whether or not this far country was something more than a dream, whether it had somehow drawn close enough to me, or drawn me close enough to it, to actually invade my soul and change my attitude—and my actions—from the inside out.

As a child, I learned to pray the prayer that Jesus taught those who followed him. One line says, "Forgive us our debts, as we forgive our debtors." This seemed consistent with other places where Jesus (as well as every kindergarten teacher in the country) taught us to "do to others what you would have them do to you." If this stuff was to be taken literally, it seemed to me that my refusal to forgive Rizgar would not only fail the test of the Golden Rule, it would rip the rug of grace out from under my feet whenever I sought to kneel upon it and ask God for any sort of forgiveness myself.

"Forgiveness and trust are not the same thing," Caleb would later say in objection. Indeed, he was right. Trust between Rizgar and me was not yet repaired. But Rizgar had asked to be welcomed back into our lives, and I knew that full restitution is exactly what I would want if I had lost my head and alienated everyone in my orbit.

To preempt the "I told you so" that was waiting to flow forth as soon as Rizgar turned on me again, I made sure that everyone knew that this was not peacenik, "let's all get along" naivety; this was the substance of preemptive love.

"I am willing to get burned again. It will not surprise me when it happens, and I do not think that because we have reconciled (for now), this is the last we will see of this. We are not done with tantrums, threats, or petulance. But there is something lacking in all the religions, sacred texts, and holy prophets of the world. We scarcely know what they mean until they are embodied in front of us. I want us to fill up what is lacking by giving ourselves over again and again to be led like lambs to the slaughter. In a country where everyone else is trying to save their own skin or take another's life, giving your life away is truly the stuff of the far country!"

Caleb did extremely well to make it on the airplane and leave the country with dignity and poise. In the end, an eleventh-hour fiasco on the day of his flight caused another uproar between Caleb, Rizgar, and local authorities, along with all the attendant threats and abuses of the previous few days. By that point, Caleb had the weight of the U.S. embassy on his side investigating Rizgar and his family, but our government's cachet and cooperation only made the threats seem that much greater. No one should have had to look over his shoulder to protect himself against the wounds of a brother.

Caleb arrived in Istanbul completely undone, unmade.

I worked hard to keep open lines of communication in an effort to work out the implications of all he went through. For weeks I was still learning of many significant, traumatizing events that contributed to the ways in which Caleb had been threatened, things that we knew nothing of until it was all too late. I offered to pay for trauma counseling and to network with others who had been through similar experiences.

Caleb gave the impression he would stay in touch, but we knew he wouldn't. His spark was gone; the lights were out.

Over the next few months we e-mailed, to little effect. Around Thanksgiving, while traveling through Ohio on a Heartmender Tour to raise money for heart surgery and share some stories in hopes of inspiring others to pursue peace, I got a quick fifteen-second call from Caleb: "Hey, man, uh, I just got a message from your neighbor across the street in Iraq . . . he messaged me on Facebook. He said police are all over your house right now. You might want to have someone check it out."

I asked some follow-up questions: "What happened? Was it a break-in? Was anything stolen? Is this connected to the situation with Ayad? What about the situation with Rizgar?" But it was clear he neither knew anything nor wanted to get into that awkward space where we had to address the distance that had grown between us.

"Sorry, man, I'm in such a rush. I gotta get to work. Bye." The line went dead.

Our house in Iraq had been broken into, and with that, the final barrier had been breached. We had let the others—tell-alls, terrorists, and madmen—through the front door willingly, but we had slept soundly knowing the locks on the door still worked. The final naivety of that comfort was gone.

Some suggested it was our neighbors, as neighbor burglaries in our area seemed to occur on the heels of catastrophic violence (with all the uncertainty that comes when people need to provide for their families) *and* with upward economic trends, in which certain neighbors begin to pull ahead of others and new wealth is more easily spotted by those who are increasingly left behind. Others suggested it was the lady we had hired to clean our home, one of Jessica's most trusted friends. Some suspected it was Rizgar retrieving a last piece of evidence that might compromise some elaborate plot against Ayad. We couldn't really know for sure.

Two things were stolen during the invasion. The first was Ayad's work computer that I had placed in the back room just minutes after he handed it to me the night I stood outside his gate and terminated his employment.

Could it have been Ayad himself who broke in? Is there something incriminating on the computer? We also wondered at length if it wasn't some tentacle of the secret security apparatus that had hired Ayad in the first place, reaching into our sanctuary to molest our family.

After Caleb called to alert us to the robbery, we entered nearly a year and a half of radio silence, entirely against my will. My philosophy— theology, whatever it was—that said we should love first had not only failed, it had deeply wounded and betrayed someone I loved. It left Caleb confused, feeling like I had chosen a lunatic over him, or worse, that I had chosen our organization and our work in the most utilitarian way, ultimately betraying all my rhetoric about doing what's right *because it is right,* even if it does not always net the most metric-friendly results. My efforts to remain in dialogue with Caleb went unheeded, and eventually Jessica and I gave up trying and let him walk away.

Only later did we discover that the other thing missing after that fateful invasion was our hope of ever fully trusting another person in Iraq the same way again.

CHAPTER 14

The Remedy

After weeks of agonizing over the fate of our team in Iraq, Ayad's betrayal, Rizgar's reactionary tirade, and Caleb's decision to make a run for the border, my red-eye flight out of Dallas was like a cocoon. I ripped the clear plastic wrapper off my airline blanket and covered my face with nary a thought as to how many snot-nosed children or airsick travelers might have previously done the same. Passengers were still settling into their seats all around me, including Cody somewhere left of the dreaded middle-middle seat.

I was exhausted from days of crying and yelling, threats made to me, and hourlong calls to ambassadors and their staffers. I was fearful of being arrested at the airport. I had every intention of holding Rizgar accountable for what he had done to damage or destroy the psyches of people I loved—Jessica, Caleb, Leigh, Cody and Michelle, other interns. But I was dreading it. On top of all of that, I feared walking into my own home, knowing that it might be full of hidden surveillance devices, and I felt a spectacle of epic proportions was looming if my medical team landed before I could patch the hole in our sinking ship.

Meanwhile, Jessica was nearly bed-bound in our disco-era "don't worry it's already furnished" rental in Texas. She felt as though every crystalline, snaking nerve in her entire body had conspired to form a flaming straitjacket of paralyzing stress and fear. Sure, a cadre of heart doctors and nurses were boarding planes from all over the world to join our very first Remedy Mission in Iraq. We were turning a page, making history. But my joining the mission meant leaving Jessica behind to fend for herself and the kids.

She had never intended to miss the launch of the very first Remedy Mission in Iraq. She had worked as hard as anyone—in most cases anonymously, behind the scenes—to see this day become a reality. But when we were given the opportunity to bring in Dr. William Novick[1] and one of his teams with too little notice for us all to make it together, we couldn't pass it up. So, in spite of the pain and the stress, Jessica helped me pack my bags and shoved me out the door, convinced that this unsung role was hers to play in changing the course of history for the children of Iraq. Keeping up with me—helping me keep my head on straight—is a full-time job in and of itself.

There was so much guilt I couldn't shake: for firing Ayad, for leaving Caleb in Iraq without a leader, for trusting Rizgar, for distrusting Rizgar, for leaving Rizgar, and most of all, for sentencing my wife to some kind of neuropathic prison when anyone else with half a heart would have certainly said, "Enough is enough!" In spite of all the pressures and threats from outside, it was becoming clear that my passion to help others and somehow create a sphere of significance for myself was the greatest enemy to my marriage. In my own way, about a decade or two ahead of schedule, I had fulfilled some kind of Courtney genetic code and become the most hyped-up version of my father and my nono, revving my engine, spinning my tires in an effort to love some distant other, but doing so at the expense of family and friends closest to home.

A wave of emotions came over me as I settled into my seat, closed my eyes beneath my blanket, and fell into the deepest sleep of my life, hoping to emerge again on the other side of the ocean transformed, no more inching around on my belly in guilt and fear.

I had billed our inaugural Remedy Mission as a classroom experience; that was to be its overarching benefit as we sought to convince the Ministry of Health and all our partners to stop wasting their money, kicking the can down the road, by sending their children outside the country for heart surgery. Remedy Mission was built to educate, but stepping off the plane in Iraq, still licking my wounds from the indictment and the mysterious disappearance of my court case just a week prior, I was entirely unprepared to be among its students.

What local doctors and nurses gained in drinking from the fire hydrant of hands-on experience, biological exploration, and protocol management, I gained in a deluge of political fallout, as competing political entities from around the country vied for public recognition for the successes of our surgical team. When parents around the country heard about the arrival of an American heart surgery team dedicated to saying yes and performing complex heart surgeries, they brought their children in droves from all over the country for a coveted spot in Dr. Novick's operating room.

Just before the team arrived, insiders and representatives from the major political parties declared our visas invalid and told me they would only be honored if we rerouted the entire team to the neighboring province, but the team was already in the air going to the regional capital. I had worked hard with the top brass to ensure that the entire team had a personal letter in hand endorsing our work and affirming the status of their visas, but given the way the recent weeks had gone, it was not out of the question that competing factions might have the clout to derail even the most prominent of our local sponsors.

But even if the visas worked out and the team was admitted to the country, the political partner, whom Rizgar suspected of turning Ayad into a spy and levying trumped-up charges against us, called me and threatened to leave Dr. Novick and his team at the airport if they did not change their plans and fly straight into our city. I was assured that thirty thousand dollars of medical machines and supplies would be confiscated at customs by loyalists to the other party when they learned of the actual sponsorship and affiliation of the mission. To their credit, our host's threats seemed motivated by their own fears of being asked to work in another city intractably seized by political disunity.

It seemed the plane carrying our very first Remedy Mission team took a nosedive in the last few hours of its flight and landed perilously on the brim of an unstable volcano. Then Dr. William Novick stepped out.

At six foot huge, "Dr. No" stepped off the plane, two parts Churchillian field marshal, here to occupy your hospital and whip you into shape, and one part Father Christmas, bringing the gift of life and the assurance that none shall be forgotten to the remotest parts of the planet. One minute he was screaming and yelling for a caravan of armored cars to be readied or a cigar to be fetched, the next he had children on his knee, making silly faces, telling Mom and Dad that he would do everything he could to ensure his team did not leave their country without operating on their child.

He didn't know it at the time, but he basically fell into the mouth of our simmering volcano, plugged it up, and forced all its boiling political froth back beneath the surface for another day.

By merely showing up, he had given us an enormous gift. Heart surgery for children has to be among the easiest-to-understand programs a government can bring to its less-developed country. For a few thousand dollars, they can hold up a sick child on the brink of death, and hours later, when the surgical high priest emerges from behind the veil of the operating room's sterile field, bespectacled and covered in blood, deliver the good news that God has intervened and another life has been saved. The cameras roll, and hand-to-mouth political incumbents earn a new lease on life. And one does not need to look any farther than Iraq to see what a decade of neglect and atrophy in surgery contributes to the "brain drain" of a once-great country. Many streams—some very violent—fed into the deterioration of the country, but when the upper and middle class cannot get access to the surgeries they need to keep their family members well, they begin making more and more trips abroad in search of solutions. Eventually, many of them find a way to stay and never come back.

So surgeries speak. And with a country of some thirty million people and between five and ten thousand *new* children each year in need of heart surgery, we had no shortage of official invitations to help in different cities pouring in from across Iraq.

In the eleventh hour, we found out that one of the major donors to the mission wanted to earmark the money "Arabs only." Kurds and Turkmen—many of whom we had already called and invited—would not be welcomed to receive their much-needed heart surgeries. Granted, Arabs made up the majority of the country, but the very notion of withholding aid and selecting patients on the basis of ethnicity, gender, ability to pay, or politics cut against everything we stood for with preemptive love. But as far as this donor was concerned, it seemed the minority could die and go to hell.

Arabs only.

In Virgil's epic *Aeneid,* Laocoön says, "I fear the Greeks, even those bearing gifts." He might as well have been talking about Iraq. Novick promptly rejected the Trojan Horse, having seen these kinds of carrot-and-stick charades too many times before in similarly divided places.

Days later, when Dr. Novick landed in southern Iraq, he was received as a guest of the vice president, paid a visit to the local hospital, and made a short road trip to the vice president's home on the banks of the Euphrates River. In short order, the veep's bodyguards and servants began stealing away for a few text messages and phone calls to family to alert them to the presence of the American heart surgeon. Before long local sheikhs, tribal leaders, and all manner of folk were at the gate asking to see the American doctor.

"Dear sir, please accept my son. He is my only son. Can you save him?"

"Sir, my child has needed surgery for four years. I have no chance without you. What can you do for me?"

Novick held a life-sized X-ray scan of a baby's chest up to the fluorescent lights on the ceiling to check the size and placement of the little heart. The vice president, a French-trained economist, intervened.

"Can you accept some of these children tomorrow into your mission?"

I had just landed, and I would later regret not being present to weigh in and speak to what happened next, but Novick was quickly learning that the latent minefields from the Iran-Iraq War were not the only explosives underfoot.

"I've already gotten into an argument with one donor who insisted, 'Arab children only.' I am not in a position to decide who is selected for surgery. If you want any spots in our surgical mission, I would suggest you call the governor or director of health."

The next day I received a phone call from my Kurdish nemesis-partner who was hound-dogging our every move. "Why have you opened the doors to all these Arabs?"

The provincial government that was hosting this first Remedy Mission, and claims a sizable Arab population, had given the money to secure the airfare for Dr. Novick's team.

"We did not make any invitations beyond what we've discussed with you. Dr. Novick spent time with the vice president, but he did not invite any patients. He knows that the surgery list is already complete. He has been reviewing it with us for weeks in preparation."

"You cannot bring Arabs! We paid for this mission from our own money. Why should our own children suffer and be displaced by outsiders?"

The message was clear: *Kurds only*.

Back in Washington, DC, the government representatives were well aware of the sudden financial need that arose when we rejected the private donor who offered "Arabs only" money. They had assured us that in taking their money, there would be no reverse discrimination.

"Look, I promise you that we did not do this. You have my word," I said, trying to assuage this guy on the phone before Rizgar and I looked up to find another police squad outside.

"It doesn't matter now. We can't stop it. We just got a call from the prime minister telling us to accept these children from the vice president.

Talib was thrilled to hear the news that his five-year-old boy, Ahmed, had been accepted for surgery by the American team. He felt so grateful that the nation's vice president—and the most prominent hometown export—would intervene on his behalf given his lack of stature. *How can I repay a man who has everything?*

Once he and his wife suspected something was wrong with Ahmed's little body, they had taken him to a variety of doctors across their city. That first visit to the cardiologist was devastating. Like most of the other pediatricians and cardiologists across the country, their doctor was forced to give Talib and his wife (whom I knew simply as "Um Ahmed," or "Ahmed's mom") the kind of news they most feared:

"There is some kind of fusion between the chambers of Ahmed's heart, and some of his arteries are attached in all the wrong places. He needs surgery, or he will die."

"Okay," Ahmed's parents said cautiously. "So when can he get surgery?"

Unfortunately, even if they drove six hours away to Baghdad's best version of a heart hospital (the one where Dr. Mohammad worked prior to its partial destruction in the early days of the war), they would find doctors already turning away eighty children per day from the lifesaving surgeries they needed. But there were always ways to jump ahead in line, whether through medical urgency or more creative means.

They had a glimmer of hope once when they heard that Ahmed had been accepted to surgery at the main heart hospital in Baghdad. They packed their bags and drove six hours north, only to arrive at the hospital to find the doctors leaving, telling them they had arrived too late and missed their chance.

In any case, Ahmed's cardiologist was not about to refer him—the

Iraqi surgeons in Baghdad could never successfully complete a surgery this complex. The risks were far too high, and he didn't want Ahmed's death on his conscience.

"He should have had surgery when he was three months old. There is no one in Iraq who can save your son's life. You *must* leave the country for this surgery."

They worked for four years to gain access to "the List" so that their little Ahmed could travel outside for his much-needed surgery. With every passing day, Talib and his wife grew more in love with their son and stored up more memories in their hearts, not knowing if today's sticky-faced ice-cream kiss or yesterday's walk through the park might have been their last. One thing I will say about parents who walk the tightrope of death with their kids each day: they give hugs and kisses and color pictures and share snack time with their kids like they really mean it. Minutes together become a currency more precious than gold.

I've stood present as close friends like Yusuf drove away from the local airport with the bodies of their baby girls in the beds of pickup trucks, protected by nothing more than a makeshift box dressed up in locks. And I've put a white-knuckled grip on the rails of the ICU bed as friends like Faraydoon lamented over the suddenly lifeless bodies of their ten-year-old boys:

Your life on earth was so difficult and full of sadness.
But it was such a joy for me to have you here.
Now you are in Joy and Happiness forever.
But I am left in difficulty and sadness without you.
You were like seven sons to me.
You were like seven brothers!
My son! My friend! What will I tell your mother?
My eldest . . . how can I live without you?

All this death has helped bring the things in my life into a more proper perspective. Thirty-two times I've come home and kissed my kids and hugged them more intensely than I might have otherwise. That perspective is a gift.

We should not compare the differences between the death of a baby and the death of an older child. But my bedside observation of far too many deaths in Iraq leads me to believe that there *are* some differences (not that one is easier or harder, better or worse than the other). On the one hand, Iraqis have grown (or are, at least, expected to have grown) somewhat accustomed to infant mortality over the preceding two decades of sanctions, bombings, malnutrition, cholera, typhoid, and terrorism. And yet the parent who loses an older child testifies to the comfort of memories—their songs, their laughter, their stories— while those who lose their smallest babies are left grasping for the fading memories of an indistinct coo or smile, of a personality not yet fully formed.

But it looked as if Talib was going to dodge that bullet with Ahmed. He had received the call: the American team was not only the first in Iraq to perform complex heart surgeries like Ahmed's, but the vice president had worked it out so that Ahmed and a few others would be included on the list. All Talib had to do now was get his family packed and hitch a ride six hundred miles north. In spite of the increase in ambushes and attacks on Shia pilgrims along the northbound highways that passed outside the eastern edge of the infamous "Sunni Triangle," Talib did what others we've known have failed to do: he looked at Ahmed and took the risks necessary to love him first, left all the nagging unknowns to God, and set out toward the site of the country's brand-new heart center.

The black asphalt road threaded like a belt through the giant khaki desert. Twenty meters ahead the road and the occasional motorist were obscured by heat waves arising from a boiling cauldron of oil beneath the desert. Herds of camels sauntered along in search of shrubs, refusing to join the millions of Muslims across the country who were fasting from water and food for the month of Ramadan.

They weren't far along, no more than an hour or two; Ahmed could have been asleep in the rear seat by then.

Suddenly, everything went white . . . black . . . nothing.

All their senses had been muted: voices arrived as if swimming in water, lights and shadows projected on an eyelid screen.

Was that a roadside bomb? Did we hit another driver?

"Mommy! Mommy! Mommy!" Ahmed cried out, terrified. He couldn't hear an answer. "Baba! Baba! Baba!"

Two more holes had ripped in Ahmed's heart.

The details are hazy. I guess that's to be expected when a five-year-old is your primary witness. But as best we could tell, the ambulance driver found Talib's phone and managed to call his brother. I knew him only as Amo—"Uncle." How the decision was made for Amo to sweep Ahmed up and stay the course northward toward surgery, choosing Ahmed's life in the face of his own brother and sister-in-law's death, is staggering.

Jesus once told a guy, "Let the dead bury their own dead; you follow me." I think Jesus was saying, "Choose life!"

Amo knew Ahmed was his brother's greatest joy in this world. He knew how proud Talib was when his son was born and how devastated he was when he learned of Ahmed's death sentence. Like most families, they had gathered the night before for an *iftar* meal to celebrate God's provision for Ahmed with the American medical team, the unlikeliest of heroes. Talib probably said, "Praise God!" like everyone else each time Ahmed's condition was mentioned, but praise like that—if you really mean it, at least—is painful.

So there was no deliberating when Amo found Ahmed. Amo chose life. He knew his brother would not want any kind of sympathy that stole from Ahmed's future.

Amo and Ahmed were a living parable when they checked in at the hospital's security station, a testament to love and courage and enduring to the end, setting your hand to plow and not turning back.

I would have had trouble getting through the hospital gates if I arrived separate from the medical team each morning, and I lived in the city, was an American, and was responsible for arranging the entire program. I'm not sure how Amo—an Arab from the south—talked his way through the various checkpoints, but we were thrilled to finally meet him and Ahmed in the basement of the cardiac center.

Ahmed was crouching on the ground with his legs pulled up to his chest, playing with an orange plastic bulldozer. I call it "first position" for kids with congenital heart disease. Somehow, without ever being taught how to do it, children around the world learn to squat into "first position" to compensate for the weaknesses of their broken hearts. Ahmed had been safely admitted to the ward, and his name was secured on the surgery list. Outside in the general waiting area, hundreds of families were gathered, respectfully accosting us at the shoe-changing station each time we entered from the outside and were forced to stop at the bottleneck where we had to cover our shoes in plastic hairnets. My phone was filling up with scores of text messages from families across the country who had seen the press conference announcing the arrival of our team:

"Is my boy going to surgery? Mr. Jeremy, just do something to help my little boy!"

Some parents were texting and calling as many as ten times per day in hopes of securing their child a spot.

There were kaffiyeh-wearing Shia Arabs from the south, Sunni Arabs in suits from the west, Turkmen from Diyala, Chaldean Christians from Mosul, and at least three different kinds of Kurds. They spent their days together talking, crying, and simply listening to one another. If a mother had to leave the room, the other mothers in the room quickly took up the responsibility of looking after her child as if she was their own. I had to say, in a country where the various ethnic and religious blocs were constantly threatening to secede or cordon themselves off from one another, the hospital looked more like a productive gathering of parliament than the dysfunctional party politics that hours before had been threatening to cut off aid at the city's borders.

And these kids were sick. Even with Dr. Novick's medical team working around the clock, the hospital had only two operating theaters and limited ICU beds. Once the team had performed two or three surgeries per day a few days in a row, there was nothing to be done except wait for the kids in the ICU to be discharged before more surgeries could resume.

Moreover, our entire reason for being there was predicated on the fact that this was a *new* heart center, that the local team had barely kicked the tires since it opened a few months prior, and that they needed help learning the various deficiencies in design, in their own knowledge and skills, and in management protocols. Their understandable ignorance and need for education meant that most procedures took two to four times longer to accomplish than they might have in the Western centers from which Dr. Novick's team had assembled.

There were far too many children to serve, at far too slow a pace, with far too many bottlenecks to get to all the children, parents, and grandparents who camped out in the hospital's waiting room. Within a few days of being in the hospital, Ahmed's surgery had already been canceled a couple of times to accommodate more urgent children, and Amo was becoming anxious. One of our American volunteers was passing through the waiting room when the first child died, but he was helpless to act before it was too late. When the second child died, there was no foreigner present. These children were not even in our system or on our radar. They were strangers who were hoping for a miracle. And though we were within inches, we fell short of helping them by a mile.

Finally the day came for Ahmed's surgery. Cody spent some meaningful time with Amo and Ahmed ahead of time, watching cartoons, praying for the surgery's success, and playing dress-up (Cody traded his purple silk tie for Amo's dirty white man-dress).

Dr. Rao, a pediatric cardiologist from Chicago, came around to perform one last checkup on Ahmed before he became the first child in the history of the country to undergo his complex correction. Dr. Rao spent a good portion of the week in a set of Batman scrubs, perhaps to help put the children at ease. *Just a goofy guy in a Batman costume.*

But I saw him as the superhero who made sense out of chaos, who worked for justice without any superhuman powers. Other superheroes seem to attain some kind of invulnerability when they don their masks and capes. We expect as much from our doctors in their white coats. Not Batman. And not Dr. Rao.

Ahmed, at five years old, still reeling from the absence of his mom and dad, while he sat in some foreign place surrounded by people speaking foreign languages, could not have possibly understood what was going on. But when the doctor worked the stethoscope across his torso to listen one last time, Ahmed stuck out his little bird chest and beamed with pride.

Dr. Rao picked Ahmed up into his arms and walked him around a bit like a special friend. Ahmed's dad, Talib, would have loved to see that moment.

Ahmed was so strong and smiley as he dressed in his turquoise surgical gown. He clearly did not know what was about to happen. Amo carried him upstairs to the "Authorized Personnel Only" double doors in front of the operating area and placed him on a rolling stretcher. That was when Ahmed lost it.

He wrenched his head backward, upward, crying as he lay on the cot and the swinging doors behind slammed back and forth. First he saw his uncle, then he didn't. Over and over again the swinging doors swung, making it seem as though his *amo* was playing the cruelest game of peekaboo in his time of need. First his mom and dad, and now his uncle, the very last person he really knew in this entire place. The porter waved his hand in front of the optical sensor, the automatic door opened, and Amo disappeared around the corner as Ahmed was wheeled into surgery.

Communication between various departments of the hospital had been anything but flawless. Labs, X-rays, the pharmacy . . . it was rare to get the information or results requested in anything approximating a reasonable amount of time. When Novick's biomedical engineer became suspicious about the symptoms of some of the children and the quality of the oxygen they were being given, he headed to an obscured room in the basement to test the oxygen and found it to be about 50 percent oxygen and 50 percent other stuff.

A lot of hospitals in Iraq made you bring your own survival gear: blankets, sheets, food, meds . . . Worst-case scenario, you might even need to bring your own gauze and a backup bag of blood!

The month of Ramadan and the widespread daytime fasting had caused a precipitous decrease in blood donations, as it did every year. But it was not every year that an international heart surgery team showed up and pushed the hospital to the edges of its capacity. Blood was needed urgently, or there was a grave risk these kids were not going to make it through their surgeries alive.

Rizgar called the provincial director of health, who, in turn, called a press conference. With cameras rolling for the evening news, Rizgar gave an impassioned speech to his compatriots about the team, about welcoming Arabs and Turkmen to the city for surgery, about love and working for God. He then asked everyone to eat a hearty *iftar* meal and come out to donate blood so that we could finish these surgeries and save as many lives as possible.

When the cameras turned off, Rizgar was first in line to donate blood.

The image of Kurdish blood pumping through the heart of a little Arab boy like Ahmed was not lost on anyone.

I was so proud of Rizgar and so glad that we had pushed through our conflict and made peace with one another. Preemptive love means putting your own blood on the line.

In surgery, Dr. Novick and his team stopped a human heart, cut it open, patched the holes, reconstructed the valves inside, and made it beat again. Ahmed's surgery went past midnight, but he came through with flying colors. We were about to send a little boy back into the world, never again to fear his heart or dream small dreams.

Amo sat by his bedside in the ICU, so grateful his nephew was alive and well. To celebrate, he returned a phone call he had received earlier in the day:

"Talib? Brother? Your son is alive! The surgery went well, praise God! He's alive!"

Talib and his wife had miraculously survived the tragic car accident that rendered them unconscious, in critical condition and on the brink of death, while their son was being whisked away to surgery at the hands of Kurds and Americans—people many of their neighbors might very well have called their enemies.

Now, just a few days down the road, Ahmed was sprawled out on his bed with potato chips and candy wrappers all around him. He was breathing well on his own, his circulation was great. No more first position for him! His heart had been remade, and everything he could want still lay ahead of him: his family, his friends, his school, and . . . soccer.

Over in the corner, a mustached man in reading glasses sat regally in what could have been a set of Brooks Brothers nighttime loungewear (a.k.a., grandpa pajamas). He turned out to be Chief Awad, an Arab tribal sheikh from the vice president's delegation of patients. His grandson was sleeping in the bed beside him, recovering from surgery like Ahmed.

"You know, you guys—you *Americans*—don't have a very good reputation among our people these days."

Chief Awad went on to tell the history of his area, providing greater context for the war stories and anecdotes about the ongoing American presence in Iraq. He talked about his hometown and the incredible history behind it. He spoke with pride, sharing what he loved about home and how strong and hope-filled his people were. We knew so little about his people and their place.

His hometown was ground zero for some of the earliest stages of the Iraq War, as the United States invaded from the southern port, fought through his area, and pressed northward to Baghdad. The fact that we were Americans would have normally made him standoffish and distrusting. I can only wonder what sort of counsel and support he had given in previous days to those who might have asked his permission to retaliate against Americans, both soldier and civilian. But he was not in his home element. He was still the chief of his tribe of hundreds of thousands—the kind of guy who could issue an edict and rally thousands of sons and cousins throughout his bloodline to do ill or do good. But no one in these parts recognized his authority or treated him with any special dignity. Except us.

He was warm and clearly very moved by the week of surgeries and the obvious efforts to create an environment for life and peace. Some of the files of sick children I looked at that week had surveys from the most war-torn areas of Iraq attached with questions that broke my heart:

1. Where did you live during the bombings?
2. Were any of your residences bombed? Were you there?
3. Do you know if your house was attacked with white phosphorus or any incendiary weapons?
4. Were you or your family ever burned, wounded, or injured in bombings?
5. Have you ever searched and recovered survivors, corpses, cleaned and prepared bodies for burial, searched bodies for identification, or transported any of these people?
6. Did you clean up, recover your things from, or rebuild your house on the rubble?
7. Have your children played in bomb craters, buildings, construction sites, or collected materials salvaged from sites that have been bombed?

Cody spent a long time talking to the chief about how we could take steps toward creating postures of preemptive love with his people and across Iraq. Cody dreamed with him about a time and place where lions lie down with lambs, where there is no more war, and where heart disease never wins.

"What if we could step into that place *here,* today?"

"You know, Americans don't have a very good name among our people. But you guys are unlike the Americans and Christians we constantly hear about."

He paused.

"I am a sheikh—the chief—so my people are sad when I am sad. And when I am *happy,* my people are *happy.* You have done so much for us here today. You are not like the others. I am going back happy. I am going back with a message of peace . . ."

He stole a look at his grandson Hussein and surveyed the effects of the most border-crossing, death-defying surgery-and-training effort to date in Iraq. Never before had a team so large and diverse descended to say yes to so many children in need of lifesaving heart surgeries. Never before had Iraqis been so widely gathered from across the lines that divide and sheltered in a safe place of healing. As Chief Awad surveyed the meaning of our inaugural Remedy Mission and our message of preemptive love, Ahmed and other "enemy" children from every warring faction in the country were laughing and playing together, recovering from lifesaving heart surgeries.

"You are truly messengers of peace. I will make my people happy over you!"

Afterword

The nationwide impact of our first Remedy Mission inside Iraq was greater than anything we had imagined. We knew that there was probably no one alive who had done more to improve heart surgery for children around the world than Dr. Novick, but we did not really understand the cascading effects of what would happen on the heels of his arrival. Interest and invitations began to pour in from around the country. The vice president allocated money from his own budget to pay for two full-blown surgical missions, fast-tracking the logistics and bypassing the bureaucracy of Baghdad. The pan-Arab news agency Al-Jazeera, which had become so famous for stoking the flames of al-Qaeda and the insurgency across Iraq, even ran a front-page story highlighting the scope of the problem and the hope of our remedy.

What had previously taken us one year and a quarter of a million dollars to accomplish now happened in just two weeks, with all the added benefits of actually training Iraqis to handle the problem on their own, at home, at a fraction of the cost. Novick's vision for the future was every bit as big and bold as our own, and the partner he had brought from Washington, DC, Mrs. Nadwa Qaragholi, was eager to form a wider coalition. We committed ourselves to an immediate, nationwide expansion.

Since then, our work together has expanded across the country, from north to south, east to west, serving every major region, every ethnic group, and every religious sect without discrimination. We have also been privileged to add a few medical partners, including our longtime friend Dr. Çiçek, from Turkey, and former U.S. Air Force flight surgeon Dr. Kirk Milhoan, the first foreign cardiologist to implement robust research protocols to determine the local and nationwide incidence of heart defects in children while providing expert diagnoses to thousands of children with heart disease across Iraq.

With these friends, we were the first to establish ongoing surgical training programs to save the lives of Iraqi children in the southern port city of Basra, where U.S. troops first entered the country; in the city of Nasiriyah, where Private Jessica Lynch was the first prisoner of war in 2003; in Najaf, the worldwide seat of Shia power, where one mercurial cleric escaped U.S. capture and went on to foment considerable violence against both Iraqi and Western interests before eventually welcoming and endorsing our restorative work years later; and so much more.

I passed through the locked-down city of Fallujah, thumbing through the pages of my passport. Ever since Fallujah became known as the bomb factory for al-Qaeda, outsiders have not been welcome without an invitation and a local sponsor. The young men with AK-47s at the city's main checkpoints look like anger and skepticism personified. It's hard to blame them after all they've been through. All around us metal scaffolding had been charred black from explosions, and buildings lay in ruins after countless aerial bombings from the much-hated U.S. military.

"Identification," the Iraqi soldier said brusquely, swinging his tattered Russian machine gun back on his shoulder.

He strained his eyes to make out the faded visa on the last page of my passport. I'm not sure where it's from myself. He gave me that accusatory "Where have you been?" look, but even when I strain to read it, I cannot quite make out the terms of the stamp myself. I can see the green entry marker, telling me I gained entrance to some far-off country, but for the life of me I cannot find any indication that I ever left.

In his line of work, it's natural to question where people have been. It helps size up the person in front of him as a threat. But it is so hard to see things for what they are. And even though it is more difficult to see them for what they could be, I'm constantly on the lookout for where people are going and how I can help get them there.

If my Arabic was more advanced, I would have better explained that I had become a citizen of the far country. I'm not sure if it would have made a difference, or made sense, but I wanted him to know that, not only had I *not* come with the upper hand to harm his people, I had actually written what might have been my final words to my wife and kids the night before, considering what it would mean to enter this terrifying city, fearing that my decision and my lack of firepower might mean that I would never return.

As I tried to string together the words to convey my love, my driver intervened and told him we had come to heal the hearts of their children—the first Americans ever to enter the city of Fallujah without guns, the lead surgeon would later tell us.

Some saw Fallujah frozen in the headlines of years gone by: barbaric, defiant, and staunchly fundamentalist. I saw those things—and I certainly feared that was all there was to Fallujah. But I also saw what Fallujah could be: forgiving, forgiven, made whole; ambassadors of goodwill; a lighthouse for anyone in the world looking for preemptive love.

After being inundated by photos and reports from doctors in Fallujah claiming an astronomical rise in birth defects after the U.S.-led battles in 2004, I collapsed in my dorm room at Fallujah General Hospital and cried over the babies I had just seen who were born with two heads, cyclops eyes, and monstrous deformities that made me seriously question the existence of God. I called my longtime adviser and friend Dr. Kirk Milhoan, a frontier cardiologist who had shaped our priorities and programs from our earliest days and had become the first foreigner to treat children with heart disease inside Iraq.

"You are never going to believe where I am!" Dr. Kirk is an Iraq War veteran, so I figured Fallujah would hold some symbolic significance for him, as it did for the rest of us.

"The doctors here are saying that something like one in every seven children is born with a birth defect. I don't know if it's entirely accurate, but it caught my attention and they are asking what we can do to help train them and treat their children. None of the other doctors we work with are willing to come to Fallujah right now. The prevailing sense is that it's just too dangerous or too underdeveloped."

As a cardiologist—a diagnostician—Dr. Kirk approached medical decisions more conservatively than his surgical counterparts. We had seen deaths in other parts of the country lead to moblike scenes outside the hospital gates and had endured the threats of tribal sheikhs inside who tried to strong-arm their way onto the surgery list. In an especially high-stakes environment like Fallujah, we would have very little room for error. Although I questioned how the people of Fallujah would accept him as a former flight surgeon, I liked the idea of hitching our reputation to Dr. Kirk and his incredibly tight-knit team.

"Will you help us launch a program in Fallujah? There is no one else I would rather work with in an environment like this."

Months later, when Dr. Kirk arrived, he proved that he was all in by bringing his wife, Kim, to train the Iraqi anesthesiologists who would work alongside her. Together, they are an amazing embodiment of what we mean when we say "preemptive love." Over the years, Dr. Kirk has helped us pioneer into some of the hardest-to-work-in places where few others are willing to go, including Fallujah and Tikrit, the hometown of former dictator Saddam Hussein.

Even with the exciting developments happening, my heart was still heavy with the difficult things that had passed and the many still to come. I had long since written off ever making up with Caleb. He wrote a brief message when we announced the death of Yahya, one of the little kids that he had become close to during his time in Iraq.

Yahya's was the most difficult death I've ever endured. A mob of extended family and tribesmen gathered outside the hospital with weapons, threatening us and accusing us of butchering their child. I couldn't help but wonder if they were right.

"Lord, forgive us for all the children we've killed while trying to help," became my daily prayer for weeks.

The death led Jessica to walk away from the emotion of this life-and-death drama for two years. She had been helping Yahya's family work toward his surgery for well over a year. She had been in their home and shared meals with them a couple of times. She wanted me to send him to Turkey just to be safe, but I had decided to pursue the surgery inside Iraq instead.

Eventually, Jessica decided to enter the fray again, but she will be the first to say that she may never be the same.

Even in New England, Caleb appeared to have a similar experience, being deeply affected, longing to reconnect with us over this loss of life that no one in America could feel the way he did.

One year later, Caleb read an international headline about our mutual friend, an American teacher, who was murdered in Iraq at point-blank range by his student. With another life lost—this one even closer to home—Caleb was finally in a place to begin the long walk back toward us, toward forgiveness, and toward community.

"I hold no record of wrongs—or supposed wrongs—against you, and I pray you would do the same for me," Caleb said at one point. I was leaving for the morgue to identify the body, terrified that three shots to the head would be more than I could bear to look at. I was supposed to call our friend's mom and dad in the States within the hour to advise them on whether to have an open or closed casket. Of all the kinds of conversations I have with parents who have lost their children, I fear this one most of all.

Before leaving, I wrote Caleb as I struggled again with loving the killer who took my friend's life and tried to faithfully lead my friends in Iraq through tragedy: "I have really tried to learn what it means to love and forgive. I certainly don't understand it all! But I'm doing my best." I was mostly talking about the past that Caleb and I had shared (and lost)—the devastation of not being able to save Ali's life after his father was arrested, the pain of betrayal by our good friend Ayad, the fear of living with Rizgar's threats, Caleb's belief that I had thrown him to the wolves. But my words were equally suitable for loving my friend's killer, struggling through the aftermath of Yahya's death, and many situations that were still to come.

The commitment Caleb, Jessica, and I had made to preemptive love made fools of us all, exposing how far we are from being the people we want to be. In the end, however, the tragedies we shared and the hopes we still held for the people of Iraq, Syria, Iran, Yemen, Palestine, Israel, and America gave us all the common ground we needed to reestablish trust and begin working together again for each other's well-being, as well as that of the precious children we hoped to save.

Where you are sitting in the world as you finish this story may influence how you interpret my idea of preemptive love. If you are in the States, you may think first in terms of American kindness toward enemy Iraqis. If you are in Iraq, however, you may be more quick to see the countless times in this story in which the Iraqis acted first, offering protection, intervening, or taking a risk to welcome us in, even though we were often cast as their enemies. The truth is, preemptive love does not begin in the heart of humanity. Neither Americans nor Iraqis are inherently better at loving first than the other. We are all tribal, programmed to protect our own.

Instead, preemptive love originates in the heart of God. The one who made the universe and holds everything in it—the one to whom Muslims, Christians, and Jews are all ostensibly pointing—is the first and the last enemy lover. And in the end, it is not our love that overcomes hate at all. It is God's. And preemptive love is not just something God does as a one-off transaction. *Preemptive love is who God is,* constantly overcoming our hateful rebellion and our lesser passions that belie the self-interest we suppose ourselves to be pursuing. In fact, if we were really self-interested, committed to our ultimate well-being, we wouldn't fill ourselves up, saying, "Eat, drink, and be merry." We would empty ourselves out and give ourselves away in service or sacrifice to others, just like Jesus did. That's where the real joy is. Whenever we spend our lives trying to preserve, protect, and shore up security for ourselves, we actually lose the very thing we were trying to save, as it daily flits away while we obsess over insurance policies, retirement plans, and dead bolts on the doors. We lose the joy of living for something bigger, something with meaning. But when we spend our lives trying to lose ourselves in love for God and love for friends and enemies, we actually gain life, no matter how much we lose in the process.

This is the paradox of preemptive love!

But I would be so afraid! I could never do what you are doing!

I hear that objection wherever I go, from Iraqis and Americans, Muslims and Christians alike. But preemptive love does not require the absence of fear. Jessica and I are not brave or courageous. That is not the take-away we want for you! If anything, we live with a chronic sense of fear: for our physical safety, for our kids, for our financial future, for our faith. In fact, even as I write this sitting in Iraq, I find all of those fears pounding on my door after a group of thugs threatened me and insisted I halt publication of this book. As I weigh the consequences of caving in to their bullying versus keeping my word and following through with the commitments I've made, I am afraid of the ways they can manufacture "evidence" that would ruin our work here once and for all and leave thousands of children without many of the immediate and midterm solutions they need to survive.

No, preemptive love is not about the absence of fear. We cannot avoid the foreboding storms that loom on the horizon, but we can learn to dance in the rain. And when we accept God's preemptive love, that Christ makes all things new, we can quit playing by everyone else's rules and pursue a long, risky journey with the God who loves his enemies—even enemies like you and me.

What Jess and I learned in that broken-down neighborhood so many years ago is still true today: we don't need power to live in peace. Because even though fear, hatred, and violence conspire to unmake the world, preemptive love unmakes violence. Preemptive love fulfills the fears of fundamentalist fatwas, making children love their enemies. And preemptive love overcomes fear.

And before all is said and done, the far country is the near-and-now country for all who enter the marathon, lean on love, and make it to the finish line.

Acknowledgments

It has been difficult to speak in terms of "I" and "me" throughout much of this book. It made the story a little cleaner and kept me from putting too many words into the mouths of people who did not sign up to be in my book. But it dwarfed a more complex, more beautiful story. The reality is, this entire thing has been one big communal effort. Even the things I did myself would have failed miserably without these friends and colleagues along the way.

To our core support team over the years: Preston and Erica; J. R. and Chelsea; Tom and Nona; Mary and David; Jim K.; Dudley and Laura; Terrill and Leigh; Bobby and Tyra; Robbie and Carissa; James and Mandi; Justin and Kaela; Scott and Abby; Ruth; Scott and Katarina; Jeff and Erin; Jen and Robert; Brett and Christina; Matt and Holly; Michael and Abby; David and Judith; Justin and Atalie; and Michelle T. None of this would have been possible without you!

To our partners in Iraq: There are too many of you to list, but without you, this would be pointless and impossible. We are honored to work with you for the peaceful future of Iraq, the Middle East, and the world.

To our medical partners from around the world who have raised their hands to join us in preemptive love:

Dr. Sertaç Çiçek, Dr. Hasan Kuş, Aslı Akyavaş, Murat Ercan, Dilek İnci, Alice Abdi, and Cana Muhallebicioğlu: Your tireless charitable efforts for the children of Iraq have healed the hearts and saved the lives of thousands. When so many others tread lightly, you proved the way of peace and loved lavishly.

Drs. Kirk and Kim Milhoan, Dr. Mary Porisch, Dr. Minnette Son, Molly King, Shannon Kyle, and Nelia Soares from For Hearts and Souls: Thank you for your years of partnership and for being the first to Sulaymaniyah, Fallujah, and Tikrit. It is an honor to walk with you.

Dr. William and Elizabeth Novick, Martina Pavanic, and the entire team at the International Children's Heart Foundation: You have given more than any other foreign medical team to the people of Iraq. You had the vision when others played it safe and pulled back. The future for Iraqi children with heart disease is much brighter because of you.

Mrs. Nadwa Qaragholi, Dr. Wieam Ahmad, and Living Light International: Without you, none of this would be possible! You work tirelessly behind the scenes, interpreting culture, bridging divides, negotiating contracts, and making connections, while the rest of us sleep soundly. Your hearts of compassion and your hope-filled vision for your country inspire us to keep going on the most frustrating days.

To Jonathan Merkh, Becky Nesbitt, Jessica Wong, and the entire team at Howard Books: it is a joy to be on the same team!

To my agent, Chris Ferebee, thanks for taking a risk on me!

Lastly a few words to my closest friends and family:

Matt and Cayla, you've always argued that the "far country" is here and now. I couldn't agree more! Thanks for pushing me toward it.

Cody and Michelle, I could not have dreamed up a better

story, or better friends to bring it to reality each day, thank you. Everything good in this story belongs to you.

Larry and Ioana, your unconditional love and encouragement make all the difference.

Nono, every time you pulled a coin out of my ear or my nose, you taught me that things are not always what they seem. You were the first to introduce me to people across the globe who were different from me. You instilled curiosity and a conviction that I, too, could make my vision into reality. Your love for God shaped every bone in my spiritual frame. You're one of my great heroes.

Dad and Mom, I caused you years of stress and headache. You said I could argue with a fencepost. But you tilled the ground, planted the seed, pulled the weeds, and sacrificially watered and fed every good part of who I am. You will never hear the thank-yous of thousands of Iraqis, but they praise God for you and bless you. I do, too!

Nicci and Rachel, I wish I knew this stuff much earlier in life. I love you both deeply.

Emma, you stole my heart the day you were born. You are bold, courageous, and strong. Even at this young age, you show all the hallmarks of a woman who walks into danger in the name of love. You long for fairness and justice for everyone, just like your mom. But an eye for an eye will never satisfy. Go beyond justice and fairness. Love your enemies; give yourself away. It will set you free.

Micah, you have the heart of a superhero: brave, full of empathy for others and an unwavering commitment to doing what's right and honorable. Some will call you naive, maybe worse. But I pray you never lose your way, and never forget what the Lord requires of you: love mercy, do justly, and walk humbly with your God.

Jessica, your love, compassion, and desire to give seem to know no limits. Surely I have been the greatest recipient of your patient grace and your pain-absorbing love. I don't deserve you, but I am daily filled with joy that you are mine, and I am yours.

To the King of the ages, immortal, invisible, the only God, be honor and glory forever and ever. Amen.

Notes

CHAPTER 2: THE SKY RAINED DEATH

1. Susan J. Schuurman, "An 'Inconvenient Atrocity': The Chemical Weapons Attack on the Kurds of Halabja, Iraq" (master's thesis, University of New Mexico, 2007).

2. Joost R. Hiltermann, *A Poisonous Affair: America, Iraq, and the Gassing of Halabja* (Cambridge: Cambridge University Press, 2007), 107–20.

3. Jeffrey Goldberg, "A Reporter at Large: The Great Terror," *New Yorker,* March 25, 2002, http://www.newyorker.com/archive/2002/03/25/020325fa_FACT1?currentPage=all.

4. Interview with Kaveh Golestan, an Iranian photographer, in Guy Dinmore, "The Enduring Pain of Halabja," *Guy Dinmore's Blog,* July 2, 2002, http://guydinmore.wordpress.com/2002/07/02/the-enduring-pain-of-halabja/. Golestan is not talking about the exact house where Nasreen took shelter, but similar scenes were repeated in homes throughout the area.

5. David McDowall, *A Modern History of the Kurds:* Third Edition (London: I. B. Tauris, 2004), note #45, 366.

6. Ibid., 362.

7. I intend to expound upon the reasons for this "deafening silence" in a forthcoming book.

8. Testimony of Dr. Christine M. Gosden before the Senate Judiciary Subcommittee on Technology, Terrorism, and Government and the Senate Select Committee on Intelligence on Chemical and Biological Weapons Threats to America: Are We Prepared?, April 22, 1998, http://www.fas.org/irp/congress/1998_hr/s980422-cg.htm.

9. Christine Gosden, "Why I Went, What I Saw," *Washington Post,* March 11, 1998, A19.

10. Middle East Watch, *Genocide in Iraq: The Anfal Campaign Against the Kurds* (New York: Human Rights Watch, 1993), 8.

CHAPTER 4: BUY SHOES. SAVE LIVES.

1. One diplomat named Peter Van Buren tells story after story of grandiose waste in his book, *We Meant Well: How I Helped Lose the Battle for the Hearts and Minds of the Iraqi People* (New York: Metropolitan Books, 2012).

2. Hassan Abolghasemi et al., "Childhood physical abnormalities following paternal exposure to sulfur mustard gas in Iran: A case-control study," *Conflict and Health* 4 (July 2010), http://www.conflictandhealth.com/content/4/1/13.

CHAPTER 5: FATWA

1. Dr. Mohammad is actually a composite of two different Iraqi doctors whose stories I represent here accurately but whose identities I would like to obscure and protect.

2. Preemptive Love Coalition was one of two or three foreign groups in Iraq at that time working together to send Iraqi children to our surgical partners in Israel. Eventually Preemptive Love Coalition discontinued our work sending children outside the country, believing that the best way forward for Iraq and its people had much more to do with providing the training necessary for Iraqi doctors and nurses

to perform these complex surgeries and the associated aftercare for themselves. Although we dreamed of bringing Israeli doctors to Iraq to begin such training, we were never able to see that to fruition before formally dissolving all of our partnerships in Israel.

Our former partners still remain actively engaged in taking children outside Iraq to Israel for surgery. Out of respect for the safety of their staff and the safety of those Iraqi families with whom they work, I have avoided naming them herein and speak broadly about "our work" together instead. In using words like *us* and *our,* I mean all the partners that labored together to bring life and hope to these children we love. Most, if not all, of our partners were involved in the opportunity long before the Preemptive Love Coalition came along.

We are deeply grateful to you for those early days we shared together! (You know who you are!)

3. Sadly, I do not have an existing authoritative source for some of these quotes and translations. Most of what I have is based on my personal journal entries and real-time translations, news gathering, and interactions we were having at the time.

Some of the things like this that were archived during the war years were archived by fundamentalist organizations that were eventually rooted out, causing their websites to go offline, change management, etc.

4. Marie Syrkin, ed., *A Land of Our Own: An Oral Autobiography* (New York: Putnam, 1973), 242.

5. Edited for length.

CHAPTER 6: THE SHEIKH

1. I have not read enough of Said's body of work or that of his critics to have a fully formed view of his critiques of "Orientalism" and the peace process or his recommendations for resolving the Israel-Palestine conflict. Quoting him here is not meant to be a full endorsement of his scholarship and activism, but rather a nod to a single statement culled from his work that affected me deeply and fueled my own moral imagination and subsequent pursuit of "capturing the imagination of the oppressor" as a natural outworking of preemptive love.

2. Edward Said, "The Only Alternative," *Al-Ahram,* March 1–7, 2001.

CHAPTER 7: SERVING HIS ENEMIES

1. See, for example, Hassan Abolghasemi et al., "Childhood physical abnormalities following paternal exposure to sulfur mustard gas in Iran: A case-control study," *Conflict and Health* 4 (July 2010), http://www.conflictandhealth.com/content/4/1/13.

2. Both the Iraqi official and the non-Iraqi partner have requested anonymity to protect their ongoing efforts to take children to Israel.

3. For example, see United Press International, "Kurdish mass grave in Turkey likely from 1990s," Kurd Net, February 9, 2012, http://ekurd.net/mismas/articles/misc2012/2/turkey3751.htm; "Discovery of Kurdish Mass Graves Leads Turkey to Face Past," Voice of America, February 08, 2011, http://www.voanews.com/content/turkey-facing-past-with-discovery-of-kurdish-mass-graves-115640409/134797.html.

4. My claims here about "average" Turks and Kurds are merely anecdotal conclusions based predominantly on scores of informal interviews with Turks and Kurds across Turkey and Iraq. For an exploration of the claims of food poisoning of Kurdish refugees in Turkish camps, see Dlawer Ala'aldeen, John Foran, Ivon House, and Alastair Hay, "Poisoning of Kurdish refugees in Turkey," *Lancet* 335 (1990): 287–88.

CHAPTER 8: "ANYONE BUT THE TURKS!"

1. Amnesty International, "Iran: Human Rights Abuses Against the Kurdish Minority," Amnesty International Publications, 2008, http://www.amnesty.org/en/library/asset/MDE13/088/2008/en/d140767b-5e45-11dd-a592-c739f9b70de8/mde130882008eng.pdf.

CHAPTER 14: THE REMEDY

1. William Novick, MD, is the founder and medical director of the International Children's Heart Foundation.

Preemptive Love

Reading Group Guide

INTRODUCTION

Preemptive Love is the true story of Jeremy and Jessica Courtney and their quest to put love before all else—no matter the risk. Jeremy Courtney shares with readers the journey he took with his wife, their friends, and sometimes even their enemies in order to start the Preemptive Love Coalition (PLC). The mission of PLC is simple: save as many Iraqi children as possible who are in need of heart surgery— a prevalent problem in Iraq after Saddam Hussein's chemical war- fare, more than a decade of sanctions, and outstanding environmental questions that many have linked to American and British weapons during the 2003 Iraq War, especially since there are few surgeons in the country willing and able to perform surgery on these gravely ill children. Faced with nearly every problem imaginable, Jeremy and his community begin saving lives and seeing glimmers of peace amid the violence and unrest of present-day Iraq.

TOPICS AND QUESTIONS FOR DISCUSSION

1. The story of *Preemptive Love* opens with a possible theme when Jeremy writes on page 3, "It can be so difficult to see things for what they are, even more so to see what they could be." Discuss this quote in light of the story. How does this reflect the mission of the Preemptive Love Coalition?

2. Jeremy and Jessica coming to grips with life without electricity in Iraq sets the stage for what would soon become their "preemptive love" way of life. Discuss the conclusion from page 3—"We don't need power to live in Peace"—and the various ways it challenges your assumptions about life in the midst of war, in marriage or the workplace, and in general.

3. The story of the Courtney family is extraordinary and heroic, but in many ways, Jeremy shares how he is just like all of us. On page 7, he writes, "Everything I do is probably motivated by some sense of guilt or out of a desire to stave off my own demise." Is this feeling true for most of us? Do we often want to partake in charity out of a sense of guilt or fear? Explain your answer.

4. *Preemptive Love* is full of surprises, from unlikely friendships to un-failing faith even in the presence of great danger. What surprised you the most in this story?

5. Did Jeremy's description of contemporary Iraq give you a new perspective on the situation there? Why or why not?

6. Discuss the irony of the grand sheikh's decree: "We must stop this treatment lest it lead our children and their parents to love their enemies, leading to apostasy" (page 57). Can you think of a similar irony that exists in the United States?

7. Jeremy Courtney introduces us to so many sick children in the book; some recover, others do not. Which child's story touched you the most and why?

8. Revisit Khadeeja's story, beginning on page 107. What lessons can we glean from it? Why was Khadeeja's father able to overcome his distrust of the Turkish doctor?

9. "Presence is sometimes a greater expression of preemptive love than any bold action or program" (page 120). Reflect on a time you were present or someone was present for you. Do you agree with Jeremy's statement? Why or why not?

10. Do you think that Rizgar's ten-year journey away from home as a child, and his subsequent return as an adult, was a matter of fate or luck? In what ways do you think his time away from home helped shape his work with the Preemptive Love Coalition?

11. Mustafa proudly displays his tattered soccer ball after his surgery, showing Jeremy and his team that miracles can happen. What do you think this soccer ball might be a metaphor for in Mustafa's life? What about for Jeremy and his friends? What "soccer ball" do you have in your life?

12. Why do you think that Rizgar chose to go to prison rather than use the "Get Out of Jail Free" card offered to him in exchange for information on Jeremy Courtney and his family? Consider this in juxtaposition to his later choices and discuss how real people can sometimes be at once a friend and an enemy. How have you seen this in your own family, workplace, etc.?

13. On page 199, Jeremy quotes the *Aeneid*: "I fear the Greeks, even those bearing gifts." How does this quote connect to the story of the Preemptive Love Coalition?

14. Discuss the afterword. On what note does this story end? What impression do you have for the future of the Preemptive Love Coalition and what it will be able to accomplish?

15. How has reading this book affected you? In what ways are you inspired to reexamine your life and your presuppositions about people? How will this change the way you approach others going forward?

ENHANCE YOUR BOOK CLUB

1. Jeremy Courtney gave a TED talk on November 12, 2011, about preemptive love and the concept of unmaking violence and remaking the world through healing. Gather with your reading group to watch: http://www.jeremycourtney.com/tedxbaghdad. Over dinner, discuss Jeremy's message. How does his story touch you? How can you make a difference in your world? What is the greatest lesson that Jeremy's story teaches?

2. Jeremy shares his approach to adapting to life in Iraq: "For the first six months, we say yes to everything" (page 68). Try this radical way of being in the world for one week. Afterward, meet as a group and discuss the results. What was it like to say yes for an entire week? How was it different than a typical week for you? Why do you think that Jeremy takes this approach in Iraq? In his life in general?

3. On page 162, Jeremy mentions the Robert Frost poem "The Road Not Taken" in order to explain the way that he and Jessica choose to live. Read the poem out loud (http://www.poetryfoundation .org/poem/173536) to your group and discuss the ways in which the poem articulates the tenets of faith, love, and joy that distinguish the Courtney family and the Preemptive Love Coalition.

A CONVERSATION WITH JEREMY COURTNEY

1. **In many ways, this is the story of your life, and as such, it is a work in progress. Why did you decide to begin *Preemptive Love* with the story of you drinking chai in an Iraqi hotel? How was this the defining moment of the Preemptive Love Coalition?**

    I am not sure I would say it was the defining moment. Your point about being a work in progress is exactly right. I could have just as easily started with lying on my grandma's lap three or four times a week as my grandpa preached and my father led the church in worship. In many ways, the story seems to begin for me when I went off to college and wrestled with nearly every aspect of life and faith as I had received it and understood it until that time. September 11 was certainly a defining moment for so many in my generation—some of us went one direction and some of us another with regard to how we would live in a world full of evil.

    But I began the story drinking chai in an Iraqi hotel, because the rest of the story lacks meaning without presence. The hotel scene establishes a few things: (1) our intentional proximity to suffering and need; (2) my conflicted, less-than-heroic response; and (3) my personal introduction to the utter lack of options for children born with life-threatening heart defects in Iraq.

2. **What surprised you most about living in Iraq? What has been the best part about your life there? The most difficult?**

    As with any place in the world, I'd guess all three of these questions have the same answer: people. The people here are complex, and that surprised me, honestly. I was reared on a relatively simple story about Arab backwardness, corruption, etc. Some of my first Muslim friends in my twenties were Turks and Kurds, and there was no love lost between them and the Arab Muslims who would soon be my neighbors in Iraq. So from all quarters, I entered Iraq with a story and a set of expectations that did not incline me to love. On the bright side, my negative perceptions primed me for the best possible response every time I saw an Iraqi break my simple mold. Their love for their children, their earnest desire for peace, their ingenuity to make it through another day—let alone so many prolonged seasons—of violence . . . all these things surprised me and caused love to well up in my heart for the people around me.

The best part of my life in Iraq has been the people. Both the individuals and society as a whole have enriched my understanding of God, my capacity to show honor and respect to others, my self-awareness, my confidence and humility about my place in the world, and my ability to be a better husband and father.

At the same time, the most difficult part of my life in Iraq has been . . . the people! Iraq would be problem-free if it weren't for all the people! But then, the same could be said for any nation, organization, or family. It seems to me that there is a direct correlation between the level of risk in relationships and the amount of joy derived from them. The people we endeavor to love the most become the ones who are most capable of destroying us. In the end—and I recognize that this may not be true for everyone in Iraq—it was not the suicide bombers, the militias, or the violent clerics who posed the greatest threat to us. It was those who were much closer, whom we loved even more and allowed to get even closer. And, ultimately, that is why I think preemptive love—and this book—is about relationships, and not primarily about Iraq.

3. **When the fatwa came out against you, you write that you sent an e-mail to your team inviting them to your house to pray. Can you share with us the power of prayer in your life? Has prayer been a defining part of your life in Iraq?**
There is a part of me that deeply wants to impress you with a mind-blowing answer of personal piety right now. But that part of me is vain and dishonest. The truth is that I have a sort of "love-hate"

relationship with prayer—especially with prayer as a means of asking God to do what I imagine God already wants to do. I do not mean to say that I am justified or right in this way of thinking, but that kind of prayer has always confused me and left me wondering why I would worship one so capricious.

While I think it is probably clear from the story that I believe in the existence, the presence, and the here-on-earth activity of God, I often struggle to live at this intersection of belief and doubt, where, on the one hand, I engage in prayer as a form of work because God has decided that the restoration of some things on this earth will depend on me and, on the other hand, I rest from work, even prayers of supplication and intercession, because of a bedrock conviction that God is ultimately in control and is far more concerned than I am with the well-being of my neighbors, the environment, war, peace, and God's own great name.

But there is at least one kind of prayer that has had a profound impact on me during my time in Iraq, and that is prayer as imagining, prayer as dreaming. This can be a spur-of-the-moment thing while driving in chaotic Baghdad traffic waiting for the next bomb to go off, or an extended morning of quiet meditation. In both extremes, the content is essentially the same, and it goes something like this: "God, give me your vision for this country, this city, this guy I'm sharing tea with right now."

That prayer resonates within me, because even while it is about Iraq, it recognizes a deficiency in myself that must change before I should expect to be let in on such treasure. This was the essence of our prayers after the fatwa came out. We said, "We already know the broad definition of our response. And we trust, God, that you have a plan in the midst of violence and chaos. So let us in on your envisioned future . . . what good things could we bring about here—and what evil things could we dismantle—as we submit ourselves to loving our enemies?"

4. **You describe the difficulty of baby Hope's death after surgery and the struggle to comfort grieving parents. What was it like for you**

personally in that moment? Was this the most difficult moment you had to face so far?

It was absolutely horrible. We had to grow up quickly in a lot of ways. I had just moved us from being a sort of distant, third party financier of other people's decisions and operations. With Hope, I made the call. I selected her for surgery, I chose the hospital, I signed off on the doctor. I was in the hot seat, in a highly contentious time in Iraq, among a people that still demand extortionary financial remuneration, or even blood for blood, in the wake of death. There are no insurance policies or lawyers to shield you in a time like that. But, to my surprise, those self-referential concerns were not anywhere near the top of my list. I've learned only over time to give consideration to those things. In the moment of Hope's death, the only thing I could think of was Yusuf, his wife, and their irreplaceable loss. I felt a deep sense of responsibility for that and wondered how many more losses we would have to endure on our way to reaching all the children we had promised to help.

In those crisis moments you form a special bond. But what I've had to learn is that those relationships (for the most part) cannot last—they are simply too painful for the parents. The trust formed is great. And we've heard repeatedly that our responses to their suffering are often much more sensitive and comforting than many of the responses they receive from their own families and friends. But at the end of the day, for most of these families who endure their greatest losses at our hands, they cannot stand to see us hovering around each week reminding them of hope gone wrong. They never "move on," of course, but they eventually relegate our status from "friend" to "service provider" so they can cope with their losses and begin to put their life back in order. For us, the loss of that friendship becomes the second great loss after a child dies.

5. **Do you hope to break any stereotypes with this book?**

Absolutely! But if I have to name them, I'm probably not doing a very good job as a storyteller!

6. **The complications of different cultures arise frequently in the story. If you could go back in time and change one decision you made, what would it be and why?**

I refuse to live in the past or entertain any notion of "wasted years." There are no wasted years, at least, not in the past. The only wasted years are in the future, and they are wasted only if we refuse to learn from our past. So, looking to the future, I have been much more determined to empower my colleagues on the ground to make the real-time decisions they deem best in order to keep themselves safe and enable PLC to continue its mission. If I cannot trust my team to make wise decisions, then they probably should not be a part of the team at all. If they are a part of the team, then they need to be free to read the situation around them and make the decisions required, in keeping with our vision and values.

7. *Preemptive Love* **depicts a part of life in Iraq that we don't often see in popular culture, that is, ordinary, everyday existence. Was it important to you to present an alternative point of view?**

Presenting everyday Iraqis in their own hues has been a central part of what we have tried to do since moving here in the middle of the war when "everyday Iraqis" began to destroy my black-and-white vision of war and its various justifications. YouTube, Facebook, Twitter, and their various copycats were all new technologies that came into their own during the Iraq War. In an age of institution-alized propaganda on all sides of the conflict stood a great opportunity to walk against the current with a more nuanced message about Iraqis, Arabs, and Muslims, in general. For some groups, the offending perspective was that we would portray Muslims in a positive light, making them the heroes of this story; for others, that we would call a spade a spade and name Islam and some of its clerics as the principals responsible for so much evil throughout Iraq.

8. **What would you name as the theme of the story? What do you hope readers will learn by reading your book?**

I was an unbearable partner in the process of writing the subtitle and designing the cover, because I am so resistant to any attempt to reduce the story to a single, isolated theme. If we say the story is about "unmaking violence" or "dismantling fear" or "overcoming hate," I am insistent that the story is even more about remaking the world through healing, building bonds of friendship in the midst of conflict, and creating an entire realm in which love of self is seen as inextricably tied up with love of neighbor and love of enemy. But even if you will allow all those previous themes to stand as a single descriptor, I cannot allow them to stand as primarily human pursuits, divorced from God, creator of the world, animator of life. That story is the story of a faith relegated to the "far country"— a sort of "by and by" existence that seems so distant that it has no bearing on life in this country today. I don't believe in that story.

Our story doesn't exist apart from the faith that energizes and causes it to happen. So it is a story about following Jesus and living with the kind of faith that dares to believe in destroying death and the works of the devil and joining God in the beautiful restoration of all things. And that makes it a story about journeying "through many valleys, toils, and snares" on our way to that far country, only to find that it has already arrived.

I hope readers will learn the same thing I hoped to codify for my family in writing it: try to save your life, and you are sure to lose it. Give your life away, and you will save it.

9. **On page 194 you discuss the robbery at your home, citing that "the other thing missing after that fateful invasion was our hope of ever fully trusting another person in Iraq the same way again." Did your trust ever return? Is trust in humankind something you think can be returned to you?**
I liken the break-in and that entire season of betrayal to a soul-rape. There was an innocence that was stolen, and things can never be returned to their previous state. But that inability to trust in exactly the same way again does not necessarily have any decisive bear-

ing on how we choose to live. Do we trust people outside of our immediate "circle of sameness" the same way we trusted outsiders before? Probably not. But we still choose to entrust our lives to them over and over again, come what may (and if there is one thing we have seriously considered by now, it's what may come). The book is peppered with the cautions of others who call this way of living naive. Other people's opinions of us are really none of our business. From our perspective, it is equally naive to think that armored cars, flak jackets, guns, tactical attack plans, and counterinsurgency theories represent the surest, safest way to live.

10. Why did you decide to write this story? Describe the journey from conception to publication.

The impetus really came after a number of conferences at which I spoke and people asked for anything I had written that could help them understand what was meant by this provocative phrase "preemptive love." This is still not that book. I hope to write that book at some point in the future. On my way to writing that book, however, I felt that our foundational story needed to be written to provide some kind of context for the theological and philosophical explanations that might follow.

My friend Gabe was kind enough to put me in touch with his literary agent, and I was humbled that Chris agreed to invest some of his time into the story and represent me to publishers across the country. Chris ran interference for a couple of interested parties, and we entertained a few offers on the book before settling on Howard.

I felt an instant connection with the team at Howard and was very humbled to hear their vision for the book, which aligned very closely with my own. We were talking the same language from the beginning, and that gave me hope for a very great partnership (which it has been!).

Throughout the fall of 2012, we took a semester-long break from Iraq to be present for the birth of Cody and Michelle's first child. But that same stretch of time was our busiest ever with surgical teams coming into Iraq to save lives and train Iraqis. So I was back and forth from the United States to Iraq every few weeks with a surgery team. When I wasn't at the hospital, I was holed up in a hotel room in Istanbul, Najaf, or Basra, writing as much as I could. I found that I was a significantly more focused person on the road than I was trying to write from my in-laws' kitchen table with "life" happening all around me!

In all, it has been an incredible, humbling experience. We don't deserve to have this story told. It would have been meaningful enough to have experienced it without much ado. But if this strange, media-saturated world we live in is willing to take a risk on an idea to put before the world, we are grateful that this risky message of preemptive love would rise to the top for this short moment in time. We will take the stage while we have it, however big or small, in hopes of unmaking violence and remaking the world, one heart at a time.

Keep up with or get in touch with Jeremy and PLC
Facebook: www.facebook.com/TheJCourt
Twitter: www.twitter.com/JCourt
Email: jeremy@preemptivelove.org

A Note from Jeremy

Now what? You've read the story and you've seen what preemptive love can do. I want you to know that *you* can help us save lives—in Iraq and wherever preemptive love takes us next.

If you were moved by these stories, there are two simple things you can do to join us in remaking the world through healing:

1) **Buy this book for a friend.** If you believe preemptive love can change the way we live, then I need you to spread the word.

   Give it as a gift or set up a reading group to discuss how preemptive love applies in your life. You can also write an honest review on Facebook, your blog, or on your favorite bookseller's website. There are countless ideas, but we need you to get the word out: *Preemptive Love* is not just a book worth reading, it's a vision and a plan worth living and sharing with others!

2) **Join the Coalition** — Coalition members are our core team of monthly sponsors. Your tax-deductible gift saves lives, builds peace, and puts your love into action immediately for children in need. Visit **www.PreemptiveLove.org/Join** for more info.

Thank you so much for your support! Send me a note any time with questions or to share your own story of preemptive love in action.

Jeremy
jcourt@preemptivelove.org
www.twitter.com/JCourt
www.facebook.com/TheJCourt